the two-week
Detox Diet

the two-week Detox Diet

Cleanse and boost your system in just 14 days

Lose weight the simple way, with 90 step-by-step recipes

Maggie Pannell

southwater

NOTES

Bracketed terms are intended for American readers.

For all recipes, quantities are given in both metric and imperial measures and, where appropriate, in standard cups and spoons. Follow one set, but not a mixture, because they are not interchangeable.

Standard spoon and cup measures are level. 1 tsp = 5ml, 1 tbsp = 15ml, 1 cup = 250ml/8fl oz.

Australian standard tablespoons are 20ml. Australian readers should use 3 tsp in place of 1 tbsp for measuring small quantities of gelatine, flour, salt, etc.

American pints are 16fl oz/2 cups. American readers should use 20fl oz/ 2.5 cups in place of 1 pint when measuring liquids.

Electric oven temperatures in this book are for conventional ovens. When using a fan oven, the temperature will probably need to be reduced by about 10–20°C/ 20–40°F. Since ovens vary, you should check with your manufacturer's instruction book for guidance.

The nutritional analysis given for each recipe is calculated per portion (i.e. serving or item), unless otherwise stated. If the recipe gives a range, such as Serves 4–6, then the nutritional analysis will be for the smaller portion size, i.e. 6 servings. Measurements for sodium do not include salt added to taste.

Medium (US large) eggs are used unless otherwise stated.

The diets and information in this book are not intended to replace advice from a qualified practitioner, doctor or dietician. Always consult your health practitioner before adopting any of the suggestions in this book. Neither the author nor the publisher can accept any liability for failure to follow this advice. A detox diet is not recommended for children, the elderly or pregnant women.

This edition is published by Southwater, an imprint of Anness Publishing Ltd, Hermes House, 88–89 Blackfriars Road, London SE1 8HA; tel. 020 7401 2077; fax 020 7633 9499
www.southwater.com; www.annesspublishing.com

If you like the images in this book and would like to investigate using them for publishing, promotions or advertising, please visit our website www.practicalpictures.com for more information.

UK agent: The Manning Partnership Ltd; tel. 01225 478444; fax 01225 478440; sales@manning-partnership.co.uk

UK distributor: Grantham Book Services Ltd; tel. 01476 541080; fax 01476 541061; orders@gbs.tbs-ltd.co.uk

North American agent/distributor: National Book Network; tel. 301 459 3366; fax 301 429 5746; www.nbnbooks.com

Australian agent/distributor: Pan Macmillan Australia; tel. 1300 135 113; fax 1300 135 103; customer.service@macmillan.com.au

New Zealand agent/distributor: David Bateman Ltd; tel. (09) 415 7664; fax (09) 415 8892

Publisher: Joanna Lorenz
Senior Managing Editor: Conor Kilgallon
Project Editor: Lucy Doncaster
Production Manager: Steve Lang
Designer: Nigel Partridge

ETHICAL TRADING POLICY
At Anness Publishing we believe that business should be conducted in an ethical and ecologically sustainable way, with respect for the environment and a proper regard to the replacement of the natural resources we employ.
　As a publisher, we use a lot of wood pulp to make high-quality paper for printing, and that wood commonly comes from spruce trees. We are therefore currently growing more than 500,000 trees in two Scottish forest plantations near Aberdeen – Berrymoss (130 hectares/320 acres) and West Touxhill (125 hectares/305 acres). The forests we manage contain twice the number of trees employed each year in paper-making for our books.
　Because of this ongoing ecological investment programme, you, as our customer, can have the pleasure and reassurance of knowing that a tree is being cultivated on your behalf to naturally replace the materials used to make the book you are holding.
　Our forestry programme is run in accordance with the UK Woodland Assurance Scheme (UKWAS) and will be certified by the internationally recognized Forest Stewardship Council (FSC). The FSC is a non-government organization dedicated to promoting responsible management of the world's forests. Certification ensures forests are managed in an environmentally sustainable and socially responsible way. For further information about this scheme, go to www.annesspublishing.com/trees

© Anness Publishing Ltd 2008

All rights reserved. No part of this publication may be reproduced, stored in a retrieval system, or transmitted in any way or by any means, electronic, mechanical, photocopying, recording or otherwise, without the prior written permission of the copyright holder.

Previously published as part of a larger volume, *The Detox Cookbook and Health Plan*.

CONTENTS

Introduction	6
The Detox Diet	**8**
What are toxins and where do they come from?	10
How diet affects health	12
Benefits of a detox	16
The body's natural detoxifiers	18
How to boost your vital organs	19
Foods to avoid	20
Foods to include	24
Exercise for body and mind	32
Complementary therapies and relaxation techniques	34
Preparing to detox	38
Following the detox programme	42
One- and two-week detox meal planners	46

Juices, Smoothies and Breakfast Ideas	50
Appetizers and Snacks	66
Simply Sensational Soups	76
Main Dish Salads	88
Vegetable Main Dishes	100
Tofu, Egg, Fish, Shellfish and Chicken Dishes	114
Simple Salads and Side Dishes	130
Delicious Healthy Desserts	144
Index	158
Acknowledgements	160

Introduction

Detox diets have become increasingly popular and no wonder, as they offer fantastic health benefits, claiming to leave you feeling relaxed, refreshed and rejuvenated. In an increasingly toxic world, a detox programme can help your body's in-built detoxifiers to counter the effects of pollution and the many potentially harmful, chemical substances with a spring-clean that leaves you looking and feeling brighter and healthier.

What is detoxing?

Detoxing is an ancient therapy that has been practised in various forms for hundreds of years. It is believed to cleanse the digestive system and help the body eliminate waste products and various toxins absorbed from the air, soil, water and food, as well as toxic substances produced by the body itself. Although this has not been medically or scientifically proven, a detox diet offers many health benefits and is useful for giving the body's own detoxification system a helping hand occasionally, especially since the body has to deal with an ever-increasing toxic load in the modern world.

Detox diets, although based on the same idea, vary in the length of time they're recommended for and the foods that are allowed or avoided. Strict detox diets allow just fruit and vegetables, ideally raw and often taken as juices, with plenty of water for just one or two days. This is a light fasting regime, designed to give the body's digestive system a rest, and it should not be continued for a longer period. A less restrictive regime is based on eating healthy meals, consisting of plenty of fruit and vegetables, home-made soups, whole grains, beans, peas, lentils, fish, skinless poultry, seeds and nuts. Wheat and dairy products, caffeine drinks and alcohol are not allowed.

The detox diet regime should also be combined with regular exercise and complementary therapies, including pampering beauty treatments and relaxing techniques, in order to gain the full holistic benefit.

Below: Raw vegetables are key detox foods, so eat them in abundance.

Above: Drinking plenty of water is essential for health at all times.

Benefits

A detox programme can improve your digestion, boost your immune system and give you a renewed zest for life. Benefits may include better sleep, improved hair, nails and skin, more energy, stress relief, weight loss and possibly even the reduction of cellulite. This is achieved by restricting the intake of toxins and chemical substances, eating a healthy diet and including regular exercise, all of which have the combined effect of making you feel and look better and adopt a positive attitude towards your health.

WHO SHOULDN'T DETOX?
Don't embark on a detox if any of the following apply to you:
- If you are pregnant, trying to get pregnant or if you are breast-feeding.
- If you are diabetic or following a special diet for another condition.
- If you have recently been ill or are recovering from an illness. Wait until you feel completely better.
- If you are under 18 years of age, or over 65 years of age.
- If you are taking any kind of medication, in which case you must first consult your doctor.

Beyond detox
For the long-term, a detox should be followed by choosing a healthy balanced diet, including a wide variety of foods, such as fresh fruit and vegetables, lean protein and wholefoods. This can aid in the prevention of chronic illnesses, such as cancer and heart disease.

Is it for you?
The checklist in the following column will tell you if you could be suffering from toxic overload. Basically if you have ticked at least five of the questions, you are likely to be feeling below par and could benefit from a detox.

As long as you are fit and healthy, it is safe for you to follow a detox programme. However, you must first check with your doctor, especially if you suffer from any health conditions or are taking any medication. Do not attempt to self-diagnose any troublesome symptoms that may have an underlying physical cause and require medical investigation.

Remember that a detox diet is not designed to be a weight-reducing diet, nor is it an elimination diet for identifying the cause of food allergies, although it may be successful in helping with weight loss or spotlighting a food sensitivity. For successful weight loss and long-term maintenance, a healthy balanced diet combined with regular exercise is essential.

How to use this book
You can choose to follow either a one- or two-week detox diet designed to give your body a full internal cleanse, and allowing a wider variety of foods than a more restrictive weekend detox. It is entirely up to you which you choose. Certainly you will feel the benefit after one week, but if you are able to continue for two weeks, the benefits will be more noticeable.

Another approach could be to follow the detox prgramme for just one week, then to reintroduce some wholegrain wheat products and reduced-fat dairy products to add greater variety to your diet for a more flexible eating plan.

It is not recommended that you follow a detox diet for longer than two weeks, since certain food groups are restricted and a healthy diet should include a wide variety of foods and not remove any foods long-term, without sound medical or health reasons.

However, once you've completed your detox, you can gradually reintroduce food and drinks that were restricted on the diet, but you should avoid junk foods, which are high in fat and sugar and have very little in the way of nutritional value. Try to maintain and build on the benefits gained by following the basic principles of leading a healthy lifestyle.

Below: Frequent headaches can be a symptom of toxic overload.

ARE YOU SUFFERING FROM TOXIN OVERLOAD?
Check how toxic you are by answering the questions below. The more questions that you answer 'yes' to, the more toxic you are likely to be and the more likely you are to benefit from a detox.

1. Are you constantly tired and lethargic?
2. Do you have difficulty getting a good night's sleep?
3. Do you suffer from frequent headaches or migraine attacks?
4. Do you suffer from bloating and wind?
5. Do you suffer from constipation or diarrhoea?
6. Do you suffer from catarrh and sinus problems?
7. Do you have difficulty maintaining concentration?
8. Do you suffer from frequent mood swings, anxiety or bouts of depression?
9. Do you frequently feel stressed and irritable?
10. Is your skin spotty or dull, or do you suffer from skin problems, such as eczema, dermatitis or psoriasis?
11. Is your hair dull and lifeless?
12. Do you sometimes have aches and pains in your joints?
13. Do you suffer from frequent colds and other minor illnesses?
14. Do you smoke, live with a smoker, or work in a smoky environment?
15. Do you drink alcohol heavily or regularly?
16. Do you drink more than 3–4 cups of coffee, tea or cola drinks daily?
17. Are you addicted to chocolate?
18. Do you crave sugary and snack foods?
19. Is your diet high in processed foods and convenience meals?
20. Have you developed any food sensitivities?

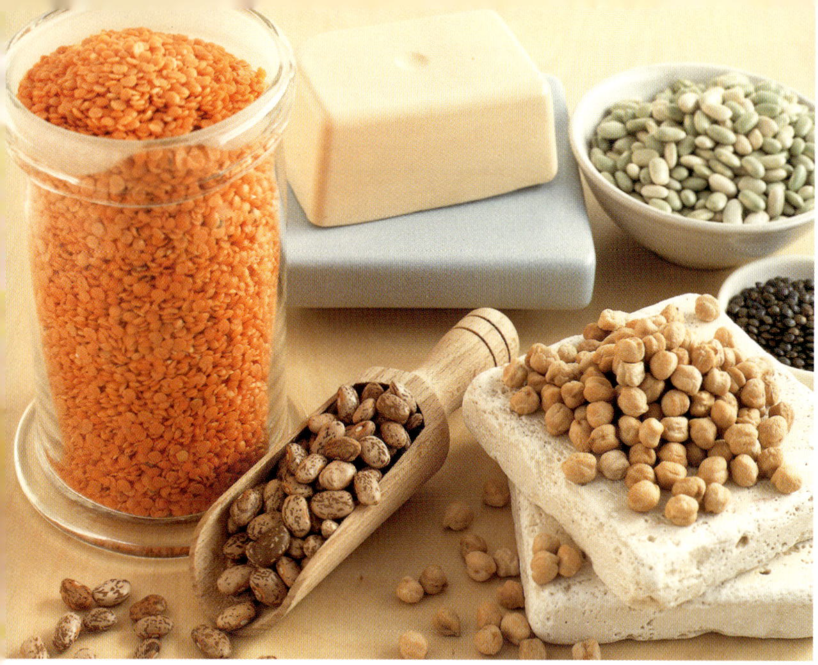
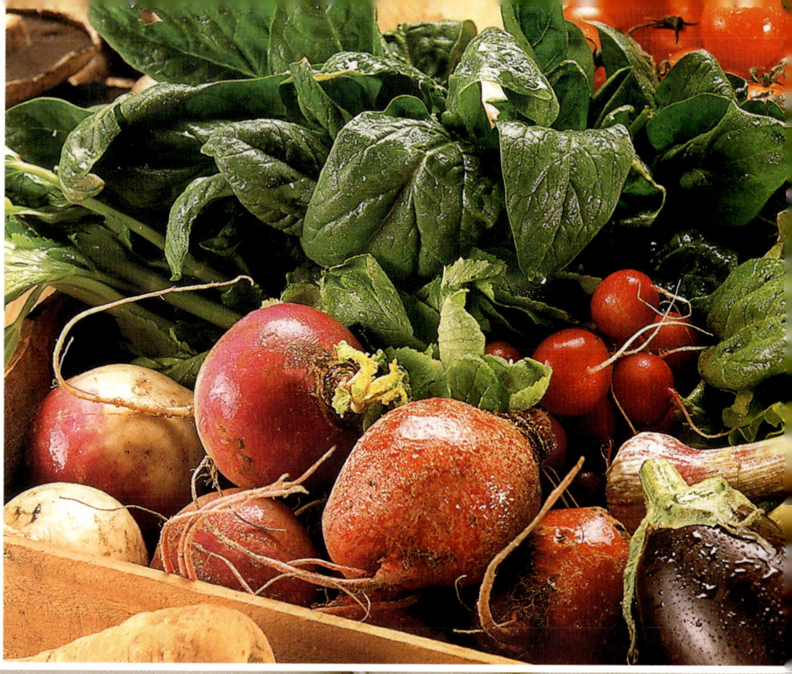
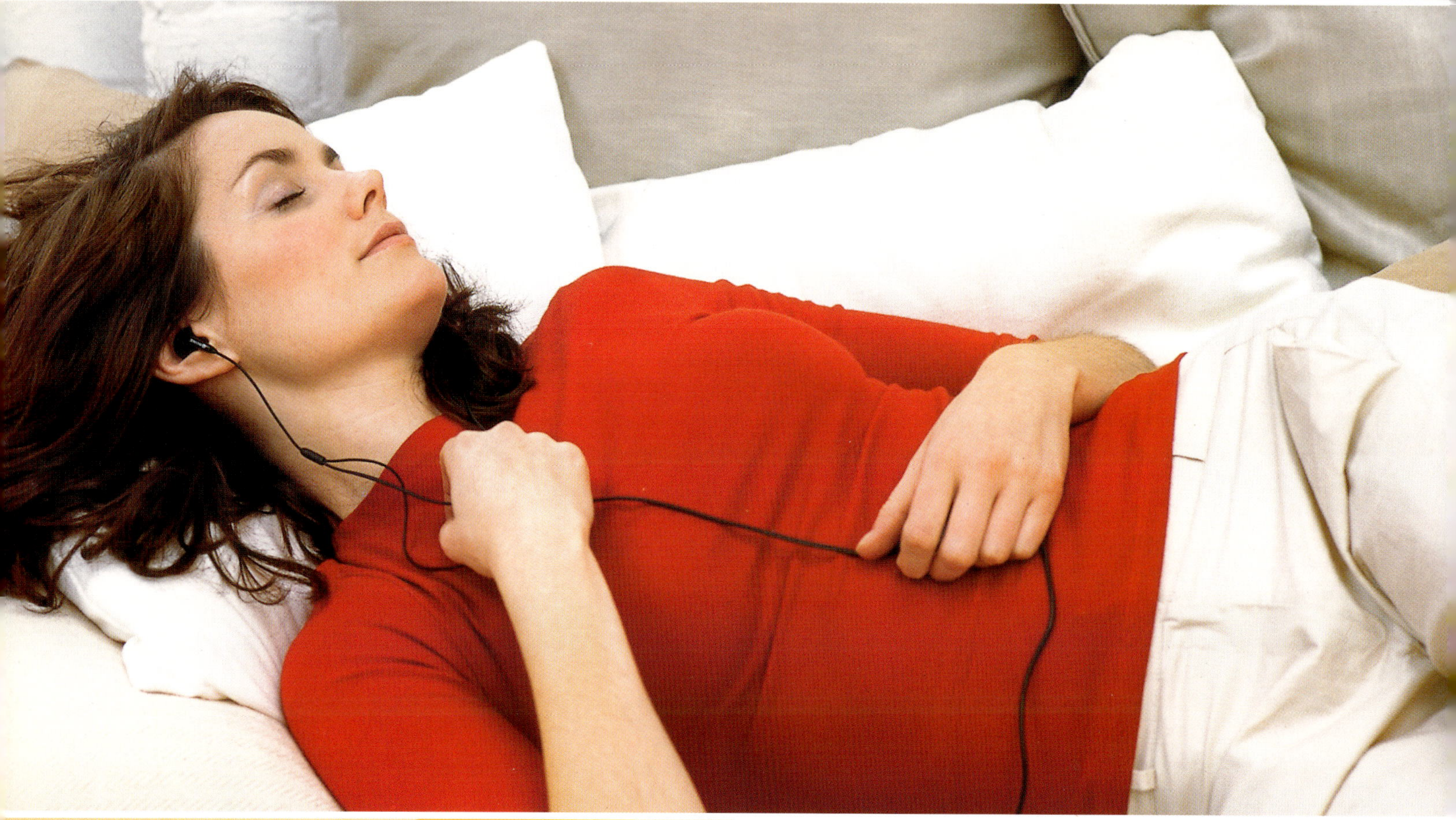
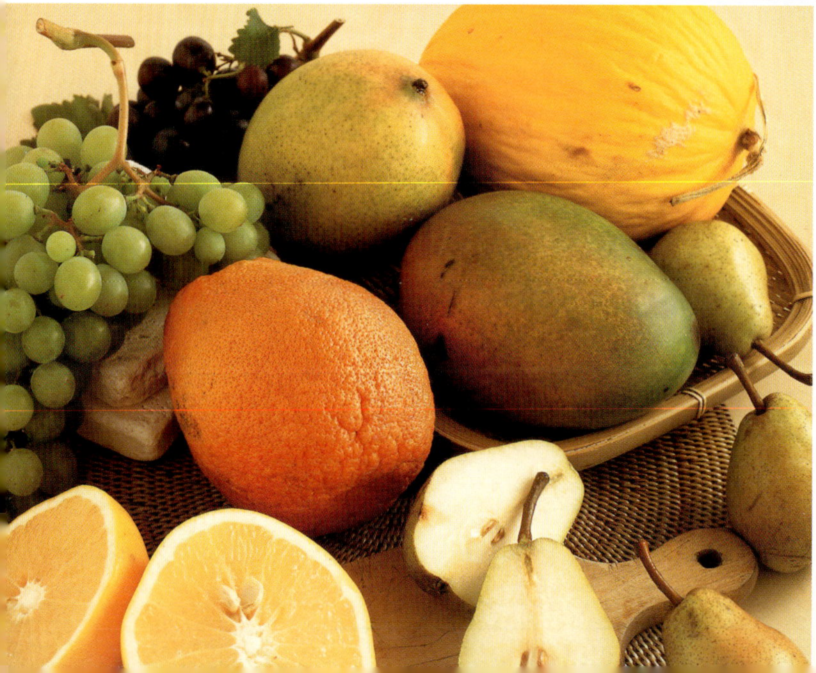
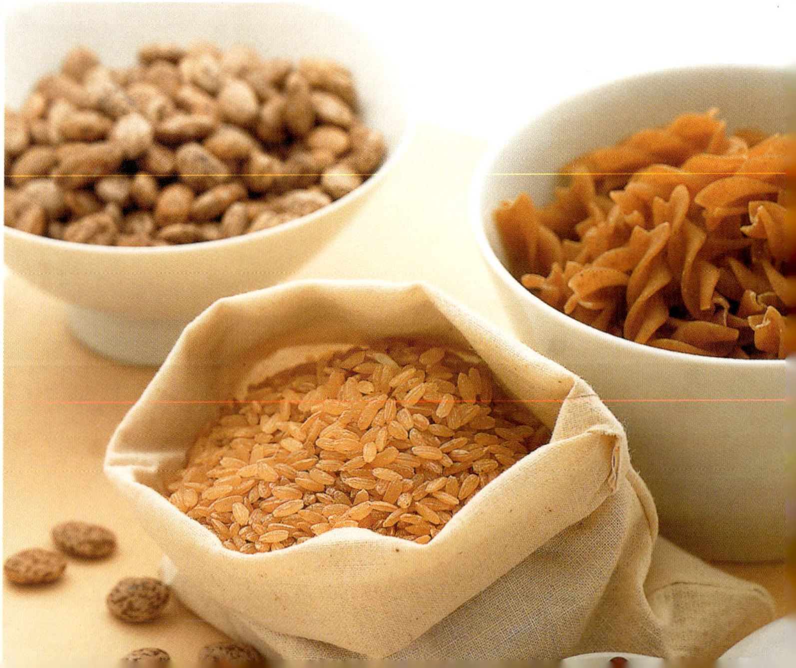

the detox diet

Discover how to detox your body and mind safely and efficiently through healthy eating combined with exercise and relaxing complementary therapies. All aspects are discussed, including advice on which foods to include and which to exclude, exercises for body and mind, complementary therapies, how to follow the programme and a day-by-day meal planner.

What are toxins and where do they come from?

Overload of toxins can be responsible for causing a range of health problems. So what are the different toxins that we are now exposed to in the modern industrial world and what can we do to restrict our exposure?

What are toxins?

Toxins are potentially harmful substances that pollute and irritate our bodies, putting a strain on the efficiency of our vital organs. There are many different kinds of toxins and they are nothing new, but we are now living in an increasingly toxic world, due to modern technology, intensive farming and food production methods, and a greater use of chemicals, all of which may affect our health and well-being.

Although the human body is designed to deal with these unwanted substances, a build-up of toxins puts an extra strain on our natural detoxifying system, especially with increasing age. This can lead to troublesome symptoms and health conditions,

Below: Traffic exhaust fumes are a major air pollutant.

particularly affecting the digestive and respiratory systems. Asthma, for example, is becoming increasingly common, and although environmental pollution is not necessarily the cause, it is certainly a contributing factor and can be responsible for making the symptoms worse. Increasing evidence and scientific research now suggest that many health conditions and chronic diseases may be linked to toxins in our world and lifestyle.

Where do toxins come from?

Toxins bombard us every day. Not only are they produced naturally in the body, but they can enter the body in the air we breathe, from pollutants in the atmosphere and our environment, and in the food, drinks, drugs and medicines that we consume. Toxic chemical substances are also absorbed through the skin from cosmetics, toiletries and household products, including everyday materials such as paint, glue and electrical products. In fact, unless you live in a sterile bubble, it is impossible to avoid everyday exposure to toxins.

Environment

Pollutants in the air include car exhaust fumes, cigarette smoke, fumes from industrial waste, air-conditioning and heating systems, cleaning fluids, air fresheners, paints, detergents, deodorants and hairsprays.

Tap water

Water quality regulations are imposed to ensure that tap water is safe to drink. It also contains valuable minerals, depending on the source and region. However, there is increasing concern about levels of pollutants, including nitrates from fertilizers, weedkillers, industrial chemicals, poisonous metals (such as lead and mercury) and oestrogen-like chemicals, that may be present (albeit in minute quantities) and their possible effect on our health. You can easily find out about the quality of water in your area. If you are concerned, buy a water filter or choose bottled water.

Chemical residues

Agricultural land is treated with fertilizers, crops are sprayed with pesticides and growth regulators, and animals and farmed fish may be fed antibiotics. All of these practices can leave artificial chemical residues either on or in our food, as well as contaminating the environment and water supplies. Increasing concern about these pollutants and a desire to move towards a greener future has led to more and more farms converting to an organic system and more people choosing organic foods.

Free radicals

The body constantly makes and breaks down free radicals, and in small amounts they are helpful as a natural defence against invading bacteria and viruses. However, certain factors such as cigarette smoke, environmental pollution and over-exposure to sunlight, can accelerate their production. In large amounts, they are thought to cause damage to cell walls and DNA (the genetic material found in cells), speeding up the ageing process and contributing to the development of heart disease and some cancers. Antioxidant enzymes and nutrients in the blood (produced naturally and ingested in food) help to neutralize and deactivate free radicals and render them harmless.

Food additives

Due to a diet that tends to be largely made up of processed foods, manufactured to suit a fast modern lifestyle, where speed and convenience are often key to the choices we make, much of our food now contains a wide array of additives. Preservatives are added to prevent the food spoiling, to protect against contamination and to increase the shelf life; emulsifiers improve the texture and consistency of foods; colours, flavourings, flavour enhancers and sweeteners are used to alter the appearance or taste of a food or drink, and various other additives may be used for miscellaneous purposes such as for glazing or as anti-foaming agents. All these additives would not be necessary if we chose to eat more fresh food that was seasonal and produced locally. Although only some people may be sensitive to certain additives, the combined effect adds up to a considerable intake, of which we don't really know the effect over a long period of time.

Alcohol

Drinking alcohol in moderation is relaxing and sociable and can be positively good for your health, but alcohol is basically a poison to the body and puts strain on the liver. Alcoholic drinks, such as wine, beer, cider and alcopops, may also contain chemical additives such as sulphite preservatives that some people can be allergic to. Sulphites can trigger an asthma attack in susceptible individuals.

Cigarettes

Tobacco smoke, which is inhaled into the lungs, contains nicotine and tar as well as many other chemical substances. Not only is the nicotine extremely addictive, but the smoke exposes the body to powerful and harmful chemical compounds that are known to cause cancer and other tobacco-related diseases, such as heart disease and bronchitis.

Left: Highly processed convenience foods are loaded with additives.

Above: Organic farming avoids the use of chemical fertilizers and pesticides.

HOW TO RESTRICT EXPOSURE TO TOXINS
- Avoid smoky environments and if you're a smoker, seek help and advice on how to kick the habit.
- Avoid walking in built-up areas, close to traffic or in industrial areas.
- If you live in a town or city, try to escape to the seaside or country as often as you can for fresh air.
- Wear a mask if you cycle in heavy traffic conditions.
- Cut down on or cease using unnecessary household chemical products, such as aerosol air fresheners and insect sprays.
- Buy eco-friendly household cleaners, washing powder and washing-up liquid.
- Choose organic produce whenever possible.
- Adopt a 'greener' lifestyle.

How diet affects health

Diet is a complex affair. Just think about all the foods you have eaten over the past few days and imagine how their substance and value may affect your body. Then consider all the other factors in your life that may influence your health and you can begin to see why it is generally so difficult to identify the causes of troublesome symptoms and conditions.

Diet in general, or a particular food or group of foods may well be at the root of the problem, but it's important to consider and examine a broad view of possibilities before eliminating foods indiscriminately from your diet.

Symptoms may be attributable to other medical conditions so it's vital to always check with your doctor in the first instance to safely rule out any possible underlying physical causes.

Below: Wheat products can cause gastrointestinal complaints.

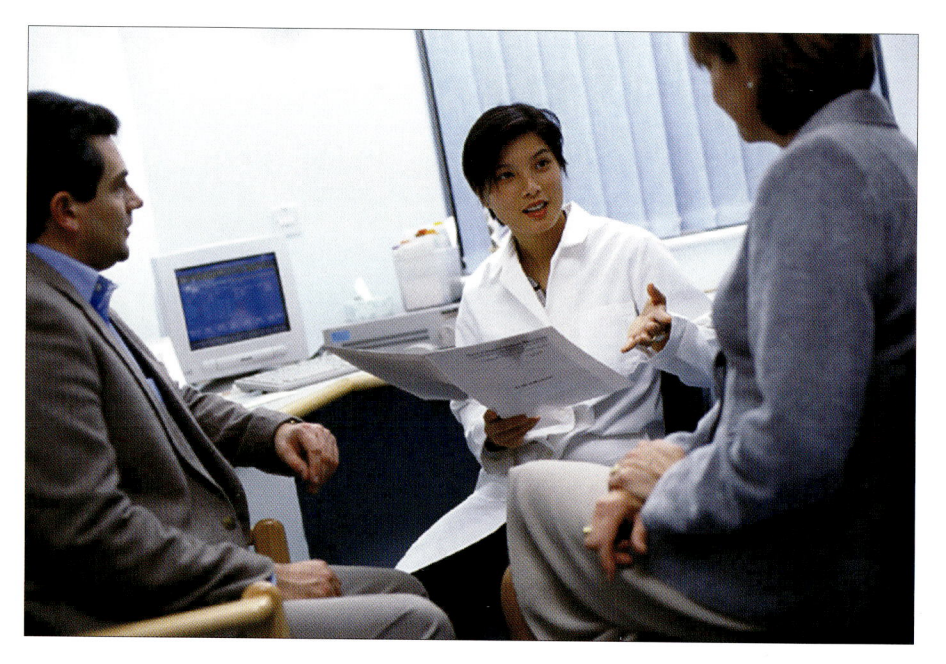

Above: Always discuss troublesome symptoms with your doctor.

Digestive problems

Wheat and dairy products are frequently suspected and sometimes identified as causing bloating, abdominal pain and wind in susceptible individuals. Symptoms of a digestive disorder may also include diarrhoea and constipation. This may be due to a true allergy or an intolerance. The degree of sensitivity may be slight, moderate or severe and there may also be other symptoms present, such as asthma, eczema, rashes and wheezing. Food intolerance or a food allergy, however mild it may seem, should always be taken seriously, so seeking professional diagnosis is very important.

Could also be due to:

• Irritable bowel syndrome (IBS). This is the most common bowel disorder in the Western world although sufferers are often too embarrassed to discuss the condition with their doctor. It is twice as common in women as in men and is most likely to affect people between the ages of 20 and 40 years. Typical symptoms include stomach-ache, bloating and wind, as well as constipation and/or diarrhoea. The condition may be triggered by stress, a hormone imbalance or different types of food. Wheat (especially bran), beans, peas, lentils and dairy products are common food culprits. There is no single effective treatment, but generally a dietician will recommend a special diet that may exclude suspected offending foods. If you think that you may be suffering from this condition, keep a food diary together with a record of your symptoms and consult your doctor for referral to a dietician.

• Coeliac disease. This life-long inflammatory condition is caused by a permanent adverse reaction to gluten, a protein in wheat, as well as other similar proteins in rye, barley and oats. Diarrhoea, abdominal pain and wind are common symptoms and adults may find that they lose weight and become anaemic. Coeliac disease used to be rare, but more and more doctors are beginning to recognize the disorder. The average incidence in the West is 1 in 100 people and about one in 1000–1500 people are affected worldwide. Once diagnosed, the condition can be controlled by following a strict gluten-free diet for life, under the guidance of a dietician. There is now a wide variety of gluten-free foods readily available, allowing you to have a less limited diet.

How diet affects health

Above: Dairy products could be responsible for sinus problems.

Respiratory problems
Dairy products can lead to excess mucus in the sinuses and nasal passages, so if you suffer from a persistent stuffy or runny nose (perennial rhinitis) or congested sinuses (sinusitis), dairy foods could be the culprit. A short detox, eliminating all dairy products from your diet, will help to highlight if this could be the cause of your symptoms.
Could also be due to: An allergic reaction to any substance that may trigger an individual reaction. This could be a food or an additive in the food, or it could be a household or cosmetic product or something in the environment that the body regards as alien and potentially harmful. House-dust mites, pollen, feathers, animal fur, air fresheners and washing powders may all be offending triggers. Allergic reactions can be responsible for triggering asthma attacks, so it is important to always seek medical advice. Some asthmatics are sensitive to sulphite preservatives, commonly used in beer, wine and cider. Labelling laws now require alcoholic drinks to be labelled if they contain sulphites.

Food cravings and addictions
The body can get hooked on certain foods that are eaten frequently and suffer withdrawal symptoms when they are not eaten. This can be caused by foods believed to boost serotonin and endorphin levels in the brain, which provide a feel-good effect, or by sugary foods that give an instant, but temporary blood-sugar fix. Addiction to caffeine is also common. Symptoms include fatigue and mood swings and binging on the culprit food, which can then cause weight gain and bad skin. In effect you can find yourself trapped in an addictive cycle of craving and withdrawal. Refined and sugary foods tend to be responsible, including cereals, cakes, biscuits, chocolate and sugar as well as tea and coffee. Sometimes a food craving can indicate a sensitivity to it, and this should be investigated by a dietician or a professional allergy specialist.

Skin problems
Common complaints include rashes, eczema and spots, and although acne is generally a teenage problem, it can strike as late as middle-age. Eczema, characterized by red, itchy, dry and flaky skin that may bleed or blister, is often brought on by allergens. This may be an external irritant, such as wool, metal or a detergent, to which the skin is sensitive, or a reaction to something eaten. Milk, eggs, fish, shellfish, tomatoes, nuts and wheat are common culprits. A medically supervised exclusion diet can identify the offending trigger, if symptoms improve or disappear when a suspect food is avoided. Drinking plenty of water daily will help improve the general condition of the skin by flushing out the body's waste products.
Could also be due to:
- Emotional stress.
- Hormonal fluctuations, especially in the week before a menstrual period.
- Nutrient deficiencies.

Above: Eggs may be a problem food and exacerbate eczema.

Right: Chocolate is a common food addiction.

Left: Drinking a cup of hot water with a generous squeeze of lemon juice in the morning will stimulate the liver and the gall bladder to kickstart the process of detoxing the body.

Headaches

These may be triggered by a food sensitivity, additives used in certain processed foods, or by consuming excessive amounts of caffeine, which alters the blood supply to the brain. Chocolate, cheese, citrus fruits and alcohol, especially red wine and port, are also commonly cited dietary culprits associated with migraine attacks. Headaches may also be due to an irregular eating pattern. Skipping meals causes blood sugar to plummet, which in turn can precipitate a headache. Try eating regular light meals, do not skip breakfast and if you often wake up with a headache, have a light snack before bedtime to prevent blood sugar levels from dropping too low overnight.

Dehydration can also trigger headaches so be sure to drink plenty of water, especially during hot weather spells, or following strenuous exercise or excessive alcohol consumption.

Could also be due to:
- Poor posture.
- Eye strain.
- Hormonal fluctuations.
- Stress and tension.
- Nasal congestion.
- High blood pressure.
- Poor liver or kidney function.

> **HEADACHES**
>
> Frequent or severe headaches should always be investigated by a medical professional to establish their cause, especially if ordinary painkillers do not help and certainly if you experience other symptoms such as blurred vision, muscle weakness, weight loss or vomiting.

Below: Frequent or severe headaches could be due to a toxic overload, and may be alleviated by making simple changes to the diet.

Tiredness and lack of energy

Sweet snacks, caffeine, alcohol and chocolate can all play havoc with your energy levels, giving you a quick energy boost followed by a rapid fall in sugar levels and an energy dive. Drowsiness may also sometimes be due to a food intolerance. While it is normal to feel sleepy after a big meal, constant lethargy is not normal, and may be due to a sensitivity to grains – particularly wheat, as the process of digestion may induce excessive sleepiness in susceptible individuals.

Could also be due to:
- Coeliac disease.
- Anaemia resulting from poor iron and folic acid absorption.
- An underactive thyroid gland or a viral infection.
- Stress in your professional and/or personal life.
- Mild dehydration resulting from insufficient fluid intake.
- Diabetes.

Mood swings and depression

There are many reasons for changing moods, and ups and downs are part of everyday life. It may be because you are unhappy, under pressure or worried. Stress makes you feel depressed and may be accompanied by various aches and pains. Over a long time, stress can lead to serious illness, including high blood pressure and heart disease. Identify the root cause and think of ways to cope and reduce the strain. Everyday foods can affect your mood and nutritional deficiencies, food intolerances and the level of blood sugar in the bloodstream can all influence your mental state. Regular meals, eating foods rich in B vitamins (which are good for the nervous system) and cutting down on caffeine and alcohol will all help to maintain a steady blood sugar level.

Could also be due to:
- Premenstrual syndrome (PMS).
- Clinical depression.

Below: Close contact with a loved one provides comfort when you are down.

Above: Snack on fresh fruit rather than processed foods when you are hungry.

Premenstrual syndrome (PMS)

This is a common female complaint brought on by fluctuating hormone levels, which can be responsible for causing bloating, headaches, breast pain and depression. Research shows that nutrition can influence hormone production, so a change of diet may help to relieve symptoms. Cutting down on saturated fats may relieve breast tenderness and lowering the intake of salt can reduce bloating and water retention. Also avoid coffee and alcohol for 1–2 weeks before a period is due. Small frequent meals, including nutritious snacks, such as fruit, nuts and seeds, will maintain blood sugar levels. Obesity can affect hormone balance so try to keep your weight within acceptable limits. Regular exercise helps to relieve symptoms.

Joint pains

An allergy or intolerance to particular foods could be a contributing factor to joint pain. Pinpointing the culprit foods can be difficult, but common suspects include dairy products, eggs and cereals. An exclusion diet, followed under medical supervision, will help to identify problem foods. Scientific evidence suggests that a diet deficient in antioxidants, particularly vitamins A, C and E and the mineral selenium, may also predispose some people to joint problems. To increase your intake of these nutrients, you should eat a healthy balanced diet, rich in oily fish and shellfish, fresh fruit and vegetables, wholegrain cereals, eggs, nuts and seeds.

Could also be due to:
- Excessive body weight. Not only can this be a cause of joint problems, particularly affecting the hips and knees, but carrying excess weight can add to the pain caused by other factors.
- Lack of exercise. Regular exercise helps to strengthen the muscles responsible for protecting the joints and helps to prevent stiffness.
- Injury or over-exertion. Cut back your exercise routine or change to a less physically demanding activity.

Benefits of a detox

The benefits you will enjoy from following a detox programme will vary depending on the length and strictness of the regime, the degree of change to your usual lifestyle and eating habits, and your current state of health and well-being. Benefits vary from person to person, but these are the main physical and mental improvements frequently experienced.

Better health
As well as helping to relieve bothersome ailments like headaches and bloating that may be due to food intolerances, a detox diet including plenty of vitamin C from fruit and vegetables can also help to boost your immune system and fight off minor infections – or at least reduce their severity. Including a wide and plentiful variety of fruit and vegetables, packed with antioxidant vitamins and minerals,

Below: Regular exercise, especially when taken in the fresh air, helps to promote mental and physical health.

and other valuable compounds called phytochemicals, also helps to protect against chronic diseases such as heart disease and cancer. Regular consumption of low-fat probiotic yogurt also tops up the good bacteria in the gut, which improves the digestion and helps to relieve disorders such as IBS and constipation, and strengthen the immune system.

Improved appearance
A diet that is rich in vitamins and minerals, with plenty of fruit and vegetables, and that avoids alcohol and cigarettes, will improve the condition of your skin, hair and nails and can help to slow down the ageing process. Fruit and vegetables provide a rich source of vitamin C, needed for the production of collagen (a protein needed for healthy skin, teeth and gums) and also betacarotene, which helps to generate new cells. Overall skin health also depends on proper hydration, so drinking plenty of water helps to promote clearer skin. Regular exercise, especially if taken in the fresh air, boosts the circulation, delivering oxygen to all body cells, and giving the complexion a healthy glow. Teeth will look brighter if not discoloured by tannins present in red wine and black tea.

Improved mood and inner calm
By choosing nutrient-rich foods, your body is better equipped for coping with stress. You will feel calmer and more relaxed and better able to concentrate and think clearly. Regulating blood sugar levels will help you to avoid mood swings, and a break from alcohol will prevent the depressive effect that dulls the brain and affects the memory. Complementary therapies, such as visualization and meditation, are excellent for helping to declutter the mind and induce a relaxed sense of well-being. Feeling happy, optimistic and having a positive outlook on life all help to boost your confidence and self-esteem and promote good health, and a long life span.

Benefits of a detox **17**

Above: A detox diet will help you to sleep better.

Restful sleep
Alcohol, cigarettes and caffeine drinks all interfere with sleep patterns and can cause insomnia. As these should all be ideally eliminated during your detox, you will begin to have a better night's sleep. Also, you will not be eating highly processed junk foods that tend to be high in fat and difficult to digest, especially if they are eaten late at night. Regular exercise and many of the complementary and relaxation therapies, chamomile or valerian tea, all of which are recommended while detoxing, will also help you to sleep.

Increased energy
Fatigue can be made worse by not eating the right foods and therefore not getting enough nutrients to promote sustained energy and vitality. Maintaining good nutrition by eating a wide variety of foods, combined with more sleep and a better ability to cope with stress through complementary relaxation techniques, will all help to banish tiredness and replenish your energy levels.

Weight loss
A detox is not designed to be a weight-reducing diet. However, because you are choosing healthy foods (whole grains, low-fat protein foods and plenty of fruit and vegetables), and cutting out foods that are high in fat and sugar, as well as alcohol, you will naturally consume fewer calories and are therefore likely to lose some weight. Also, gentle but regular exercise will encourage weight loss as well as improving muscle tone.

Reduction of cellulite
Some women also notice a reduction in the appearance of cellulite, although there's no sound scientific evidence to support the claim that cellulite is actually caused by a build-up of toxins, and therefore by following a detox diet the appearance of cellulite can be reduced or removed. Cellulite has a dimpled, orange-peel-like appearance on the skin and can affect women's thighs, buttocks and upper arms – even if you are slim. The female hormone oestrogen is responsible for women acquiring fat in these areas, and because it is stored just under the skin, it can affect its appearance. Many naturopaths and beauticians claim that a diet high in processed and refined foods and low in fruit and vegetables can be to blame for causing cellulite. Certainly a low-fat diet that includes plenty of fruit and vegetables may help to reduce it, and regular exercise will definitely help too. Dry skin brushing and massage treatments can also help to improve the appearance of cellulite.

Improved long-term diet
Although certain foods and drinks are restricted temporarily while following a detox programme, the basic principles of the diet should help you to kick bad habits and adopt a pattern of healthy eating that you will be able to maintain afterwards. It is important to remember that a restrictive diet is not recommended as a continued or long-term eating plan.

Below: A slimmer, more toned figure results from cutting out foods that are high in fat and sugar.

The body's natural detoxifiers

The body is a remarkable system of organic engineering, working to eliminate undesirable substances via the liver, kidneys, lungs, skin, and digestive and lymphatic systems. Generally toxins are dealt with and cleared out routinely and efficiently, but a detox 'spring clean' provides the body with extra help in coping with an increased toxic load.

The digestive system

Your health is often governed by your digestive system. Everything you eat travels from the stomach to the intestines where nutrients are absorbed and waste is eliminated via the bowel. Food is broken down by digestive enzymes and 'friendly' bacteria in the gut. If these are out of sync, due to poor diet, stress, over-use of antibiotics, food intolerances or toxin overload, food remains semi-digested and problems such as constipation, leaky gut, irritable bowel syndrome (IBS), nausea and bloating arise. Food itself can also become toxic if not digested properly.

The liver

This is the most complex human organ and it is responsible for handling almost everything that enters the body. It has hundreds of functions including the removal of toxins from the bloodstream. It is the body's main detoxifier, removing and neutralizing poisons, drugs, alcohol and nicotine. Once made 'safe', these substances can then be eliminated from the body via the kidneys, lungs and bowel. The liver also converts the energy from food into the metabolic nutrients that are needed for cells to function efficiently.

Optimum health depends on the efficient functioning of the liver. If it becomes overloaded with toxins, these are not eliminated and are instead stored in the liver and in fat cells throughout the body. Signs that may indicate an unhappy liver range from: headaches, IBS, poor digestion,

Above: Exercise aids the effective functioning of the internal organs.

bloating, depression and mood changes to the more serious problems of hepatitis and cirrhosis.

The kidneys

These organs basically act as filters to clean the blood. They are responsible for the removal of urea (a toxic waste product from the liver), removal of excess ions (such as sodium) and adjustment of water content in the blood. These waste products are then eliminated in urine, via the bladder. During this filtration process, the kidneys reabsorb useful nutrients and recycle them for further use. It is very important to drink plenty of water at all times to help the kidneys carry out their function efficiently.

The lymphatic system

This system carries toxins, unwanted waste, dead cells and excess fluid to the lymph nodes, where the waste is filtered before being passed into the bloodstream. Poor circulation and a weakened immune system may be signs that the lymphatic system is not functioning efficiently. Higher levels of toxins are believed to slow down your lymphatic system.

The lungs

When we breathe, the lungs deal with air-borne pollutants, such as carbon monoxide from traffic pollution. They allow oxygen to enter the bloodstream and waste products to be removed as carbon dioxide.

Correct breathing is essential if the body's metabolism and organs are to work properly. However many of us do not inhale enough oxygen and so do not expel all the unwanted waste gases. Catarrh, blocked sinuses and a constant runny nose are signs of a poorly functioning respiratory system.

The skin

This is the body's largest organ. Every pore eliminates waste and sweat, and the sebaceous glands help to remove toxins. The skin reflects what is happening inside our bodies. If we are stressed, run down, or have over-indulged, this can show up in a dull, lifeless complexion, or as rashes, spots and blemishes. A healthy diet and drinking plenty of water help to promote clear skin.

Below: Clear skin reflects a healthy digestive system.

How to boost your vital organs

Like a car, the body benefits from a regular service to ensure it runs efficiently and has sufficient energy to fight and eliminate toxins. There are a number of simple, common-sense steps that can help to improve the overall functioning of your vital organs.

The digestive system
- Only eat when you are hungry, and do not overeat or eat large meals late in the evening.
- Take time over meals to eat each mouthful properly and slowly.
- Cut down on refined carbohydrates and foods with a high fat content.
- Do not drink too much with meals as this can dilute your digestive juice.
- Start the day with fruit juices or fruit to boost your digestive system.
- Herbal teas, such as chamomile, peppermint or fennel can be soothing.
- Improve the overall condition of the gut by regularly eating low-fat probiotic yogurt.
- Many herbs and spices are an aid to digestion, so use bay, caraway, cardamom, cinnamon, cumin, dill, fennel, ginger, marjoram, mint, parsley and tarragon in cooking.

The liver
- Drink plenty of water – at least 2 litres/4 pints/8–9 cups a day.
- Eat plenty of fresh fruit and vegetables, in particular apples, citrus fruits, garlic, beetroot (beets), carrots, broccoli, cabbage, globe artichokes, ginger, green leafy vegetables, and bitter leaves, such as dandelion, as well as whole grains, nuts, seeds and beans.
- Avoid processed, salty, sugary, high-fat and very spicy foods.
- Try to eat mainly organic foods.
- Cut down on alcohol and caffeine.
- Exercise regularly.
- Liver-boosting supplements can help to neutralize free radicals that damage cells. Try an antioxidant supplement containing betacarotene, vitamins C and E and selenium.
- Artichoke extract supplements (containing the compound cynarin) claim to help boost a sluggish liver.

The kidneys
- Drink plenty of water.
- Reduce your intake of animal protein foods, such as meat and dairy products, as these can put a strain on the working of the kidneys.
- Cut down on alcohol.
- Dandelion leaves, tea or supplements can be helpful as a diuretic to treat fluid retention and to help to prevent common kidney problems.

The lymphatic system
- Exercise regularly.
- Stimulate the lymphatic system by exfoliating and skin-brushing.
- Have a massage to encourage the efficiency of the lymphatic system.

Left: Citrus fruits stimulate the digestive system and are powerful cleansers. They are also rich in vitamin C.

BREATHING EXERCISE
Use this exercise to check that you are breathing correctly.

1 Lie with your back on the floor, bend your knees and place your feet on the floor a comfortable distance from your buttocks. Rest your hands flat on your stomach, just below the ribs.

2 Breathe in slowly through your nose, filling your lungs. The lower part of your stomach should rise first. If your chest moves first, you are breathing incorrectly and are not using your diaphragm – this is known as shallow-breathing.

3 Exhale slowly though your nostrils, emptying your lungs – notice your abdomen flattening.

The skin
- Drink plenty of water.
- Eat plenty of fresh fruit and vegetables – preferably raw or juiced. They provide betacarotene (the plant form of vitamin A) and vitamin C, both essential for maintaining healthy skin.
- Choose whole grains, lean protein foods and a moderate intake of polyunsaturated essential fatty acids, found in oily fish, vegetable oils and nuts and seeds.
- Ensure that your diet is not lacking in the mineral zinc. Lean meat, skinless poultry, shellfish and nuts are all good sources and yogurt and skimmed milk also supply useful amounts.
- Restrict convenience foods, high in saturated fats.
- Cut down on chocolate, sweets, highly salted snacks and soft drinks.
- Restrict alcohol intake.
- Boost your circulation by exercising and skin-brushing.
- Get plenty of restful sleep.
- Take regular exercise in the fresh air and breathe deeply.

Foods to avoid

Successful detoxing relies on making both dietary and lifestyle changes in order to allow your body to cleanse itself readily and efficiently. Some of the foods that are off-limits during the detox programme are those known to commonly cause digestive problems and other side effects in susceptible individuals. Others are those widely recognized as best limited or avoided in order to promote a healthy body, thus helping you to retrain your eating habits and make healthy food choices for the long term. These restrictions are only suggested for a detox period of up to two weeks to give your body a break and can be reintroduced in moderation afterwards if you like, unless advised otherwise by a doctor or dietician.

Alcohol

Drinking in moderation can be relaxing and sociable and indeed is reputed to help lower the risk of coronary heart disease if it is kept at a 'sensible' level, but you need to give up drinking alcohol completely while following a detox programme.

Below: Alcoholic drinks in excess place unnecessary strain on the liver.

Alcohol is basically an extremely toxic compound, and although the liver acts as an efficient detoxifier, breaking down alcohol and converting it into harmless components, this process puts unnecessary strain on the liver, which can become damaged with regular or heavy drinking. Alcohol metabolism also depletes many valuable nutrients, particularly essential fatty acids, vitamins A, C and E, thiamin and zinc, and it acts as a diuretic, causing the kidneys to excrete more fluid along with vital minerals, such as calcium and potassium. This has a dehydration effect on the body.

Alcoholic drinks are also loaded with 'empty' calories (nearly twice as many as sugar) and therefore provide little nutritional value. They may also contain various additives. Sulphites and sulphur-based preservatives are commonly added to wines, beers, ciders and ready-mixed cocktail drinks, which can trigger reactions such as asthma in certain people. Colours and artificial sweeteners may also be added, all increasing the toxic load.

Above: Tea, coffee, cola drinks and chocolate are all high in caffeine.

Caffeine

Particularly high levels of caffeine are found in coffee (especially ground coffee), but it is also present in tea, chocolate, colas and some fizzy drinks and in some cold and pain relief tablets. Caffeine is a potent substance that stimulates the brain, heart and central nervous system helping to keep us awake, think clearly and feel brighter. It is also a diuretic, causing loss of calcium and an increased risk of osteoporosis. While it is the stimulant effect of caffeine that makes drinks containing it popular, caffeine can also act as a laxative and may cause migraines, insomnia, irritability and palpitations, especially if consumed in excessive amounts. More than six cups a day could give rise to high blood pressure and kidney problems. It is also highly addictive, so to avoid withdrawal symptoms you need to cut back on your intake gradually before starting on a detox programme.

Foods to avoid 21

Above: Avoid processed meat products such as sausages.

Meat and meat products
Red meat, and meat products especially, are also generally high in saturated fat, although farmers are now breeding animals to be leaner and modern butchery methods have produced leaner cuts. Meat products, such as burgers and sausages, may also contain additives and may be made with low-quality meat, depending on the manufacturer. Moreover, meat creates extra work for the digestive system, so while detoxing it is advisable to take a break from eating it, then to only eat lean cuts of quality meat in moderation after your detox.

Dairy products and eggs
Cow's milk and dairy products can be difficult to digest for many people and can often cause excessive production of mucous in the sinuses and nasal passages. Yogurt, however, is usually tolerated by most people and provides a good source of calcium. Low-fat probiotic yohurt has a calming effect on the digestive system and can help to maintain a healthy balance of bacteria in the gut. Dairy products, especially butter, cheese and cream, are also the main source of saturated fats in the diet, which healthy eating guidelines advise most people to cut down on.

Eggs may also cause an allergic reaction in susceptible individuals, in which case all eggs and egg products should be excluded from the diet. However, for the majority of people, eggs (ideally organic) can be eaten occasionally and provide an excellent source of protein as well as a range of valuable minerals and vitamins.

Above: Dairy products can be high in saturated fats.

Left: Red meat should be avoided during a detox programme, and eaten in moderation at other times.

Above: Cream is very high in saturated fat and should be eaten sparingly. Eat low-fat probiotic yogurt instead.

Wheat products

Coeliacs need to avoid all sources of gluten (the protein found in wheat and also present in barley, rye and oats) permanently. Other individuals may be less seriously intolerant of wheat, but still suffer a mild sensitivity, finding it difficult to digest, and experiencing bloating, constipation and/or diarrhoea. Other grains may be consumed without causing problems. Common wheat products include bread, flour, pasta, breakfast cereals, couscous and bulgur wheat. Wheat flour is used for making cakes, pies and puddings and is widely used in the manufacture of many processed foods, such as sauce mixes, soups and stuffings. This can make it quite difficult to cut out, although other grains can be substituted. However, it is important to remember that wheat products, especially wholegrain varieties, are nutritious foods and play an important role in a healthy balanced diet. It should therefore not be eliminated from the diet long-term, unless coeliac disease or a true wheat allergy has been diagnosed.

Above: Wheat flour is used in the manufacture of bread, cakes, cookies and pastries.

Salt

A very small amount of salt is a vital constituent of our diet, but we eat far more than our bodies actually need. Most of the salt that we eat is hidden in processed foods; the rest is either added at the table or during cooking. It's now known that our high salt intake has many potentially adverse effects on our health. It is linked with high blood pressure, kidney disease, strokes, stomach cancer and osteoporosis and may play an aggravating role in asthma. It is not a direct cause of asthma, but a high consumption of salt may make the condition worse. High salt intake also increases fluid retention and the tendency to suffer from bloating and swollen ankles and fingers. Simply restricting salt intake to a much lower level can cause fluid loss of up to 2 litres (4 pints) or 2 kg (4½ lb) in body weight. Lemon juice, garlic and herbs and spices can be used instead.

Sugar

This is a very concentrated source of energy that is quickly absorbed into the blood stream, however it has little nutritional value and is high in calories. Avoiding sugary foods and added sugar is therefore a relatively easy way of cutting calories without adversely affecting nutrient intake, especially if you are overweight.

Sugar and refined carbohydrates (as found in chocolate and confectionery, cookies, cakes and pastries) can also be responsible for causing tiredness. This is because they provide a sudden surge of energy, as the enzyme insulin is released and the blood sugar level shoots up, before tumbling again soon afterward – with a resulting feeling of tiredness. The key to maintaining maximum energy is to keep your blood sugar levels constant by eating regular, satisfying meals with a good balance of nutrients and to choose healthy snacks such as fruit, nuts or seeds if peckish in between. Learn to enjoy the natural flavours of food without adding sugar and try not to use artificial sweeteners as an alternative.

Below: Cakes and biscuits contain high amounts of fat and refined sugar.

Foods to avoid

Above: Fast foods are usually very high in saturated fat.

Processed foods
Foods that are processed are not intrinsically unhealthy. When you cook, you are processing food at home, but much of the manufactured food that we eat includes large amounts of unhealthy saturated and trans fats, sugars, salt, and chemical additives, which may build up and produce harmful effects in the body. Also the more a food is processed, the more likely it is to have lost some of its nutrient value, particularly vitamins and fibre.

While following a detox programme you should aim to choose fresh, natural food, avoid all additives and to eat as much raw food as possible. Some quality canned foods, not including those packed in brine (high in salt) or syrup (high in sugar), are acceptable as well as being very convenient. So are frozen fruits and vegetables, as they are quickly processed at source and can be more nutritious than fresh food that has been transported over a long distance and displayed for days, or that has been treated after harvesting to lengthen its shelf life.

Fatty and fried foods
Fats provide essential fatty acids, which are vital to the body's metabolism. They also provide a concentrated source of energy, make food more palatable and enable the body to make use of the fat-soluble vitamins, A, D, E and K. However most of us eat too much unhealthy saturated fat, which can raise blood cholesterol levels and increase the risk of heart disease. Calorie-rich, high-fat diets can also lead to obesity. While following the detox programme, and for long-term healthy eating, you need to cut down on saturated fat and replace some of it with the healthier unsaturated types. This includes using olive oil (or other vegetable oils high in unsaturates) for cooking, rather than hard fats, and choosing oil-rich fish in preference to red meat. A simple guide is that saturated fats are usually solid at room temperature.

Below: If you can buy only processed food at work, take in a lunch box instead.

Take-away meals
A take-away (take-out) meal makes an enjoyable treat and occasionally gives you a break from cooking, especially when you are time pressured. However, curries, pizzas, burgers, fried chicken, fish and chips and Chinese dishes are generally loaded with fat and can be difficult to digest. They are also likely to be high in salt, yet lacking in a wide variety of nutrients, especially vitamin C, B group and E, and fibre, and may well contain additives, such as food colours and flavour enhancers that can trigger allergic reactions.

So take a break from these meals while detoxing, although you can still make dishes such as lighter curries and stir-fry dishes, packed with healthy vegetables during the programme, following the recipes in this book. After your detox, take-away meals needn't be banned. Many fast food outlets now offer healthier alternatives, such as grilled chicken salad or chargrilled vegetable kebabs.

Foods to include

You can enjoy a wide variety of foods while following a one- or two-week detox diet, so you should never feel hungry or find the diet difficult to stick to. It is not designed to be a starvation diet, but includes selected foods that help and encourage the detoxification process while providing a healthy balance of nutrients.

Fruit and vegetables
These are an essential part of a healthy, balanced diet, and all types should be included in abundance on a detox diet. They are highly nutritious, packed with antioxidant vitamins A (as betacarotene), C and E, minerals, fibre and other natural plant compounds, called phytochemicals, which together protect against illness and disease. Antioxidants neutralize free radicals that can damage body cells and increase the risk of cancer.

Be sure to buy fresh-looking produce, ideally that is seasonal and that has been grown locally. Always wash fresh produce before using to remove any chemical residues and choose unwaxed citrus fruits – wash in warm water before use if not unwaxed.

Choose a wide variety of different coloured produce to make sure you are getting a range of nutrients. Eat as snacks, in salads or lightly cooked. Limit potatoes and bananas to no more than 3 times a week, as they are high in fast-releasing sugars.

Right: Fresh pineapple aids the digestive system.

Super fruits
Apples Studies have revealed that pectin can help protect against the damaging effects of pollution by helping to remove toxins and purify the system. The malic and tartaric acids in apples also benefit the digestion. Apples – if unpeeled – are also a good source of vitamin C, and fibre.

Berries This group includes strawberries, raspberries, blackberries, blackcurrants, cranberries and blueberries. They are rich sources of vitamin C, which helps to fight infection and boost the immune system. Cranberries and blueberries fight harmful bacteria in the kidneys, bladder and urinary tract.

Citrus fruits All are an excellent source of vitamin C. Lemons have a strong cleansing effect and can help relieve gastric problems.

Melons Their high water content is thought to stimulate the kidneys to work more efficiently. Orange-fleshed cantaloupes have the highest vitamin C and betacarotene content.

Left: Fresh melon has a high water content and can stimulate the kidneys.

Papayas Contain an enzyme called papain, which aids the digestion of proteins and benefits the digestive system. It is rich in fibre, betacarotene, vitamin C and phytochemicals with antioxidant properties.

Pineapples Contain the enzyme bromelain, which aids digestion by breaking down proteins and which also has anti-inflammatory properties, which may help relieve arthritis and speed recovery from injuries. It has also been shown to help to relieve sinus congestion and urinary tract infections. Pineapple must be eaten fresh for its healing powers, as bromelain is destroyed in canned pineapple.

Pomegranates Offer good vitamin C and fibre value, and compounds believed to fight disease. New research suggests that the juice may offer many health benefits.

WAKE-UP DRINK
A glass of warm water with some freshly squeezed lemon juice and sliced fresh root ginger added makes the ideal start to the day.

DRIED FRUITS

Excellent snack foods, dried fruits can also be used for making delicious compotes, or as a cooking ingredient in both sweet and savoury dishes to add sweetness and replace added sugar. Dried fruits provide a concentrated source of valuable nutrients and fibre, although they should not be eaten too freely, as due to their natural sugar content, they are quite high in calories, and if eaten between meals, can increase the risk of tooth decay. There is now a fantastic range to choose from, including common favourites like raisins, sultanas (golden raisins), apricots, prunes, figs and dates as well as cranberries, blueberries, cherries and strawberries and mango, apple, papaya, banana and pineapple pieces. Apricots, in particular, are one of the richest fruit sources of iron, a mineral that is frequently lacking in many women's diets. Prunes are well known for their laxative properties, and can help to relieve constipation.

Much dried fruit is treated with sulphur-based preservatives in order to prevent discolouration and to enhance its colour. Apricots and peaches, for example, are a less attractive brown colour if they are left untreated, but if you want to avoid additives, particularly during a detox, choose unsulphured fruit. It is also important to note that sulphured foods can trigger asthma attacks in susceptible people. Potassium-based preservatives are also sometimes added to ready-to-eat dried fruit (which is partially hydrated to be softer than normal dried fruit) to prevent fungal and bacterial spoilage. The best policy is to always check the ingredients' label, as all additives must be listed.

Right: Carrots are good for the immune system and help to maintain healthy skin and eyes.

Carrots Rich in the antioxidant betacarotene (as evident in their bright orange colour) which is good for the immune system as well as for skin and eye health. Unlike the vitamin and mineral content of many vegetables, the betacarotene is better absorbed if the carrots are cooked.

Celery A good, low-calorie diuretic that helps the kidneys to function efficiently and so hastens the excretion of waste. It may also help to lower cholesterol levels and blood pressure. Use in soups, salads and stir-fries.

Below: Broccoli is packed with goodness and is a powerful antioxidant.

Super vegetables

Beetroot (beet) A powerful blood cleanser and tonic and valued for its value to the digestive system and the liver particularly. It is rich in potassium and provides plenty of folate and iron, essential for the formation of red blood cells and helping to prevent anaemia. It has a reputation for stimulating the immune system and may also help to combat cancer, although this has yet to be proved scientifically. Choose fresh raw or cooked beetroot, but not the type packed in vinegar, because as well as being acidic and therefore an irritant to a sensitive gut, pickling reduces the level of nutrients.

Broccoli A cruciferous vegetable – along with cauliflower, kale cabbage, spring greens (collards), turnips, Brussels sprouts, kale and radishes – rich in carotenoids (phytochemicals), which are powerful antioxidants thought to suppress the formation of free radicals and protect against certain cancers. Broccoli also provides iron and is an excellent source of folate, vitamin C and potassium.

Left: Beetroot contains many beneficial substances that can cleanse the blood and aid the digestive system.

Above: Garlic is one of the most potent natural healers.

Garlic Highly valued for its anti-viral and anti-bacterial properties and many therapeutic benefits. It is a natural decongestant, helps to fight infections and eliminate toxins and may lower cholesterol levels, reduce blood pressure and help to prevent cancer.
Ginger Knobbly-looking, fresh root ginger is valued as an aid to digestion as well as being good for combating colds, stimulating the appetite, improving circulation and helping to alleviate nausea. It's also reputed to help relieve rheumatic pains.
Globe artichokes A substance called cynarin, found in the base of the vegetable leaves, may help liver function and control cholesterol levels.
Onions Like garlic, well known as a cure-all, with an impressive reputation for helping with all kinds of ailments. They have powerful antibiotic properties and are great natural decongestants.
Pumpkin and other squash Supplies a good source of the antioxidants beta-carotene and vitamin E. The flesh is easily digested, and they rarely cause allergies, which makes them an excellent detox food.

FRESH GINGER TEA
Infuse 1 tbsp peeled and grated fresh root ginger in boiling water for 5 minutes. Strain before drinking.

Spinach This and all salad leaves provide antioxidants, vital for healthy immune function. The darker the leaves, the higher their nutrient value.
Tomatoes A rich source of the antioxidant lycopene. Cooking and processing releases this lycopene, so there is even more in tomato products such as tomato purée (paste), passata (bottled strained tomatoes) and canned tomatoes. All can be included on the detox diet, although tomatoes can aggravate eczema and trigger migraine in some people.
Watercress Rich in antioxidant vitamins and minerals and reputed to help speed up the body's detoxification process and purify the blood. It is a natural antibiotic, can help to promote a clear skin and is reputed to help relieve stomach upsets, respiratory problems and urinary tract complaints. Eat in generous portions.

Above: Watercress is a natural antibiotic and can relieve a number of complaints.

SEA VEGETABLES
Seaweeds, or sea vegetables as they are now known, are highly nutritious. They absorb and concentrate nutrients present in the sea and provide a rich supply of minerals, such as calcium, iodine and iron, and vitamins, including vitamin B12, which is not found in land vegetables. In Japan, where sea vegetables are widely produced in the coastal waters, they are highly valued for the protection they provide against toxic substances, for their intestinal-cleansing qualities, and for helping to combat acidity in the body, which is caused by over-consumption of coffee and alcohol.

Much of the seaweed sold is in a cleaned, dried and packaged form, under its Japanese species name, such as nori, wakame or kombu, but varieties are also harvested in coastal areas around Europe, including Welsh laverbread and Irish carragheen. Dried types are convenient for keeping in the store cupboard (pantry), and then can be soaked before using (including the soaking water). Nori is most commonly used for making sushi, but sea vegetables generally can be added to soups, stews and salads. They go well with rice and potato dishes and have a special affinity with fish.

Kelp tablets are a convenient way of including some seaweed in the diet. They can be readily bought from most health food stores.

Foods to include **27**

SPROUTS

All sprouts can be eaten raw in salads and provide a rich source of vitamins and minerals, as well as protein. Some are easy to buy, but you can also grow your own The easiest are mung and aduki beans, chickpeas, whole lentils, mustard and cress (fine curled cress), fenugreek and alfalfa seeds. Soak beans overnight, then place in a sprouter or jar topped with muslin (cheesecloth) for a few days, rinsing twice daily. Don't use red kidney beans, as these contain a toxin that needs to be destroyed by cooking.

Dried beans, peas and lentils

These are a great source of low-fat, vegetable protein as well as B vitamins and a wide range of minerals, including iron and magnesium. They also have a high fibre value, which helps to prevent and relieve constipation and lower blood cholesterol, reducing the risk of heart disease and stroke. There is a wide variety of different beans, peas and lentils to choose from, and they can all be included on a detox diet. Dried beans and peas (but not lentils) require soaking overnight. Soak in cold water, then drain, rinse and cook in fresh, unsalted water. Bring to the boil, then boil rapidly for 10 minutes to destroy any toxins, then simmer gently for 1–1½ hours, or as advised on the packet instructions. If using canned varieties, choose those canned in water or with reduced salt and rinse thoroughly before using. They are very versatile and satisfying to eat and present all kinds of delicious detoxing recipe possibilities, including soups, salads, dips and casseroles. They can be mostly interchanged in recipes.

Above: A wide range of nutritious grains provide variety in the diet.

Left: Do not add salt to the water when cooking dried beans, peas and lentils as this prevents them from softening.

Whole grains

These provide slow-releasing carbohydrate for sustained energy and should be eaten regularly. During a detox, it is advised that wheat and wheat products are avoided, but there are many other cereal grains that can be substituted. These can include rye, barley and oats (unless a gluten intolerance is diagnosed), millet, corn, buckwheat or quinoa and rice. Whole grains make the best choice as they have a higher fibre value than refined types, as well as providing a good supply of B and E vitamins, minerals and small amounts of essential oils. Brown rice is particularly efficient at cleansing the digestive system. It is also anti-allergenic and helps to stabilize blood sugar levels. Quinoa is another easily digested cleansing grain that is a good source of protein, B vitamins, minerals and fibre. It has a nutty flavour and can be steamed or boiled and eaten like rice. Corn, millet or buckwheat pastas, or rice noodles can all be substituted for wheat pasta.

Mycoprotein (Quorn)

Quorn is made from mycoprotein, a plant that is related to mushrooms and truffles. It makes a versatile and nourishing alternative to meat that is easily digested, although it is best to choose the mince, pieces or fillets as an ingredient, rather than ready-prepared recipe dishes, while following a detox diet. Quorn is high in quality protein, low in fat and contains no cholesterol, yet provides a good source of fibre, which helps to fill you up. It is quick and easy to use and versatile for a range of dishes from salads to stir-fries. Note that Quorn contains egg albumen, so it is not suitable for people with a true egg allergy.

Tofu

Made from soya bean curd, tofu provides a healthy and versatile rich source of dairy-free, vegetable protein. It contains all eight essential amino acids making it an excellent alternative to meat. It is also low in saturated fat and sodium, cholesterol-free and provides useful amounts of calcium, iron and B-group vitamins. It is a completely natural product and contains no artificial additives. Furthermore, soya products are rich in phytoestrogens, which can help to lower blood cholesterol and relieve menopausal symptoms and may help to prevent breast and prostate cancers and osteoporosis.

Tofu is sold in a variety of forms, the most common of which are chilled firm tofu, and silken tofu, which has a silky, smooth texture like yogurt or custard. Firm tofu can be sliced or cut into cubes and used for dishes such as salads, kebabs and stir-fries, or blended for soups, dips, dressings, spreads and desserts.

Silken tofu is best suited for making desserts, soups, dressings and smoothies. Tofu has an ability to absorb and enhance whatever flavour or other ingredients it's mixed with. Other forms of tofu are available, including smoked, marinated and deep-fried tofu, but these are best avoided during a detox.

Above: Nutritious tofu is a wonderfully versatile ingredient.

Left: Mycoprotein has a meat-like texture, yet in contrast to animal protein, it contains dietary fibre in addition to high protein levels.

IDEAS FOR USING TOFU

- Mash the tofu and make it into burgers with onion, herbs, spices and garlic.
- Use as a salad dressing: blend with chopped fresh coriander (cilantro) leaves and lemon juice.
- Thread cubes on to skewers with mushrooms, tomatoes and (bell) peppers; marinate in soy sauce and mustard before grilling.
- Whip with fresh herbs and Tabasco sauce as a dip for carrot sticks and other crudités.
- Blend with fresh fruit, such as strawberries or raspberries, to make a fruit fool.
- Stir-fry with Chinese mushrooms, bamboo shoots, pak choi (bok choy) and cashew nuts.
- Poach in a clear broth with seafood and vegetable strips for a simple, light meal.

Foods to include 29

Nuts

All kinds of unsalted nuts can be included in a detox diet. They are packed with important nutrients that assist detoxification. Nuts provide protein, B vitamins and many minerals and are an excellent source of vitamin E, which helps to support the immune system and protect against heart disease. Almonds are an especially useful source of calcium, walnuts are rich in the essential omega-3 and omega-6 fatty acids and Brazil nuts are a good source of the antioxidant mineral selenium, essential for the proper functioning of the liver, hormone production and healthy hair and skin. However nuts are high in fat, and although this is largely in the healthy form of unsaturated fatty acids, they are high in calories so should only be eaten in moderation.

Seeds

All kinds of seeds are a good source of vitamin E and the B group vitamins, many useful minerals and fibre. They provide antioxidant defence against cancer, help lower cholesterol levels, prevent and relieve constipation as well as soothe digestion. Pumpkin, sunflower, flaxseeds (linseeds) and sesame seeds all make nutritious snacks, eaten in moderation, or can be sprinkled on to soups, salads, muesli (granola) or casseroles, or stirred into smoothies. Sesame seeds are used to make a paste called tahini, which is included in hummus.

STORAGE

Nuts and seeds can turn rancid fairly easily, so they should be bought in small quantities, stored in a cool dark place in airtight containers and eaten before the 'best before' date. Also, be aware of potential allergies.

Above: Unsalted nuts make a good alternative to animal protein foods.

Poultry

You can include some chicken and turkey on a one- to two-week detox diet, provided it is skinless and simply cooked by a low-fat cooking method. Poultry provides a low-fat source of high-quality protein and is also rich in most of the essential B vitamins. Do not eat duck or goose while following your detox as they have a higher fat content. Organic birds are not fed antibiotics or other drugs so should be free from drug residues.

Below: Trout is a good source of omega-3 fatty acids and tastes delicious baked or grilled.

Fish

Healthy-eating guidelines recommend that we should eat at least one to two portions of fish a week – one of which should be an oil-rich fish, such as sardines, mackerel, herring, salmon or trout. This is to boost levels of omega-3 polyunsaturated fatty acids, which are believed to help provide protection against coronary heart disease, as well as offering many other health benefits. Oily fish is also a good source of the fat-soluble vitamins A and D. White fish, such as cod, haddock and plaice contain low levels of omega-3 fatty acids, but they provide an excellent source of low-fat protein, minerals and vitamins. Shellfish are low in fat and they are also an extremely rich source of minerals.

Fish is easy to digest provided that it is simply cooked using low-fat cooking methods. Canned fish is just as nutritious and provides economical and convenient options. Look out for those packed in natural spring water or oil, rather than brine.

Fish farming in general is often criticized for its use of 'toxic chemicals', but responsible fish farms only use veterinary medicines that are necessary for fish welfare and ensure that their use is strictly monitored and controlled. You can choose to buy wild or organically-farmed fish if you prefer. What is important is that you make sure that you include fish, particularly oily varieties, regularly in your diet. Although there has been an increase in the pollution of sea and river waters, which means that even fresh fish may contain contaminants, it is mainly the longer living fish, such as sharks and swordfish, that are most likely to be affected.

Above: Non-dairy alternatives to cow's milk can be used for drinks and all kinds of recipes.

Non-dairy milk choices

It is important to include an alternative milk in a detox diet because not only will it provide essential calcium and added vitamins, provided the milk is fortified, but it is usually needed to serve with muesli (granola) and porridge and for making low-fat smoothies.

Choose from a wide range of alternative milks, including rice, almond, oat or soya 'milks', readily available in fresh chilled, long-life and organic varieties. These milks are not only free from animal protein and lactose, but they are low in fat and contain no cholesterol. They taste good too, and may be preferred even after detoxing. Soya 'milks' may be unsuitable for people with an allergy to soya.

Yogurt

Although primarily made from milk, yogurt is easier to digest, and can usually be safely consumed by people with a lactose intolerance. Yogurt provides an excellent source of calcium as well as protein and certain B vitamins. Most fresh, chilled yogurt is 'live' (although it may not be labelled as such), which means it contains living bacteria that are helpful to the digestive system. Yogurt labelled as 'bio' or 'probiotic' is particularly beneficial to the digestive system, helping to redress the natural balance of the gut flora frequently upset by poor diet, too much alcohol, stress, food-poisoning bacteria, antibiotics and foreign travel. Evidence suggests that regular consumption of probiotic yogurt,

Above: Probiotic yogurt can help to restore to the gut healthy bacteria that have been destroyed by antibiotics.

providing sufficient friendly bacteria to the gut, may help with conditions such as candida, IBS and stomach upsets as well as helping to strengthen the immune system.

Eggs

A very convenient source of protein, eggs also supply many minerals and vitamins, especially vitamin B12, making them an important food, particularly for vegetarians. Choose organic, free-range eggs to be sure that they come from hens that have ample access to land that is free from chemical fertilizers and pesticides and are guaranteed to be free from yolk colorants.

Below: Boiled, poached or cooked as an omelette, eggs provide a nourishing and easy detox meal.

Foods to include **31**

Above: A light oil and vinegar dressing perks up a simple leafy salad without adding masses of fat and calories.

Oils and vinegars

Vegetable oils provide essential fatty aids (omega-6 and omega-3) and are also a good source of vitamin E. They are made from nuts, seeds, beans, peas and lentils, the most common being sunflower, safflower, rapeseed, corn, olive and soya bean, and consist of varying ratios of monounsaturated and polyunsaturated fatty acids. Any of these can be used in small quantities while following a detox diet. Speciality oils, including walnut, sesame and hazelnut oils can also be lightly sprinkled over salads and stir-fries.

Cold-pressed oils, where the oil has been pressed out rather than extracted by heat, retain more vitamin E, but these oils especially must not be kept for long periods, as they do not keep well, lose their vitamin E when exposed to sunlight and are prone to rancidity. Store oils in a cool dark place and buy in small quantities. Also, do not reuse cooking oils because constant reheating sets off a chemical reaction that can create free radicals.

Cider vinegar makes the best choice of vinegar during a detox. It is made from fermented apple juice and is reputed to have many therapeutic properties including helping to ease arthritic pains and stimulating the liver to produce more bile. It may also help the digestion, regulate metabolism, cure gastro-intestinal infections and diarrhoea, and help to relieve chronic fatigue.

Vital water

Drink at least 2 litres/4 pints/8–9 cups of water each day to help flush out toxins and waste products and to avoid fluid retention. Drinking sufficient water also helps to prevent urinary infections, constipation, headaches and bloating and helps to keep your skin clear. It can be drunk as herbal teas or with freshly squeezed fruit or vegetable juice. Drink plenty of fluids throughout the day, but do not drink to excess. There is no benefit in doing so, and it will just be an inconvenience if you need to visit the toilet frequently.

Herbal teas

Also called tisanes or infusions, herbal and fruit teas provide a refreshing, alternative hot drink to coffee, regular black tea and hot chocolate or cocoa, while following a detox diet. These drinks are naturally caffeine-free as well as sugar-free and contain virtually no calories. They are usually enjoyed without milk or added sugar, and are equally good drunk chilled. The myriad of flavours available is a bonus too, ensuring that the taste buds will never be bored, and you can choose various flavours to suit different moods and times of the day, depending on whether you need to perk up or calm down. Some teas are also reputed to help ease common complaints such as a queasy stomach or an aching head.

HEALTH BENEFITS OF HERBAL TEAS

- Chamomile tea is well known for helping to promote a good night's sleep. You could also try adding a chamomile tea bag to your bath to help yourself relax.
- Lemon verbena, peppermint and fennel are all valued for their calming digestive properties, making them ideal as an after-meal soother.
- Mixed fruit, rosehip, cinnamon, ginger and orange blossom offer awakening, revitalizing properties for when you need a pick-me-up.
- Rooibosch (Redbush) tea, made from a South African herb, contains highly beneficial flavonoids and trace minerals and has been scientifically proved to possess both anti-inflammatory and anti-spasmodic properties, offering relief to many allergy sufferers. It may help to relieve both digestive and skin complaints.
- Parsley tea is a great general aid for the kidneys. Infuse fresh parsley in boiling water for 5 minutes.

Below: Herbal teas make a perfect detox drink choice.

Exercise for body and mind

Although making changes to your diet is the most effective way of eliminating toxins, any diet should also incorporate regular exercise to be really beneficial. Also build in some complementary therapies and relaxation techniques, which are therapeutic and make the diet all the more enjoyable.

The importance of exercise

Regular gentle exercise is essential for promoting a healthy body, mind and spirit. It is vital to living a healthy lifestyle and a valuable part of a detox as it stimulates the metabolism and the lymphatic system as well as improving circulation – efficiently transporting oxygen and nutrients to cells while removing waste. It also provides an opportunity to unwind and reflect.

Above: Gentle jogging, especially through water, is a great way to keep fit.

Exercise shouldn't be anything too strenuous or demanding, especially if you are not used to taking much exercise, but should be something you enjoy and can easily fit into your life. Aim to exercise at least three times a week for a minimum of 20 minutes, choose different types of exercise and if you lack motivation, get a friend to exercise or join a class with you. Generally, be as active as you can, walking whenever possible rather than taking the car or using public transport.

The following forms of exercise are excellent at all times, and particularly while you are following one of the detox programmes:
- Brisk walking or jogging
- Rowing
- Swimming
- Cycling
- Skipping
- Dancing
- Golf
- Tennis
- Exercise class
- Gardening
- Yoga
- Pilates

> **KEY BENEFITS**
> - Speeds up the metabolism.
> - Helps to burn fat and control cholesterol levels.
> - Muscular movement enables your body's systems to work more efficiently, removing toxins.
> - Stimulates the heart and lungs, improves circulation and helps to reduce blood pressure.
> - Helps to combat fatigue and boost energy levels.
> - Boosts the immune system.
> - Helps to keep bones strong and healthy.
> - Improves strength, stamina and suppleness of the major muscles and helps to prevent back pain.
> - Promotes deep breathing which is key to relaxation.
> - Triggers the release of endorphins – chemicals in the brain that lift your spirits and reduce anxiety, and make you feel calmer and more clear-headed.
> - Improves self esteem.
> - Aids a good night's sleep.
> - Helps to prevent a variety of health problems.

Above: Gardening is therapeutic as well as good, gentle exercise.

Above: Cycle with a friend for added enjoyment and motivation.

Relax your mind

Relaxation, de-stressing and clearing the mind of negativity are just as important as physical exercise and diet during a detox. Body and mind are fully integrated, and stress, anger, fear and negative thoughts can be damaging to the system, reducing its ability to eliminate toxins.

Stress can wear you down making you more susceptible to infections and disease. As well as affecting your health, prolonged stress will make you tired, depressed, irritable and affect your concentration. In a stressful situation, the body produces the hormone adrenalin, which induces a 'ready for action' state in the body.

When there is no outlet for this, it can affect the internal organs, manifesting itself as a headache or causing tense shoulders, indigestion or skin problems. Deep relaxation will therefore benefit not just your mental state, but your body too. There are many kinds of relaxation techniques such as massage and meditation. These are discussed in detail in the following pages.

WAYS TO REDUCE STRESS
- Take time out from work and the pressures of daily life at least once a week.
- Delegate to ease the burden of everyday tasks.
- Share problems with a partner or close friend, or talk to a professional counsellor.
- Face up to problems and do something to resolve them.
- Plan a holiday or outing so that you have things to look forward to.
- Eat regular and healthy meals.
- Build regular physical exercise into your life.
- Put on some calming music and sit back with a good book.
- Watch a comedy film that makes you laugh and smile.
- Treat yourself to a massage, facial, manicure or pedicure.
- Learn, practise and master different relaxation techniques.

Below: Make sure you take time out to relax regularly.

Above: Sleep is a great antidote to daily stresses and strains.

How to get a good night's sleep

Diet can play an important role in affecting your sleep. During a detox, you should find that you sleep better anyway, as caffeine drinks, chocolate and alcohol are eliminated from your diet, and hopefully you will not be smoking. All of these are stimulants (except alcohol which is a depressant), and can keep you awake and interfere with sleep patterns.
- Anxiety, stress and depression can all cause insomnia. Find ways to reduce or cope with stress.
- Never go to bed hungry, and never go to bed on an over-full stomach. Detox meals are not heavy or rich and include complex carbohydrates that have a calming effect on the brain.
- Chamomile tea and valerian are the best herbal teas to help promote sleep and can act as mild sedatives. Stir in a little honey, if liked.
- Regular exercise will promote deeper sleep, but avoid anything too strenuous late in the evening.
- Don't over-stimulate your mind before bedtime. Instead of watching television, try listening to some gentle music or read a book (not one related to work).
- Relaxation therapies, including a soothing bath, will help you sleep well.
- Love-making is also conducive to good sleep.

Complementary therapies and relaxation techniques

Complementary therapies have become increasingly popular and are now widely available in holistic therapy practices, beauty salons, health clinics, and sports and fitness centres. Not only can these help with the detox process, but because they aim to treat the body as a whole, they are beneficial for correcting your emotional, mental and spiritual state and inducing a state of balance and harmony in the body. Aim to treat yourself to at least one complementary therapy during your detox.

Massage

Not only is a massage pleasurable and relaxing, but it can offer a great many physiological and psychological benefits. These include:
- Stimulating the lymphatic system helping to reduce fluid retention and eliminate toxins.
- Increasing the oxygen and nutrient supply to the tissues by increasing the blood circulation.
- Helping to restore balance and to regulate hormone production in the body.
- Stimulating the body's natural immune system.
- Reducing bodily tensions and easing stiff, tight muscles that can result from being stressed.
- Helping to increase energy levels.
- Promoting a general state of happiness and well-being.
- Calming and soothing the mind.

Massage can also be helpful for conditions such as asthma, depression, neck and back pain, insomnia and immune-deficiency disorders.

There are many kinds of massage, including Swedish, therapeutic, aromatherapy and acupressure, but they all apply the same technique of using the hands to perform stroking, kneading and pummelling movements, usually directly on the skin, to promote relaxation, healing and well-being.

LYMPHATIC DRAINAGE MASSAGE

One of the most gentle forms of massage is lymphatic drainage massage. It works on the lymphatic system (the body's drainage system, which carries nutrients into cells and removes waste products), and since lymph vessels are positioned close to the surface of the skin there is no need for heavy pressure.

The lymphatic system of the body is a secondary circulation system, which supports the work of the blood circulation. The lymphatic system has no heart to help pump the fluid around the vessels, and therefore it must rely on the activity of the muscles to aid movement.

Lymphatic massage involves using sweeping, squeezing movements along the skin. The action is always directed towards the nearest lymph node. The main nodes used when treating the foot are located in the hollow behind the knee.

Lymphatic drainage massage is hugely beneficial in helping to eliminate waste and strengthen the body's immune system and leaves you feeling wonderfully relaxed.

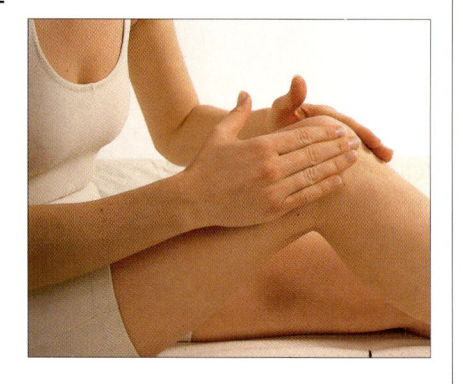

1 To improve lymphatic drainage to the feet and legs, try a daily skin "brush" using your fingertips. Begin by working on the thigh. This clears the lymphatic channels in this region so that it is ready to receive the lymph flood from the lower legs. Briskly brush all over the thigh from knee to top, three or four times.

2 Work on the lower leg in a similar way. Brush either side of the leg from ankle to knee, then treat the back of the leg. Follow this by brushing along the top of the foot, continuing up the front of the leg to the knee. Brush over each area twice more, making three times in total.

This facilitates the flow of blood and lymphatic fluid and relaxes the muscles. Massage strokes are light and move rhythmically towards the heart. A light oil, lotion or talcum powder is used so that the hands can glide smoothly and easily over the skin. For an aromatherapy massage, blends of specially selected essential oils are used. Treatments that involve a whole body massage usually take about one hour and should only be performed by a qualified practitioner.

Right: Performing a simple head massage can help to reduce the tension that can lead to headaches.

SIMPLE SHOULDER MASSAGE

If you are unable to visit a practitioner for a full body massage, a simple shoulder massage is easy to perform with a partner, either sitting on an ordinary kitchen chair or lying face-down on a bed, with your partner standing behind or at the side of the bed. Place your hands on his or her shoulders, close to the neck. Your fingers should be to the front over the top of the shoulders. Using your thumbs, press down and firmly roll the flesh upwards, working outwards across the shoulders and taking great care not to dig in with your fingernails. A massage should be relaxing and pleasurable, not painful.

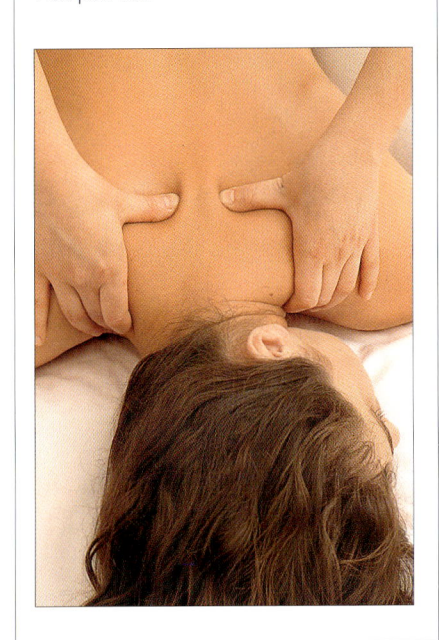

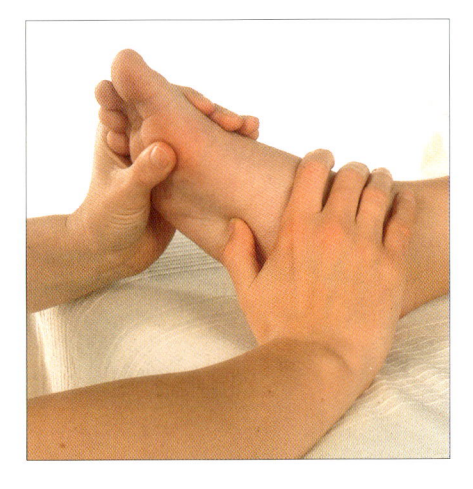

Above: Foot massage stimulates the body's natural healing powers.

Reflexology and shiatsu

This treatment, also sometimes called 'zone therapy', massages the acupressure points on the feet, and sometimes the hands, and has been shown to help remove blockages and eliminate toxins, and to rebalance the body. Reflexology is based on the belief that there are reflex areas on the feet (and hands) corresponding to all the parts of the body, including major organs. The therapist stimulates and works these organs and systems through the reflexes, applying pressure to the feet with thumb and fingers.

Not only is reflexology a very relaxing therapy, but it can also help with digestive disorders, asthma, migraine, sinus problems, hormone imbalances (including menstrual and menopausal problems), poor circulation and muscular pains, and relieving tension and stress. With regular treatments, many conditions can be alleviated without the need for medication.

Shiatsu is based on similar principles to those of reflexology but incorporates the whole body and uses pressure, stretching and manipulation to stimulate the healing process and restore a sense of well-being.

Aromatherapy

Aromatherapists use the purest plant essences in the form of organic essential oils extracted from plants, fruits, flowers, leaves, berries and roots. These aromatic oils contain powerful, complex natural chemicals with therapeutic properties that can be used to treat a wide range of ailments and conditions. Based on individual consultation, a qualified aromatherapist will select the most appropriate essential oils for each client. These oils are quite potent and should not be used directly on the skin, but are blended with a carrier/base massage oil – sweet almond or grapeseed oil are commonly used. This aromatherapy blend is usually applied to the skin with traditional body massage, then penetrates the skin and travels round the body via the bloodstream and lymph vessels. Lightly warming the oil increases absorption.

A few drops of diluted essential oil can also be added to your bath water, sprinkled on a pillow to help promote a good night's sleep (lavender is particularly good), used in an oil burner or vaporizer as an air freshener, or added to a bowl of hot water for steam inhalation. Lean your face over a bowl, drape a towel over your head to completely enclose the bowl, then breathe in the steam deeply and slowly for 3–4 minutes.

Book an appointment with a practitioner for an aromatherapy massage or for advice on choosing aromatherapy oils.

Left: Essential oils should be used sparingly and must be diluted.

Right: Moisturizing your skin straight after a warm bath leaves it soft and supple.

Hydrotherapy

Water therapy is not only relaxing but boosts the circulation, opens and unblocks the pores and encourages the removal of toxins. A bath or sauna taken before a massage will help to relax the muscles and encourage further elimination of toxins.

Aromatherapy bath Run a warm bath and add drops of your chosen essential oil or oil blend, stirring the oil into the water to disperse it. Calming oils include chamomile, myrrh, lavender, sandalwood, frankincense, patchouli and ylang-ylang. Stimulating oils include rosemary, geranium, rose, lemon and juniper. (Note that many oils are not suitable for use during pregnancy.)

Epsom salts bath This encourages the elimination of toxins through your skin. The salts are high in magnesium, which is good for tired muscles. Pour 450g/1lb Epsom salts into a warm bath and lie back for 20 minutes, adding more hot water if the bath becomes cool. Afterwards, pat yourself dry, wrap yourself in a warm towel and go to bed or relax for an hour. You may sweat during the night, so drink plenty of water before you retire. In the morning, have a bath or shower to remove any salty residues.

Sitz bath Spend a few minutes in a warm bath, then have a very brief icy-cold shower, or dip into cold water. The temperature change stimulates the circulation and internal organs, encouraging the removal of toxins.

Sauna and steam (Turkish) baths These encourage sweating and boost the circulation, which aids the removal of toxins. Spend 5-10 minutes in the sauna or steam room at a time, taking a cold shower or swim in between. Finish with a cold shower. Relax for 30 minutes to allow your body to adjust to its normal temperature.

Note If you suffer from heart problems, avoid any of these baths. If you suffer from eczema or high blood pressure, avoid the Epsom salts bath.

SKIN BRUSHING

Dry skin brushing, using a natural bristle brush or loofah, is a wonderful way to boost your circulation. It makes your skin smooth and soft and helps to get rid of cellulite, because it encourages the lymphatic system and the expulsion of toxins through the skin. The whole process should take less than 10 minutes and it is a great way to start a detox day before taking a bath or shower. It also increases the effectiveness of an aromatherapy bath.

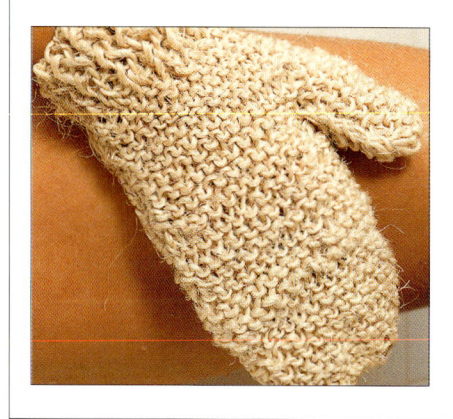

1 Start at your feet and toes, brushing up the front and back of your legs using long, firm strokes (always brush towards your heart to encourage blood flow). Move up to your thighs and groin area.

2 Brush over your buttocks, up to the lower back. Now brush your hands and arms, moving towards the heart, using long, smooth strokes.

3 Brush your stomach using circular, clockwise movements.

4 Move across your shoulders, down over your chest, then down your back, towards your heart.

Complementary therapies and relaxation techniques **37**

Meditation
This uses the same technique as visualization, by focusing the mind on a word or phrase (a mantra), and on an object, or a visual symbol, which has a special meaning for you. Your mantra can be any calming word you choose, such as 'peace', 'love' or 'joy'; an object could perhaps be a flower or a candle; the visual symbol could be a memory of a particularly happy time in your life. Choose a quiet place to meditate where you will not be disturbed, close your eyes and breathe slowly and deeply. If distracting thoughts arise, bring your attention back to what you are meditating on. To begin with, you will find that your mind constantly wanders, but the more you practise, the easier it becomes. During the day, whenever you feel stress building, simply contemplate your word, object or symbol – this will help your mind to relax.

Below: Ensure you are not going to be disturbed, wear comfortable clothes and sit in an airy room when meditating.

Deep breathing
Learn to breathe slowly and deeply, through your nose rather than your mouth, and you will immediately feel more relaxed. All too often, and especially when stressed, breathing tends to be shallow, and if you don't take in enough oxygen, it is harder for the lungs to expel waste products and harmful toxins.

This exercise costs nothing and will help your body to detox as well as to reduce blood pressure, levels of stress hormones and tiredness.

CALMING VISUALIZATION
This is a very simple and effective relaxation technique, which will have the added bonus of heightening your senses.

1 Lie or sit down in a quiet place and close your eyes. Try to clear your mind and relax your muscles.

2 Imagine yourself in an idyllic, peaceful place, where you feel comfortable and safe, such as a sandy beach or the countryside. Use your senses to visualize the colours, smells, sounds and feel.

3 Think of a short and positive statement such as 'I am calm and relaxed' and repeat it a few times. You can escape to this favourite place whenever you feel stressed.

Preparing to detox

Following a detox diet should be a relaxing and rejuvenating experience, so it is essential that you are in a positive, stress-free state of mind. However, before starting, you should be fully prepared as this is the key to a successful detox. Here are some tips and guidelines for things you need to plan and think about before you embark on a detox diet.

Timing

You can detox at any time of the year, although popular times tend to be at the start of spring or summer, after the Christmas and New Year excesses, or in preparation for a holiday or a special occasion. There is nothing like a big incentive to spur you on, but the most important factor is to start with a positive attitude.

Choose a time when you are not too busy and can allow yourself plenty of time to relax, exercise and prepare suitable meals. Delegate as many tasks as you can to others so that you do not feel pressured. When you are planning to follow the detox programme for one or two weeks, you should ideally make sure there are no important dates like dinner parties or holidays that could make it difficult to stick to a prescribed eating plan.

It is also not a good time to detox if you are going through any kind of particularly stressful major life change, such as moving house, changing your job, or divorce or separation. Wait until your life is calmer, when a detox may be just what you need for a new lease of life following a particularly demanding or worrying occasion or point in time.

> **WHEN NOT TO DETOX**
> As long as you are fit and healthy, it is safe for you to follow a detox programme. However, if you have any concerns, you must check with your doctor first. Do not embark on a detox if any of the following conditions apply to you:
> • If you are pregnant, breast-feeding or trying to become pregnant.
> • If you are diabetic or following a special diet for any other medical condition.
> • If you have recently been ill, or are recovering from an illness. Wait until you feel completely better.
> • If you are under 18 years of age or over 65 years of age.
> • If you are taking any kind of medication, you must first consult your doctor.

Clear away temptations

Remove from your kitchen cupboards items of food that should be avoided during a detox, such as processed and refined foods, and particularly sweet or salty snack foods that you might be tempted to grab in a weak moment. Pack away and certainly do not buy any biscuits, crisps or chocolate. Out of sight, out of mind is the best policy, which will make it so much easier for you to stick to the diet. Then restock your cupboards with the healthy choices you plan to eat.

Fill bowls with fresh fruit and place them on a sideboard in the living room, on the kitchen work surface and/or on a desk at work, to be readily available for healthy snacks.

Fill a jar with a selection of herbal tea bags and place it next to the electric kettle, ready for making refreshing hot drinks whenever you like.

Left: Making an action checklist and planning your detox in advance will help you to be much better prepared and to achieve your goals.

Preparing to detox 39

Kitchen essentials
Clear kitchen work surfaces of all equipment and gadgets that you will not be needing, such as toasters, coffee-makers and sandwich toasters. This will give you more space to create healthy dishes that are suitable for a detox regime, and will also help you to resist the temptation of a piece of toast or a cup of coffee.

Put out on display all types of equipment that will be useful, such as chopping boards, knives, peelers, graters, weighing scales, a blender, a food processor and a juicer or smoothie-maker. This will encourage you to use the time during a detox to experiment with dishes and equipment that you have not tried before, or that you do not use very often.

You should also make sure that you have plenty of airtight containers in which to keep dried foods – such as dried beans, peas and lentils – and to transport suitable lunchtime foods to work. It is recommended that you buy a water-filter jug and a steamer for cooking vegetables, if you do not have these already. A wok and/or griddle pan are useful but not essential pieces of equipment – you can use a large non-stick frying pan in place of both.

Use the detox as an opportunity to have a good spring-clean in the kitchen, and clear the refrigerator of any foods that are not appropriate so that it is ready to be stocked up with all the foods that are suitable for the detox regime.

Left and below: A blender or food processor is ideal for making soups and smoothies using fresh fruit and vegetables, and a juicer is useful for making a wake-up drink of warm water and freshly squeezed lemon juice.

Above: Create a luxurious sanctuary in your bathroom by cleaning and decluttering it before you embark on a detox programme.

Bathroom essentials
Clean, clear and tidy the bathroom, giving yourself a relaxing and calming environment where you can retreat for some time to pamper yourself each day, and where you will be able to relax in undisturbed peace.

Stock up with bathroom beauty products, such as luxurious bubble bath, moisturizing cream, exfoliating scrub, face masks, hair treatments and a new loofah or flannel mitt (towelling or natural fibre). Try to choose pure, natural skin care products and treat yourself to some good quality aromatherapy oils.

Position some scented candles around the bathroom so that you can enjoy their warm and scented glow while you are in the bath. Select large, thick cotton bath towels and a soft and cosy bathrobe to wrap yourself up in when you get out of the bath. In fact, why not use the opportunity to treat yourself to something new? It is all about pampering yourself without the expense of booking into a health farm.

Setting the Mood

Clear out clutter Physical disarray adds to the tension of life, so have a good tidy up and either put away or give away what you don't need. Clearing clutter is an orderly way to help you feel calm. Also, you do not want to spoil your detox time by having to do very much housework.

Buy fresh flowers Studies have shown that fresh flowers can help to relieve stress, soothe away anxieties and help trigger feelings of happiness. So choose some pretty favourite blooms to enhance your living and working environment.

Choose greenery Plants pour oxygen into the environment and soak up carbon dioxide and pollutants. Keep plants where you work, live and sleep and you will enjoy more oxygen, allowing you to breathe better.

Bring in fresh air Open at least two windows in two different rooms to let fresh air sweep away any stale air in your rooms, particularly if the air is polluted with cigarette smoke. If you live on a busy road, open windows at the back of the house or at a time when there is the least traffic. Do not use air fresheners, although pot pourri and incense can be a pleasant, non-toxic way of scenting the air.

Turn down the lights Electric lighting can be harsh and cold, so although bright lights are often needed for many daily activities, candles can provide a more soothing glow for when you want to wind down and relax, especially after a hectic day. Choose from a range of scents to suit your mood.

Music therapy Music is also brilliant for helping you to relax and unwind. It can produce a sense of well-being and stimulate the production of endorphins, the body's natural painkillers. During a detox, calming music is likely to be the best choice. You may wish to buy or borrow some suitable cassette tapes or CDs, such as some of the New-Age music styles especially suited to meditation, yoga, relaxation, massage and reiki.

Reading material Since you are unlikely to be going out wining and dining or partying and will have time to relax more at home, collect some good books and magazines for leisurely reading.

Miscellanious Ensure that you have a notepad and pen for creative writing or suitable artist's materials for drawing or painting.

Below: Enhance your bedroom environment with fresh linen, and declutter.

Preparing to detox 41

Detox your home
Give your home a quick detox and improve your environment.
• Open windows regularly.
• Turn the central heating down by a few degrees.
• Put water-filled bowls on windowsills or next to fireplaces.
• Don't overuse appliances like computers and mobile phones.
• Choose natural fabrics and materials.
• Buy some pot plants. They are natural air filters and can effectively enhance and freshen air quality.
• Keep pet allergens at a minimum by making certain rooms, such as the bedroom, a pet-free zone, and remember to wash and groom pets regularly to prevent shedding.
• Use a vacuum cleaner that has a high efficiency filter. Dusting with a damp cloth will reduce air-borne particles, and use a natural beeswax type polish rather than aerosol sprays.
• Have your boiler and any gas fires checked regularly.
• Filter your tap water if you are concerned about the quality.

Below: Houseplants can detox and freshen stuffy air.

Light up your life
Your detox living space should ideally be light and airy. Light makes you feel happy and energized, whereas dark rooms and a lack of natural sunlight can make you feel depressed. So make sure that your windows are sparkling clean, do not block out natural light with fussy window dressings and make the most of mirrors, especially opposite windows, to reflect light.

Colour too can affect your mood. For detoxing, light shades of blue are calming and relaxing, and pale green can make us feel cooler and more comfortable. Pastel shades are ideal for a tranquil bedroom atmosphere, and the tones of the sea work well in a bathroom for a feeling of freshness and cleanliness.

Gather support
Tell friends and family that you are setting aside some time to detox. With their support in helping to share healthy meals, helping with household chores and not making demands on your time, it will be so much easier to stick to the programme. Real enthusiasts may even like to join you, and following any kind of diet is so much more enjoyable with support than attempting it alone.

Above: Enlist friends and family for motivation and support.

Easing in gently
In the weeks preceding a detox, choose healthy meals, avoid junk food, wean yourself off alcohol and cut back on tea, coffee and fizzy drinks, gradually substituting with decaffeinated coffee or tea, or herbal infusions .

If you're a smoker, certainly cut back, and if possible, think about trying to give up completely. Speak to your doctor for advice or investigate the various alternative methods such as acupuncture and hypnosis.

Take some regular gentle exercise, such as a brisk 15–20 minute walk at least three times a week, to stimulate the circulation and metabolism.

Book any complementary treatments. See what's available in your area and treat yourself.

Following the detox programme

Whether you wish to follow a one- or two-week programme, you will need to incorporate the programme into your lifestyle so that the changes to your diet are relatively easy to make and adhere to. It is a good idea to plan for all eventualities so your detox runs as smoothly as possible.

How long for?
You can choose to follow either a one- or a two-week detox diet, which allows you to eat a wide variety of foods. You will feel the benefit after following the programme for just one week, but if you are able to continue for two weeks, this will reward you with an even greater boost to your health and general well-being.

The two-week detox diet is based on a regime of light and healthy eating, incorporating wholefoods and a wide variety of fruit and vegetables, and avoiding foods that commonly cause sensitivities. Some light fish, poultry and egg dishes have been included to ensure that you obtain all the nutrients you need while encouraging your body to flush out toxins.

It is not advisable to follow a detox diet for longer than the time specified. This is because certain food groups are restricted and a healthy diet should include a wide variety of foods, unless you have sound medical reasons for excluding a particular food.

Detoxing should not be viewed as a time of deprivation, but rather as an opportunity to spring-clean your body and to restore balance. Do not worry too much if you lapse on occasional days. Simply resolve to get back on track the following day.

Once you have completed your detox regime, try not to slip back into unhealthy habits. Gradually reintroduce the foods and drinks that were temporarily restricted, while continuing to eat healthily and exercise regularly, in order to maintain the benefits gained by following the healthy-eating guidelines set out by the diet.

Above: Detox dieting encourages you to freely eat a wide range of fresh fruit and vegetables, and is a good way to experiment with produce you have not tried before.

Flexible Eating
Menu plans are suggested in this book, although you can vary the recipes, swap meals around and substitute ingredients to suit your own food preferences and according to availablity and what is in season. However, be sure to choose a wide variety of foods, within the detox guidelines, to ensure that you get a balance of food groups and do not get bored.

Eat in abundance A wide range of all fresh fruit and vegetables.

Eat in moderation Rice, beans, peas, lentils, grains and grain products (including oats, barley, rye, millet, buckwheat, corn and quinoa), nuts and seeds, tofu, low-fat probiotic yogurt, fish, skinless poultry and eggs.

Avoid Red meat and meat products, dairy products, wheat products, processed and refined foods, ready meals and fast food, crisps (potato chips) and savoury snacks, chocolate and sweets (candies), sauces and pickles, caffeine drinks and alcohol.

Plan meal times
Eat three meals a day – breakfast, lunch and dinner. Do not skip any meals and make time for breakfast. Even if you do not feel hungry in the morning and do not usually eat a breakfast, get into the habit of doing so. There are lots of delicious choices suggested in the chapter on 'Juices, smoothies and breakfast ideas'. Breakfast kick-starts the metabolism after resting overnight and the body needs fuel for energy so that you do not feel tired and unable to concentrate.

Eating regularly also helps to keep your blood sugar levels stable and helps prevent binge eating or snacking between meals. Aim to have breakfast before 9am, lunch between midday and 2pm and dinner before 8pm, allowing a reasonable time between meals for comfortable digestion. If you have a busy work schedule, try to arrange your appointments around meal-times rather than letting your diary rule when you have time to eat.

Following the detox programme **43**

Above: Canned beans in water are healthy, versatile and convenient.

Be prepared
Keep the kitchen cupboards well stocked with staples like rice, beans, lentils, canned tomatoes, nuts and dried fruit, so that you always have the basics to hand for making a healthy detox meal. Also keep a selection of frozen fruit and vegetables, fresh home-made stock and fish and chicken in the freezer. Read through the recipes and buy ingredients that keep well so that you are prepared if you don't have much time to shop.

Coping with family meals
All of the recipes in this book make healthy choices and can be enjoyed by everyone, but a detox diet is not suitable for children or certain other members of the family, as discussed under 'When not to detox' on page 38. If you can follow a detox with a partner so much the better, as this will make food shopping and meal preparation easier, plus you will be able to support and encourage each other. Most of the recipes serve four, but quantities can easily be halved if just cooking for two.

For children or other members of the family who are not detoxing, you can remove your portion from the pan or dish and then simply add bread, pasta, meat and dairy products to their portions. The recipes in this book can be useful for helping all of the family to follow a healthier diet. They encourage the use of a wide range of different fruits and vegetables, whole grains and oily fish, in preference to highly processed and refined foods, which are usually loaded with unhealthy fats, sugar, salt and chemical additives as well as being low in fibre. Try to sit down for a social and structured meal rather than grabbing food on the move.

Below: Make meal times an occasion for talking and relaxing.

Eating out

You should try to avoid eating out altogether while following a longer-term programme as it will be harder to control exactly what goes into the food. However, should you for some reason have to dine out, here are some suggestions for healthy dishes that you could choose:
• Tzatziki, guacamole, salsa or hummus with raw vegetable crudités.
• Vegetable soups (non-creamy).
• A simple bean and young vegetable salad, without any mayonnaise.
• Grilled, baked or steamed fish or chicken with plain boiled rice or new potatoes and a large green leafy salad on the side.
• Baked potato, without any butter, topped with beans, hummus, tuna or mixed salad.
• Vegetable, chicken or tofu stir-fries with rice or rice noodles.
• Casseroles made with vegetables, beans or chicken.
• Lentil or vegetable curry with plain basmati rice.
• Plain or herb omelette with salad.
• Fresh fruit or fruit salad.

Above: Spring Vegetable Omelette would be an ideal light meal in a restaurant. Order with a large serving of fresh salad on the side.

Below: Tomato and Lentil Soup is quick and easy to make and perfect for a working lunch.

Working lunches

If you are out at work or away from home during a one- or two-week detox, you will need to take a packed lunch with you so that you have something suitable to eat and do not end up resorting to a food that should be avoided. Sandwiches made with wheat bread will be off the menu during a detox, although you can make sandwiches with rye bread, or add toppings to rye crispbreads, rice cakes or oatcakes. Good detox lunch choices include:
• Soups (home-made or good-quality fresh store-bought soup). Pack in a vacuum flask.
• Salads (large, mixed or a selection of simple salads).
• Dips with vegetable crudités.
• Slice of Spanish omelette made with vegetables, with side salad.
• Half an avocado filled with tuna or prawns and salad.
• Chopped fresh fruit and low-fat probiotic yogurt.
• Falafel (spiced chickpea patties) with salad and yogurt raita.

IDEAS FOR HEALTHY SNACKS

On the detox diet you should never feel hungry if you eat regular meals. This is because the meals are packed with fruit, vegetables, whole grains and beans, which are high in dietary fibre, so they are filling and satisfying. However, if you are ever peckish between meals, or need to eat something quick on the run, here are some ideas for healthy snacks to keep you going. Ensure that you do not snack to excess. Nuts, seeds and dried fruit especially are high in calories, and eating them too frequently or in large quantities can easily lead to weight gain.

- Small handful of sunflower or pumpkin seeds.
- Piece of fresh fruit or a handful of raw vegetable crudités.
- Oatcakes or rice cakes spread with Hummus or Pea Guacamole.
- Small handful of unsalted nuts or dried fruit.
- Small pot of low-fat probiotic or soya yogurt (preferably unsweetened if possible).
- Home-made unsweetened fruit or vegetable juice or smoothie (or choose good quality fresh, chilled store-bought varieties).
- Handful of olives (rinsed if packed in brine).

Above: Herbal tea makes a caffeine-free alternative hot drink.

Possible side effects

While detoxing, your health should gradually start to improve, but you may experience temporary side effects, known as 'healing or cleansing crises'. Symptoms may include headaches, tiredness, nausea, feeling cold, spots on the skin, bad breath, a furry tongue or irritability. Do not be concerned or think about giving up the diet. This is perfectly normal and a positive sign that the body is getting rid of accumulated toxins that were previously stored. The severity of any symptoms you experience will depend on the level of toxins present in your system, and on how strictly and for how long you follow a detox programme. These symptoms may also be a reaction to withdrawing foods, such as coffee or alcohol, to which you may be allergic or dependent on.

There is no need to take painkillers or other medicines, as the symptoms will soon pass. Painkillers can also be detrimental to detoxing. Simply drink plenty of water or herbal teas to flush the toxins out, and get plenty of rest.

You may also lose weight on a detox because you've cut out eating fatty and sugary foods and alcohol, all of which are high in calories, as well as removing foods that have encouraged water retention. Weight loss is not the main aim of a detox, but if you are overweight, it can be an added benefit.

A well-balanced diet is vital for good health. Detox diets are restrictive and should only be followed occasionally and for no longer than the maximum time recommended.

CAFFEINE WITHDRAWAL

Sudden removal of caffeine can cause the same symptoms as regularly drinking too many caffeine drinks. If you regularly drink six or more cups a day, cut down gradually over a couple of weeks to avoid withdrawal headaches and irritability.

One- and two-week detox meal planners

WEEK 1	Monday	Tuesday	Wednesday
Breakfast	• Raspberry and Oatmeal Blend • 1 banana	• Pineapple and Ginger Juice • Dried Fruit Compote with low-fat probiotic yogurt	• Cranberry juice • Luxury Muesli with non-dairy milk
Lunch	• Bean Salad with Tuna and Red Onion • Pear or apple	• Chilled Tomato and Fresh Basil Soup • Hummus with rice cakes and vegetable crudités • Handful of blueberries	• Citrus Fruit Salad with Avocado • Low-fat probiotic yogurt with fresh strawberries
Evening Meal	• Stir-fried Vegetables with Cashew Nuts • Wholegrain rice • Fresh fruit salad	• Tagine of Yam, Carrots and Prunes • Quinoa • Fresh pineapple	• Slice of melon • Turkish-style New Potato Casserole • Mixed Green Leaf and Herb Salad

One- and two-week detox meal planners **47**

Thursday	**Friday**	**Saturday**	**Sunday**
• ½ fresh grapefruit • Porridge made with water or non-dairy milk	• Fresh chilled unsweetened apple juice • Granola with non-dairy milk or probiotic yogurt	• Tropical Scented Fruit Salad • Scrambled egg with red pepper and fresh basil	• Mango and Lime Lassi • Porridge with Dates and Pistachio Nuts
• Country Mushroom, Bean and Barley Soup • Rye or pumpernickel bread • Handful of dried fruits	• Roasted Peppers with Sweet Cicely • Orange or banana	• American Red Bean Soup with Guacamole Salsa • Minted Pomegranate Yogurt with Grapefruit Salad	• Pan-fried Chicken with Pesto • Roasted Plum Tomatoes with Garlic • New potatoes • Strawberry and Lavender Sorbet
• Seared Tuna Steaks with Tomato Salsa • Wild Rocket and Cos Lettuce Salad with Herbs • Poached Pears in Scented Honey Syrup	• Rice Noodles with Vegetable Chilli Sauce • Fresh fruit salad	• Teriyaki Salmon • Herby Rice Pilaf or basmati rice • Steamed broccoli • Nectarines Baked with Nuts	• Stir-fried Vegetables and Seeds • Orange or banana

The detox diet

WEEK 2	Monday	Tuesday	Wednesday
Breakfast	• Apricot and Ginger Smoothie • Handful of mixed unsalted nuts and seeds	• Figs and Pears in Honey • Boiled egg with rye crispbread, spread with yeast extract or nut butter	• Strawberry and Tofu Smoothie
Lunch	• Baked potato topped with stir-fried vegetables • Orange or satsuma	• Warm Chicken and Tomato Salad with Hazelnut Dressing • Banana or apple	• New Spring Vegetable Salad • Fresh seasonal fruit salad or piece of fruit
Evening Meal	• Aromatic Chickpea and Spinach Curry • Wholegrain rice • Strawberries with Passion Fruit Sauce	• Roasted Cod with Fresh Tomato Sauce • Green beans and new potatoes • Papaya and Green Grapes with Mint Sauce	• Brown Rice Risotto with Mushrooms • Mixed Green Leaf and Herb Salad • Baked Apples with Figs and Walnuts

One- and two-week detox meal planners **49**

Thursday	Friday	Saturday	Sunday
• Lime and Watermelon Tonic • Porridge made with water or non-dairy milk	• Fresh raspberries layered with low-fat probiotic yogurt and sprinkled with granola	• Fruit salad • Luxury Muesli with non-dairy milk	• Summer Fruit Smoothie • Mushroom omelette with grilled tomatoes
• Salad Niçoise • Oatcakes or rice cakes • Grapes or other fresh fruit	• Warm Mixed Seafood and Herb Salad • Summer Berry Frozen Yogurt	• Artichoke and Cumin Dip with vegetable crudités • Roasted Peppers with Sweet Cicely • Green salad	• Tagliatelle with Vegetable Ribbons • Lemon Grass Skewers
• Penne with Green Vegetable Sauce • Rose Water-scented Oranges with Pistachio Nuts	• Griddled Chicken with Tomato Salsa • Minty Broad Beans with Lemon • Baked Peaches	• Chinese-style Steamed Trout • Stir-fried Broccoli with Sesame Seeds • Orange Granita with Strawberries	• Greek Salad • Baked potato topped with a spoonful of low-fat probiotic yogurt

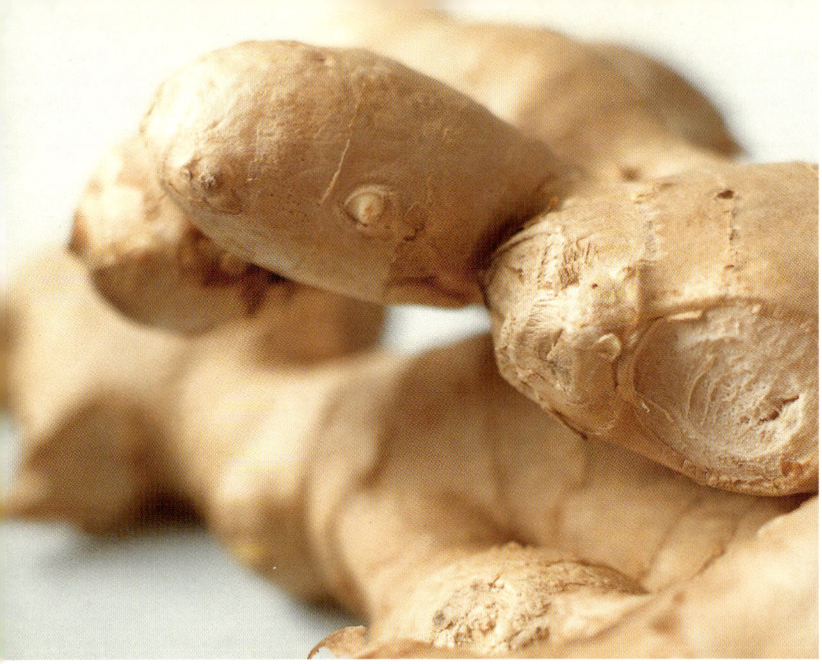
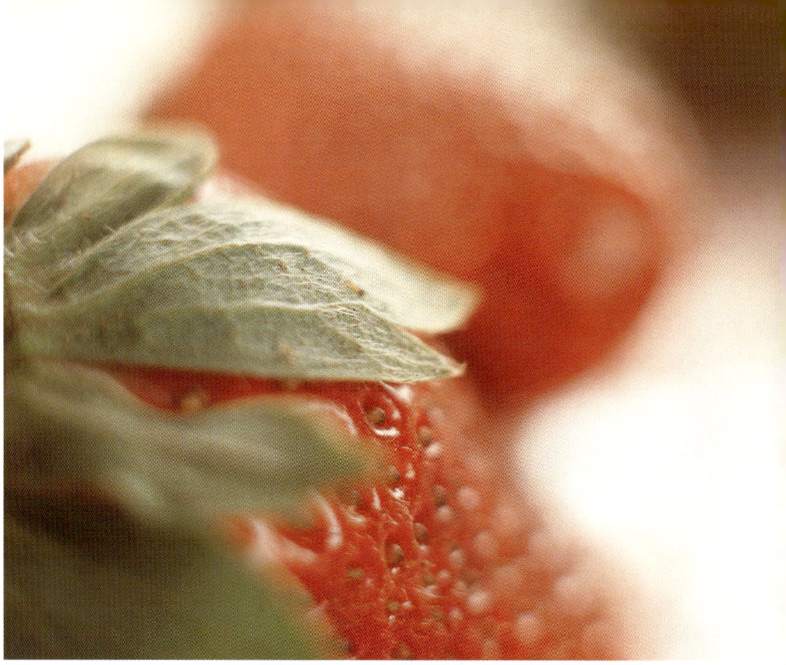
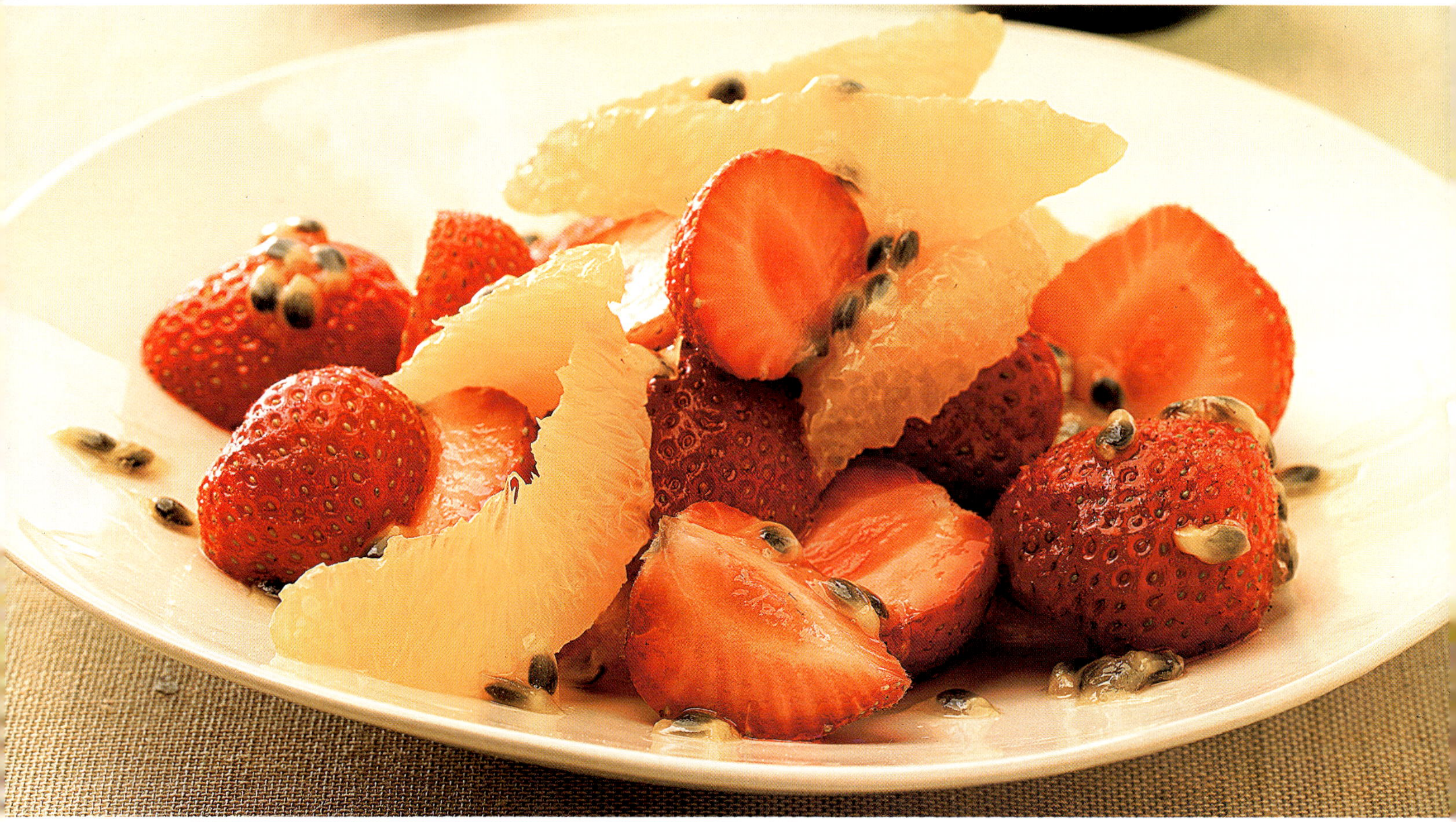
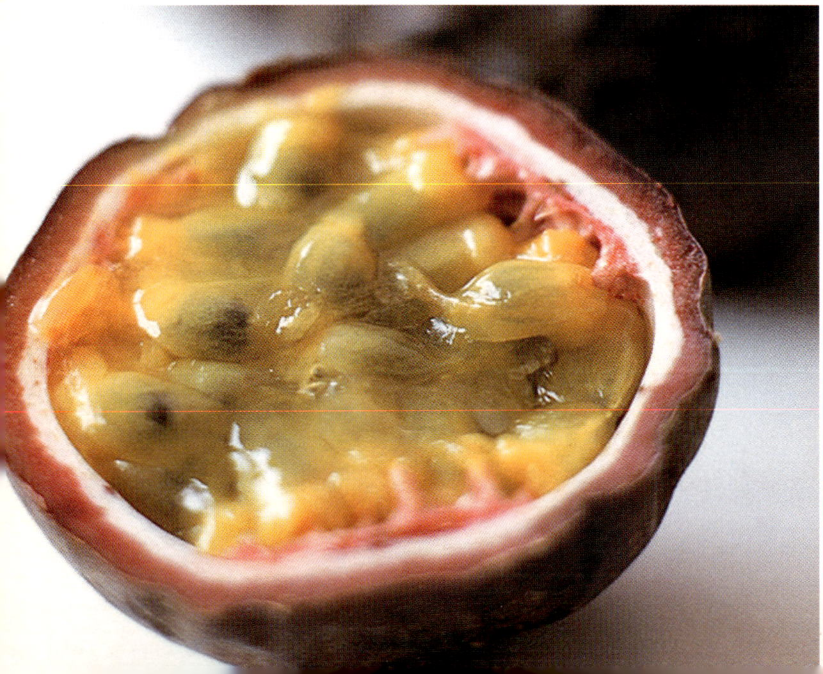
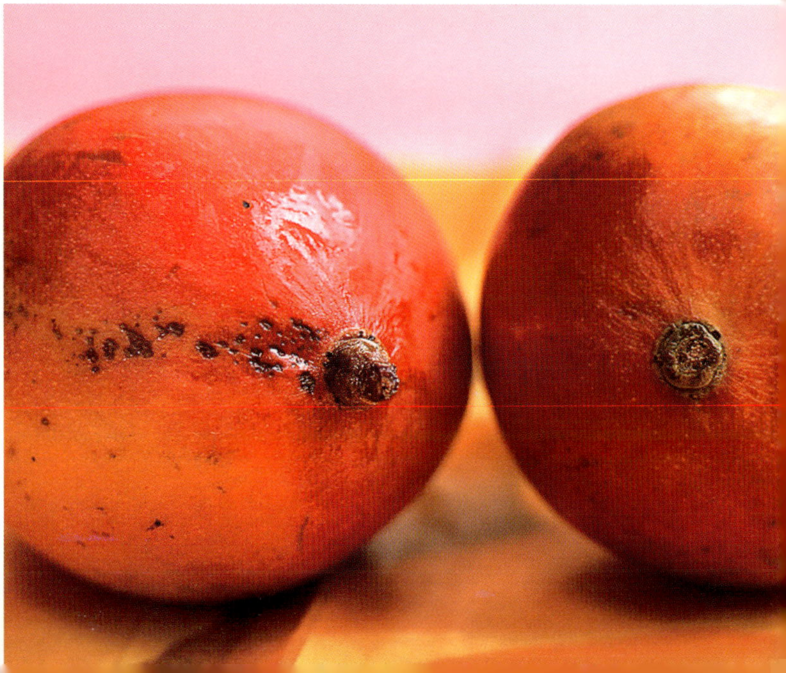

juices, smoothies and breakfast ideas

Start each day with a nourishing and sustaining breakfast. Many traditional breakfast foods such as wheat cereals and toast will not be an option while following a detox diet, but there are plenty of other delicious alternatives. Fruit and vegetables are rich in vitamins and high in fibre and have a powerful effect on the body, stimulating the digestive system. Enjoy them as juices, smoothies and fruit salads, or, for a more substantial meal, tuck into muesli, granola or porridge.

52 juices, smoothies and breakfast ideas

Pineapple and ginger juice

Fresh root ginger is one of the best natural cures for indigestion and it helps to settle upset stomachs, whether caused by food poisoning or motion sickness. In this unusual fruity blend, it is simply mixed with fresh, juicy pineapple and sweet-tasting carrot, creating a quick and easy remedy that can be juiced up in minutes – and which tastes delicious too.

Serves 1

½ small pineapple
25g/1oz fresh root ginger
1 carrot
ice cubes

Cook's tip
Before preparing the pineapple, turn it upside down and leave for 30 minutes – this makes it juicier.

1 Using a sharp knife, cut away the skin from the pineapple, then halve and remove the core. Roughly slice the pineapple flesh. Peel and roughly chop the ginger, then chop the carrot.

2 Push the carrot, ginger and pineapple through a juicer and pour into a glass. Add ice cubes and serve immediately.

Energy 120Kcal/516kJ; Protein 1.1g; Carbohydrate 30.2g, of which sugars 29.9g; Fat 0.4g, of which saturates 0.1g; Cholesterol 0mg; Calcium 33mg; Fibre 1.2g; Sodium 33mg.

juices, smoothies and breakfast ideas **53**

Lime and watermelon tonic

This refreshing juice will help to cool the body, calm the digestion and cleanse the system – and may even have aphrodisiac qualities. What more could you ask from a juice? It even looks enticing. The real magic of this drink, however, lies in its flavour. The light, watermelon taste is fresh on the palate, while the honey warms the throat – but it is the tart lime that gives it the edge.

Serves 4

1 watermelon
1 litre/1¾ pints/4 cups chilled water
juice of 2 limes
clear honey, to taste
ice cubes, to serve

1 Using a sharp knife, chop the watermelon into chunks, cutting off the skin and discarding the black seeds.

2 Place the watermelon chunks in a large bowl, pour the chilled water over and leave to stand for 10 minutes.

3 Strain the watermelon chunks, then push them through a juicer.

4 Stir in the lime juice and sweeten to taste with honey. Pour into a jug (pitcher), add ice cubes and stir. Serve in wide, chunky glasses.

Cook's tip
If the weather is really hot, why not enjoy this as a frozen slush? Freeze, stirring often, and when crystals begin to form, serve immediately.

Energy 114Kcal/486kJ; Protein 1.3g; Carbohydrate 27.3g, of which sugars 27.3g; Fat 0.8g, of which saturates 0.3g; Cholesterol 0mg; Calcium 18mg; Fibre 0.3g; Sodium 7mg.

Raspberry and oatmeal blend

A spoonful of oatmeal gives substance to this tangy, invigorating drink. If you can, prepare it ahead of time because soaking the raw oats before you blend them helps to break down the starch into natural sugars that are easy to digest. Yogurt provides a useful source of calcium when detoxing, as other dairy foods are temporarily avoided.

Serves 1

25ml/1½ tbsp medium oatmeal
150g/5oz/scant 1 cup raspberries
5–10ml/1–2 tsp clear honey
45ml/3 tbsp low-fat probiotic yogurt

Health benefits

Probiotic yogurt is especially beneficial to the digestive system. However, all live yogurt helps to restore the balance of healthy bacteria in the gut and to reduce most gastro-intestinal problems.

1 Spoon the oatmeal into a large heatproof bowl, then pour in about 120ml/4fl oz/½ cup boiling water. Leave the mixture to stand for about 10 minutes or until the water has been completely absorbed.

2 Put the soaked oats in a blender or food processor and add all but two or three of the raspberries, the honey and about 30ml/2 tbsp of the yogurt. Process until smooth, scraping the mixture down from the side of the bowl if necessary.

3 Pour the raspberry and oatmeal smoothie into a large glass, swirl in the remaining yogurt and top with raspberries. Chill the smoothie in the refrigerator until you are ready to drink it – it will thicken up so you might need to add a little juice or mineral water before serving.

Cook's tips

- If you don't like raspberry pips (seeds) in your smoothies, simply press the fruit through a sieve with the back of a wooden spoon to make a smooth purée, then process with the oatmeal and yogurt as before. Alternatively, you could try using redcurrants instead of the raspberries.
- Although a steaming bowl of porridge cannot be beaten as a warming winter breakfast, this smooth, oaty drink makes a great, light alternative, particularly in warmer months. It is a good way to make sure you get your fill of wholesome oats for breakfast.

Energy 177Kcal/756kJ; Protein 7.5g; Carbohydrate 32.3g, of which sugars 14.1g; Fat 3.1g, of which saturates 0.4g; Cholesterol 1mg; Calcium 137mg; Fibre 5.5g; Sodium 51mg.

juices, smoothies and breakfast ideas 55

Strawberry and tofu smoothie

This energizing blend is simply bursting with goodness. Not only is tofu a great source of protein, it is also rich in minerals, particularly calcium, and contains nutrients that help to protect against diseases. Tofu is naturally bland in flavour and therefore makes an ideal, versatile ingredient for including in smoothies, as it will blend with many different fruits.

Serves 2

250g/9oz silken tofu
200g/7oz/1¾ cups strawberries
45ml/3 tbsp pumpkin or sunflower seeds, plus extra for sprinkling
15–30ml/1–2 tbsp clear honey
juice of 2 large oranges
juice of 1 lemon

1 Roughly chop the tofu, then hull the strawberries and chop them. Reserve a few strawberry chunks to garnish.

2 Put all of the ingredients into a blender or food processor and blend until completely smooth and creamy, scraping the mixture down from the side of the bowl, if necessary.

Cook's tips
• Almost any other fruit can be used instead of the strawberries. Those that blend well, such as mangoes, bananas, peaches, plums and raspberries, are especially good substitutes. Frozen mixed berry fruits would also work well and are handy for keeping in the freezer.
• Tofu can be bought fresh or in a long-life pack. Try to find silken tofu, as it has a satiny texture that blends particularly well in a blender or food processor.

3 Pour into tumblers and sprinkle with extra seeds and strawberry chunks.

Energy 289Kcal/1204kJ; Protein 15.7g; Carbohydrate 21.2g, of which sugars 16.9g; Fat 16.1g, of which saturates 1.7g; Cholesterol 0mg; Calcium 684mg; Fibre 2.5g; Sodium 18mg.

Summer fruit smoothie

Long after summer is over you can still summon up the glorious flavours of the season by making this fruity and refreshing drink from frozen summer fruits. This low-fat fruity delight will pep up even the darkest mornings. Revitalize yourself with this blend before you leave for work in the morning to give your body a well-deserved boost.

1 Take the frozen fruits straight from the freezer and tip them into a blender or food processor.

2 Blend until the fruits are finely crushed, scraping down the side of the bowl, if necessary.

3 Add the yogurt to the crushed fruit, then blend again until the mixture is smooth and thick.

4 Taste and add a little honey to sweeten, if necessary.

5 Serve the smoothie immediately, decorated with fruit.

Cook's tip
You can use any mixture of soft berries and currants for this smoothie, either home-grown or bought frozen in bags.

Serves 2

250g/9oz/2 cups frozen summer fruits, plus extra to decorate
200g/7oz/scant 1 cup low-fat probiotic yogurt
clear honey, to taste

Energy 90Kcal/378kJ; Protein 6.1g; Carbohydrate 15g, of which sugars 15g; Fat 1.2g, of which saturates 0.5g; Cholesterol 1mg; Calcium 210mg; Fibre 1.4g; Sodium 91mg.

Apricot and ginger smoothie

Enjoy the perfect option for a healthy and nourishing breakfast in bed without the crumbs. This smoothie is packed with valuable vitamins and minerals and the dried apricots provide natural sweetness – so no added sugar is necessary. Choose whichever non-dairy milk you prefer, such as a rice, almond or soya alternative.

Serves 2

1 piece preserved stem ginger, plus 15ml/1 tbsp syrup from the ginger jar
50g/2oz/¼ cup ready-to-eat dried apricots, halved or quartered
40g/1½ oz/scant ½ cup unsweetened muesli
about 200ml/7fl oz/scant 1 cup non-dairy milk, chilled

1 Chop the preserved ginger and put it in a blender or food processor with the syrup, apricots, muesli and milk.

2 Process the mixture until smooth, adding more milk if necessary. Serve immediately in wide glasses.

Energy 167Kcal/706kJ; Protein 6g; Carbohydrate 29.3g, of which sugars 19g; Fat 3.3g, of which saturates 0.6g; Cholesterol 0mg; Calcium 42mg; Fibre 3.1g; Sodium 65mg.

Mango and lime lassi

A tangy, fruity blend of ripe mango, cooling probiotic yogurt, and sharp fresh lime and lemon juice makes a wonderfully satisfying, flavoursome drink that's refreshing and packed with energy. Mango makes a thick purée when it is blended, so chilled mineral water is added to dilute the mixture to a consistency that is suitable for drinking.

Health benefits
Mango is a rich souce of both betacarotene (which the body can convert into vitamin A) and vitamin C. Both these vitamins act as antioxidants, boosting the immune system and helping to prevent cell damage by free radicals.

Serves 2

1 mango
finely grated rind and juice of 1 lime
15ml/1 tbsp lemon juice
clear honey, to taste
100ml/3½fl oz/scant ½ cup low-fat probiotic yogurt
mineral water, to dilute
1 extra lime, halved, to serve

1 Peel the mango and cut the flesh from the stone (pit). Put the flesh into a food processor or blender and add the lime rind and juice.

2 Add the lemon juice, honey to taste and probiotic yogurt. Whizz the mixture until completely smooth, scraping down the sides once or twice.

3 Stir a little chilled mineral water into the mixture to thin it down to the required consistency for drinking. Serve immediately, with half a lime on the side of each glass so that more juice can be squeezed in if desired.

Energy 71Kcal/302kJ; Protein 3.1g; Carbohydrate 14.3g, of which sugars 14.1g; Fat 0.7g, of which saturates 0.4g; Cholesterol 1mg; Calcium 104mg; Fibre 2g; Sodium 43mg.

Tropical scented fruit salad

This fresh fruit salad makes a perfect start to the day. For extra flavour and colour, try using two small blood oranges and two ordinary oranges. Other fruit could be added, such as pears, kiwi fruit or bananas. Oranges and strawberries are both great sources of vitamin C, and the passion fruit adds an intense exotic fragrance, as well as further vitamin value and fibre.

Serves 4

400g/14oz/3½ cups strawberries, hulled and halved
4 oranges, peeled and segmented
2 passion fruit
120ml/4fl oz/½ cup fresh, chilled tropical fruit juice

Cook's tip
Passion fruit should feel heavy for their size and have a dimpled skin. If the skin is smooth, the fruit is not quite ripe.

1 Put the hulled and halved strawberries and peeled and segmented oranges into a bowl.

2 Halve the passion fruit and using a teaspoon scoop the flesh into the bowl.

3 Pour the tropical fruit juice over the fruit and toss gently. Cover and chill in the refrigerator or serve immediately.

Energy 87Kcal/371kJ; Protein 2.4g; Carbohydrate 20g, of which sugars 20g; Fat 0.3g, of which saturates 0g; Cholesterol 0mg; Calcium 78mg; Fibre 3.5g; Sodium 14mg.

Figs and pears in honey

A simple breakfast idea that combines lightly cooked fresh figs and pears. Both fruits have good fibre value and therefore help to promote the digestion and to cleanse the system. This makes a tempting combination of fruits for the autumnal months, when pears are at their seasonal best. Alternatively, serve this dish as a dessert.

Serves 4

1 lemon
30ml/2 tbsp clear honey
1 cinnamon stick
1 cardamom pod
2 pears
8 fresh figs, halved

Cook's tip
To vary the flavour, substitute the pears with eating apples or add a kick to the syrup by adding 2.5cm/1in peeled, bruised fresh root ginger in step 2. You could also omit the cardamom or cinnamon stick if you don't like their flavours.

1 Pare the rind from the lemon using a zester or vegetable peeler, avoiding the white pith, then cut into very thin strips.

2 Place the lemon rind, honey, cinnamon stick, cardamom pod and 350ml/12fl oz/1½ cups water in a pan and bring to the boil. Boil for 10 minutes until reduced by about half.

3 Cut the pears into eighths, discarding the cores. Place the pears in the syrup, add the figs and simmer gently for about 5 minutes until the fruit is tender.

4 Remove and discard the cinnamon stick and cardamom pod, then transfer the fruit to a serving bowl. Serve warm or chilled.

Energy 143Kcal/606kJ; Protein 1.7g; Carbohydrate 34.4g, of which sugars 34.4g; Fat 0.7g, of which saturates 0g; Cholesterol 0mg; Calcium 109mg; Fibre 4.7g; Sodium 28mg.

Dried fruit compote

Dried fruit, although slightly higher in sugar – and therefore calories – than fresh, supplies significant amounts of minerals, notably iron and potassium, and fibre as well as useful amounts of energy. This makes a satisfying and sustaining bowlful to start the morning and can be served with low-fat probiotic yogurt if you like.

Serves 4

350g/12oz/2 cups mixed dried fruits, such as apples, pears, prunes, peaches
1 cinnamon stick
65g/2½oz/½ cup raisins
30ml/2 tbsp clear honey
juice of ½ lemon
mint leaves, to decorate (optional)

Cook's tip
This compote will keep well, chilled in the refrigerator. If you are following the longer detox plan, for one or two weeks, it is well worth making enough for several servings that you can eat as and when you are ready. Look for unsulphured fruit, which is available from health food stores, especially if you suffer from asthma.

1 Put the mixed dried fruit in a large pan with the cinnamon stick and pour over 300ml/½ pint/1¼ cups water.

2 Heat gently until almost boiling, then cover the pan, lower the heat and cook gently for 12–15 minutes until the fruit is plumped up and softened.

3 Remove the pan from the heat, add the raisins and honey and stir gently.

4 Cover the pan with a lid and leave the compote to cool. Once cooled, remove the cinnamon stick and stir in the lemon juice.

5 Transfer the compote to a serving bowl, cover with clear film (plastic wrap) and keep refrigerated until needed.

6 Before serving, remove the fruit compote from the fridge and allow to return to room temperature.

7 Decorate with a few fresh mint leaves before serving, if you like.

Energy 189Kcal/807kJ; Protein 2.6g; Carbohydrate 46.8g, of which sugars 46.8g; Fat 0.4g, of which saturates 0g; Cholesterol 0mg; Calcium 38mg; Fibre 5.3g; Sodium 20mg.

Luxury muesli

The benefit of making your own muesli at home is that you can combine a wide variety of seeds, grains, nuts and dried fruits to make a nutrient-packed breakfast, which is also free from added sugar. Use this recipe as a basic guide, but you can alter the balance of ingredients, or substitute others, according to your personal preferences.

Serves 4

50g/2oz/½ cup sunflower seeds
25g/1oz/¼ cup pumpkin seeds
175g/6oz/1½ cups porridge oats
175g/6oz/1½ cups barley flakes
115g/4oz/1 cup raisins
115g/4oz/1 cup chopped hazelnuts, roasted
115g/4oz/½ cup dried apricots (preferably unsulphured), finely chopped
50g/2oz/2 cups dried apple slices, halved
25g/1oz/⅓ cup desiccated coconut

1 Put the sunflower and pumpkin seeds in a dry frying pan and cook over a medium heat for 3 minutes until golden, tossing the seeds regularly to prevent them burning.

2 Mix the toasted seeds with the remaining ingredients and leave to cool. Store in an airtight container. Serve with non-dairy milk – this can be a rice, almond or soya substitute.

Granola

Oats, nuts and seeds, combined with sweet dried fruits, make an excellent and nutritious start to the day – without any of the additives often found in pre-packed cereals. Serve the granola with your choice of non-dairy milk or low-fat probiotic yogurt and top with plenty of seasonal fresh fruit. It can also be eaten as a healthy snack at any time of the day.

Serves 4

115g/4oz/1 cup porridge oats
115g/4oz/1 cup jumbo oats
50g/2oz/½ cup sunflower seeds
25g/1oz/2 tbsp sesame seeds
50g/2oz/½ cup hazelnuts, roasted
25g/1oz/¼ cup almonds, roughly chopped
50ml/2fl oz/¼ cup sunflower oil
50ml/2fl oz/¼ cup clear honey
50g/2oz/½ cup raisins
50g/2oz/½ cup dried sweetened cranberries

1 Preheat the oven to 140°C/275°F/Gas 1. Mix together the oats, seeds and nuts in a bowl.

2 Heat the oil and honey in a pan until combined, then remove from the heat. Add the oat mixture and stir, then spread out on one or two baking sheets.

3 Bake for about 50 minutes until crisp, stirring occasionally to prevent the mixture sticking.

4 Remove from the oven and mix in the raisins and cranberries. Leave to cool, then store in an airtight container.

Health benefits
Oats have been the focus of much publicity in recent years; numerous scientific studies have shown that their soluble fibre content can significantly lower blood cholesterol levels.

Variation
Include any unsalted nuts you like in this granola. Try roughly chopped walnuts, cashews, pecans or Brazil nuts. You can lightly toast the nuts before chopping, if you like.

Top: Energy 813Kcal/3411kJ; Protein 20.8g; Carbohydrate 100.9g, of which sugars 33.4g; Fat 39g, of which saturates 5.5g; Cholesterol 0mg; Calcium 145mg; Fibre 12.4g; Sodium 55mg.
Above: Energy 638Kcal/2674kJ; Protein 14.4g; Carbohydrate 72.3g, of which sugars 27.9g; Fat 34.3g, of which saturates 2.9g; Cholesterol 0mg; Calcium 132mg; Fibre 6.9g; Sodium 39mg.

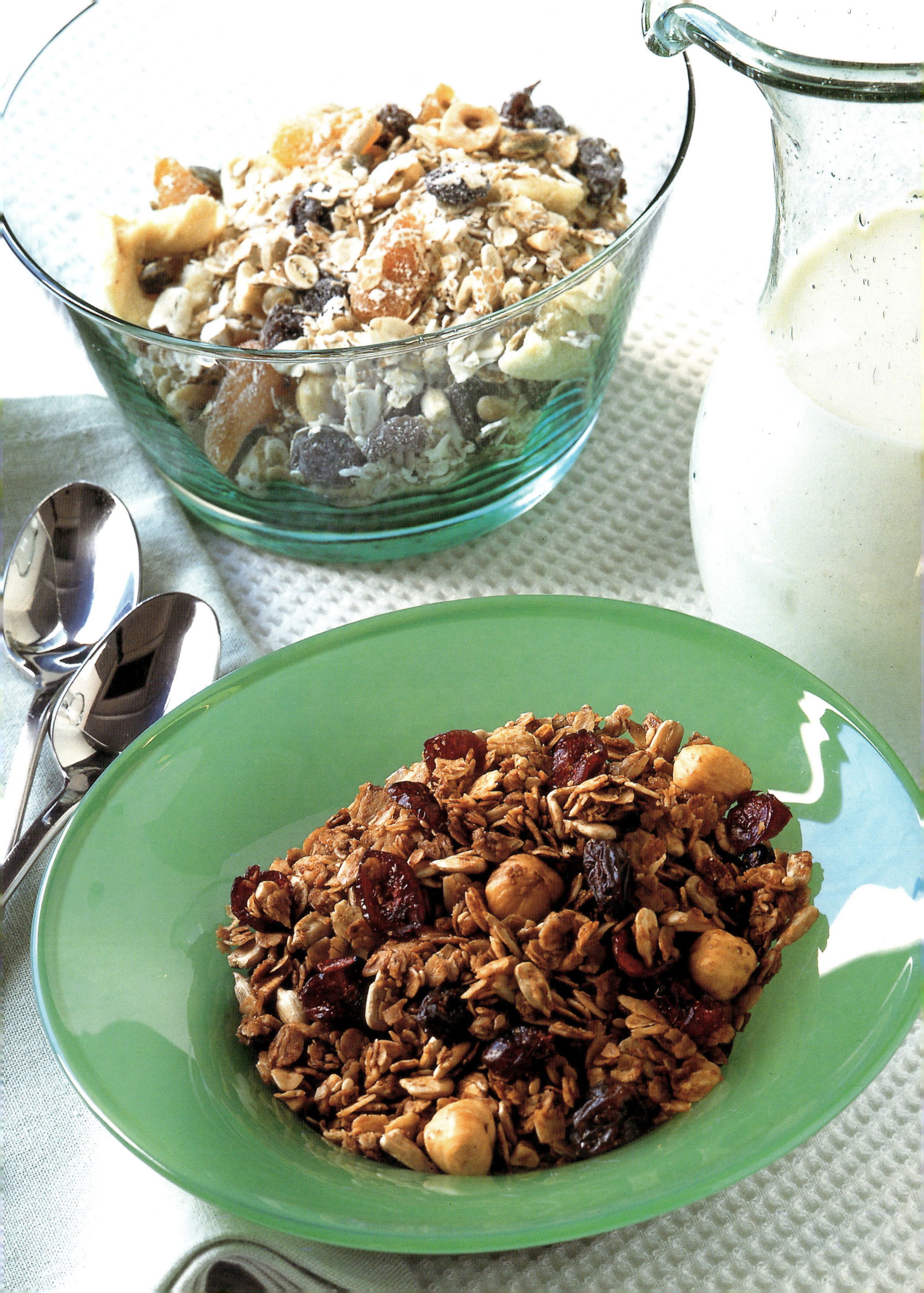

Traditional Scottish porridge

One of Scotland's oldest foods, oatmeal porridge gets your day off to a super-healthy start. This recipe uses traditional pinhead oatmeal, but you can use rolled oats if you prefer. Oats contain gluten and are therefore unsuitable for people with coeliac disease. If this is the case, millet flakes can be used instead to make a good alternative porridge.

Serves 4

1 litre/1¾ pints/4 cups water
115g/4oz/1 cup pinhead oatmeal
pinch of salt
clear honey, to taste
non-dairy milk, to serve

Variation
Rolled oats can be used, if preferred. This cooks more quickly than pinhead oatmeal. Simmer, stirring to prevent sticking, for about 5 minutes.

1 Put the water, pinhead oatmeal and salt into a heavy pan and bring to the boil over a medium heat, stirring with a wooden spatula. When the porridge is smooth and beginning to thicken, reduce the heat to a simmer.

2 Cook gently for about 25 minutes, stirring occasionally, until the oatmeal is cooked and the consistency smooth. Sweeten to taste with honey, and serve hot with non-dairy milk. Top with fresh fruit, such as banana (optional).

Energy 115Kcal/488kJ; Protein 3.6g; Carbohydrate 20.9g, of which sugars 0g; Fat 2.5g, of which saturates 0g; Cholesterol 0mg; Calcium 16mg; Fibre 2g; Sodium 10mg.

Porridge with dates and pistachio nuts

Full of valuable fibre and nutrients, puréed fresh dates give a natural sweet flavour to this warming winter breakfast dish, so there is no need for any added sugar. The addition of this fruit and nut topping makes your porridge all the more nourishing and exciting. You could use prunes or dried apricots in place of the dates, and any unsalted nuts in place of the pistachios, if you prefer.

Serves 4

250g/9oz/scant 2 cups fresh dates
225g/8oz/2 cups rolled oats
475ml/16fl oz/2 cups non-dairy milk
pinch of salt
50g/2oz/½ cup shelled, unsalted pistachio nuts, roughly chopped

Health benefits
Oats have a reputation for being warming foods due to their fat and protein content, which is greater than that of most other grains. As well as providing energy and endurance, particularly in the colder months, oats are one of the most nutritious cereals.

1 First make the date purée. Halve the dates and remove the stones (pits) and stems. Cover with boiling water and soak for 30 minutes, until softened. Strain, reserving 90ml/6 tbsp of the soaking water.

2 Remove the skin from the dates and purée them in a food processor with the reserved soaking water.

3 Place the oats in a pan with the milk, 300ml/½ pint/1¼ cups water and salt. Bring to the boil, then reduce the heat and simmer for 4–5 minutes until cooked, stirring frequently.

4 Serve the porridge in warm serving bowls, topped with a spoonful of the date purée and sprinkled with chopped pistachio nuts.

Energy 416Kcal/1754kJ; Protein 13.6g; Carbohydrate 62.5g, of which sugars 21.2g; Fat 13.8g, of which saturates 1.3g; Cholesterol 0mg; Calcium 75mg; Fibre 5.7g; Sodium 127mg.

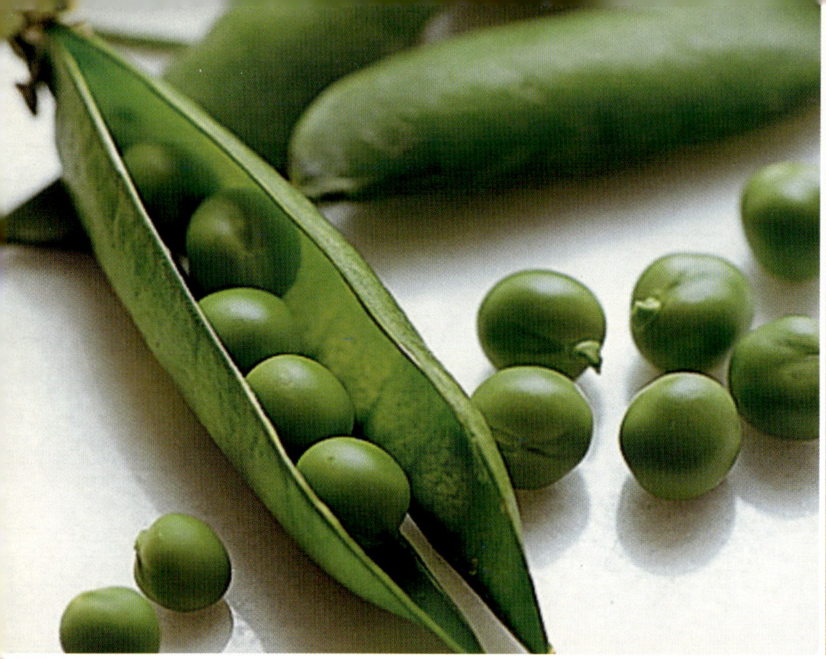
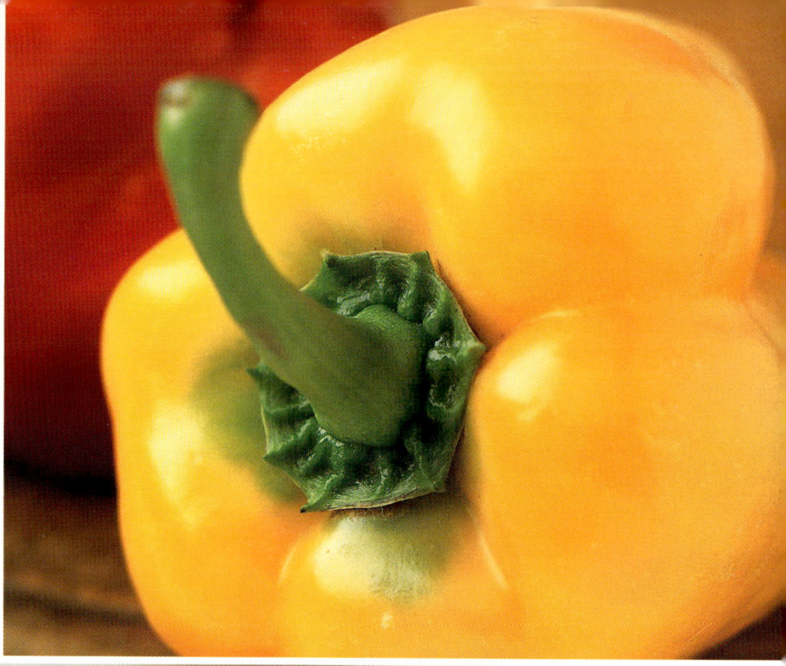
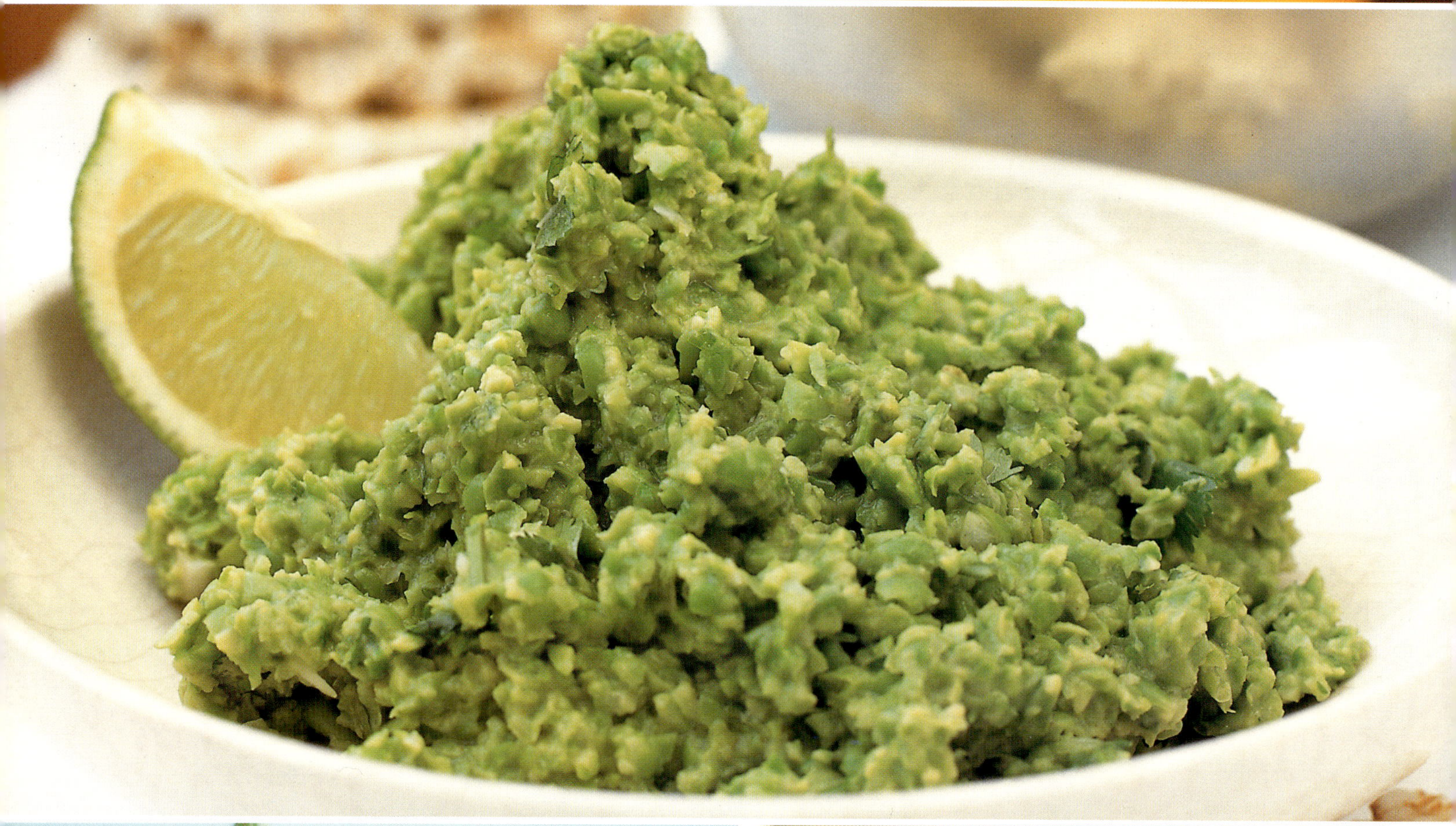
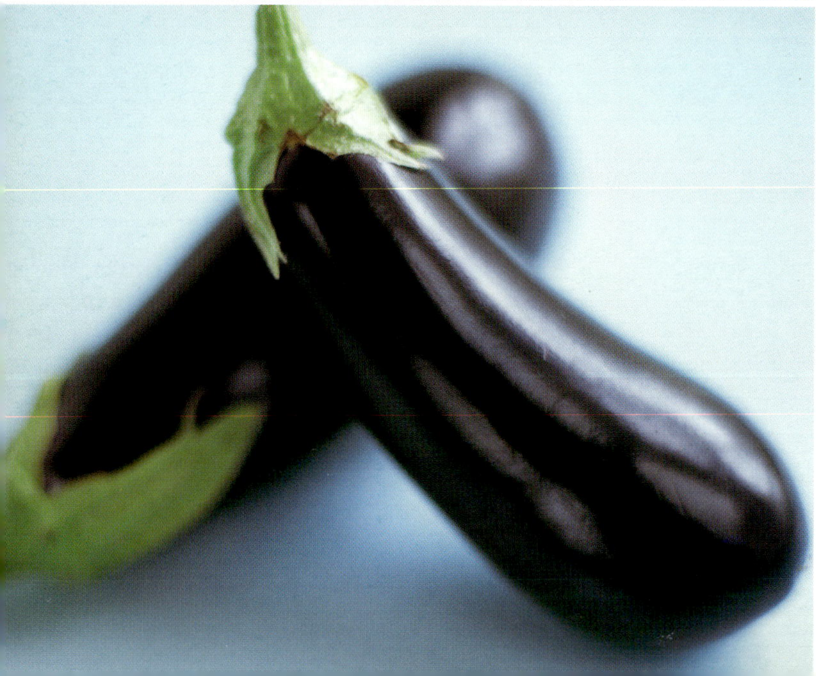
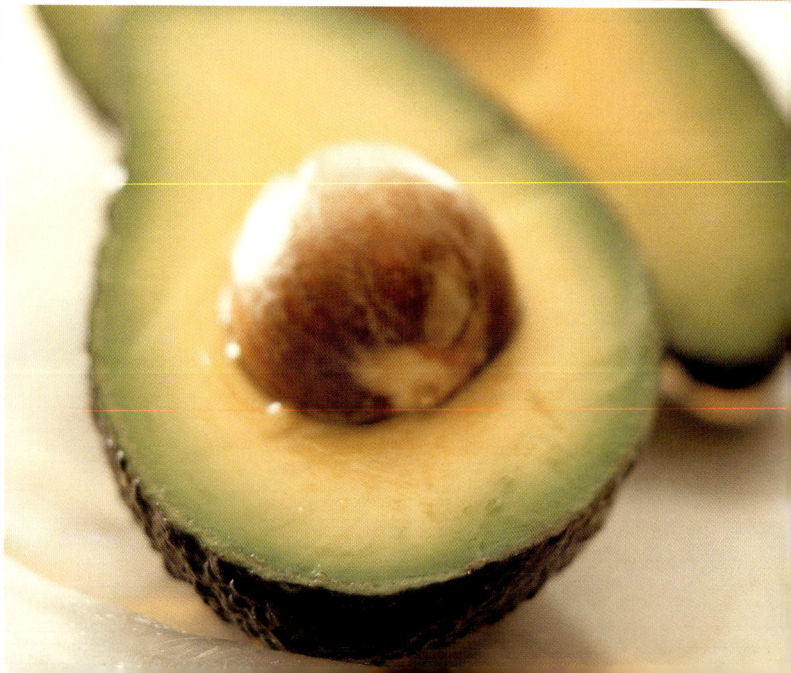

appetizers and snacks

Whether you want a light lunch or supper dish, a healthy snack or a tempting appetizer to lead into a main meal, this section includes delicious ideas for both everyday and special occasions. Vegetable dips served with crudités or rice cakes make a good detox choice, or how about stuffed, roasted peppers or griddled polenta?

Hummus

This creamy purée combines chickpeas, garlic, lemon juice, olive oil and tahini to produce a tasty snack, appetizer or light meal that is rich in vegetable protein. Serve with a selection of raw fruit and vegetable crudités for extra fibre and vitamin value.

1 Put the chickpeas in a bowl, cover with plenty of cold water and leave to soak overnight.

2 Drain, place in a pan and cover with fresh water. Bring to the boil and boil rapidly for 10 minutes. Reduce the heat and simmer gently for about 1 hour until soft. Drain.

3 Process the chickpeas in a food processor or blender until smooth. Add the lemon juice, garlic, olive oil, cayenne pepper and tahini and blend until creamy. Season with pepper and transfer to a serving dish. Sprinkle with oil and cayenne pepper. Garnish with parsley and serve with cherry tomatoes.

4 To make the crudités, trim and peel the carrots and quarter lengthways. Halve the celery sticks lengthways and trim to the same length as the carrots.

5 Core, quarter and thickly slice the apple and pear, then dip into the lemon or lime juice. Arrange with the baby corn in a bowl or on a platter.

Serves 4

150g/5oz/¾ cup dried chickpeas
juice of 2 lemons
2 garlic cloves, sliced
30ml/2 tbsp olive oil
pinch of cayenne pepper
150ml/¼ pint/⅔ cup tahini
freshly ground black pepper
extra olive oil and cayenne pepper, for sprinkling
flat leaf parsley, to garnish
cherry tomatoes, to serve

For the crudités
6 baby carrots
2 celery sticks
1 eating apple
1 pear
15ml/1 tbsp lemon or lime juice
6 baby corn

Cook's tip
You can use a 400g/14oz can of chickpeas if you prefer.

Energy 453Kcal/1887kJ; Protein 15.7g; Carbohydrate 32.1g, of which sugars 13.8g; Fat 30g, of which saturates 4.2g; Cholesterol 0mg; Calcium 345mg; Fibre 10.5g; Sodium 49mg.

Pea guacamole

This is a variation on the more classic avocado guacamole and provides another delicious idea for including more vegetables in your diet. It's based on frozen peas, which are a good source of vitamin C and fibre, as well as being convenient to use, straight from the freezer.

Serves 4

350g/12oz/3 cups frozen peas, completely defrosted
1 garlic clove, crushed
2 spring onions (scallions), trimmed and chopped
5ml/1 tsp finely grated rind and juice of 1 lime
2.5ml/½ tsp ground cumin
dash of Tabasco sauce
15ml/1 tbsp extra virgin olive oil
30ml/2 tbsp roughly chopped fresh coriander (cilantro)
ground black pepper
pinch of cayenne and lime slices, to garnish
brown rice cakes, to serve

1 Put the peas, garlic, spring onions, lime rind and juice, cumin, Tabasco sauce, olive oil and ground black pepper into a food processor and process for a few minutes until smooth.

2 Add the chopped fresh coriander and process for a few more seconds.

3 Spoon into a serving bowl, cover with clear film (plastic wrap) and chill for about 30 minutes.

4 Sprinkle over the cayenne, garnish with the lime slices and serve with brown rice cakes.

Energy 103Kcal/425kJ; Protein 6.5g; Carbohydrate 10.4g, of which sugars 2.5g; Fat 4.3g, of which saturates 0.7g; Cholesterol 0mg; Calcium 45mg; Fibre 4.8g; Sodium 5mg.

Avocado guacamole

A highly nutritious dip, based on avocados, onion and tomatoes spiked with fresh chilli, garlic, toasted cumin seeds and lime. The avocados are half mashed and half diced for an interesting texture. This makes a great dish to serve with lightly salted corn chips as an appetizer or light meal, or it could be served as a salsa on the side of plain grilled fish or chicken.

Serves 4

2 large ripe avocados
1 small red onion, finely chopped
1 fresh red or green chilli, seeded and very finely chopped
1 garlic clove, crushed
finely shredded rind of ½ lime and juice of 1–1½ limes
225g/8oz tomatoes, seeded and chopped
30ml/2 tbsp roughly chopped fresh coriander (cilantro)
2.5–5ml/½–1 tsp ground toasted cumin seeds
15ml/1 tbsp olive oil
ground black pepper
lime wedges and fresh coriander (cilantro) sprigs, to garnish
lightly salted corn chips, to serve (optional)

1 Cut one of the avocados in half and lift out and discard the stone (pit). Scrape the flesh from both halves into a bowl and mash it roughly with a fork.

2 Add the onion, chilli, garlic, lime rind, tomatoes and coriander and stir well. Add the ground cumin seeds and pepper to taste, then stir in the olive oil.

3 Halve and stone the remaining avocado. Dice the flesh and stir it into the guacamole.

4 Squeeze in fresh lime juice to taste, mix well, then cover and leave to stand for 15 minutes so that the flavour develops. Serve with lime wedges and garnish with fresh coriander sprigs.

Energy 187Kcal/771kJ; Protein 2.4g; Carbohydrate 4.7g, of which sugars 3.3g; Fat 17.6g, of which saturates 3.5g; Cholesterol 0mg; Calcium 41mg; Fibre 4g; Sodium 14mg.

Artichoke and cumin dip

This dip is easy to make and unbelievably tasty. Globe artichokes contain compounds, including a substance called cynarin, believed to have a range of medicinal properties, including helping to give a boost to a sluggish liver. Serve with raw vegetable crudités for dipping, during your detox, or breadsticks or wholemeal pitta after your detox.

Serves 4

2 x 400g/14oz cans artichoke hearts, drained
2 garlic cloves, peeled
2.5ml/½ tsp ground cumin
olive oil
ground black pepper

Cook's tip
For extra flavour, add a handful of fresh basil leaves to the artichokes before blending.

1 Put the artichoke hearts in a food processor with the garlic and ground cumin, and a generous drizzle of olive oil. Process to a smooth purée and season with black pepper to taste.

2 Spoon the purée into a serving bowl and serve with an extra drizzle of olive oil swirled on the top. Serve with a selection of raw vegetable crudités, for dipping.

Energy 76Kcal/315kJ; Protein 2g; Carbohydrate 3.9g, of which sugars 2g; Fat 6g, of which saturates 0.8g; Cholesterol 0mg; Calcium 85mg; Fibre 2.7g; Sodium 121mg.

Spiced carrot dip

This delicious and unusual dip combines the sweet flavour of carrots and oranges with the light spiciness of a mild curry paste. The addition of low-fat yogurt creates a creamy texture and mellows the spice flavour. Serve with crisp raw celery and cucumber sticks for dipping as an appetizer or as a healthy snack at any time of the day.

Serves 4

1 onion
3 carrots, plus extra to garnish
grated rind and juice of 2 oranges
15ml/1 tbsp mild curry paste
150ml/¼ pint/⅔ cup low-fat
   probiotic yogurt
handful of fresh basil leaves
15–30ml/1–2 tbsp fresh lemon juice,
   to taste
Tabasco sauce, to taste (optional)
ground black pepper
celery and cucumber sticks,
   to serve

1 Finely chop the onion. Peel and grate the carrots, then place the onion, carrots, orange rind and juice, together with the curry paste in a small pan. Bring to the boil, cover and simmer gently for 10 minutes, until the vegetables are tender.

2 Process the mixture in a blender or food processor until smooth. Leave to cool completely.

3 Stir in the yogurt. Then tear the basil leaves roughly into small pieces and stir them into the carrot mixture so that everything is well combined.

4 Add the lemon juice and Tabasco, if using, and season with pepper to taste. Chill in the refrigerator until shortly before serving.

5 Garnish lightly with some grated raw carrot. Serve with raw celery and cucumber sticks for dipping.

Energy 60Kcal/248kJ; Protein 2.6g; Carbohydrate 9.9g, of which sugars 9.2g; Fat 1.4g, of which saturates 0.4g; Cholesterol 1mg; Calcium 94mg; Fibre 2g; Sodium 50mg.

Aubergine dip

Another idea for a vegetable dip, this time made with grilled aubergines flavoured with garlic, tahini, cumin, mint and lemon for a Middle Eastern taste sensation. The dip can be enjoyed with raw vegetable crudités while you are following the detox diet, but afterwards, Lebanese flatbread makes an ideal and complementary accompaniment.

Serves 6

2 small aubergines (eggplants)
1 garlic clove, crushed
60ml/4 tbsp tahini
25g/1oz/¼ cup ground almonds
juice of ½ lemon
2.5ml/½ tsp ground cumin
30ml/2 tbsp fresh mint leaves
30ml/2 tbsp olive oil
ground black pepper

LEBANESE FLATBREAD
4 pitta breads
45ml/3 tbsp toasted sesame seeds
45ml/3 tbsp chopped fresh thyme
45ml/3 tbsp poppy seeds
150ml/¼ pint/⅔ cup olive oil

1 Split the pitta breads through the middle and open them out.

2 Mix the sesame seeds, chopped thyme and poppy seeds in a mortar. Crush them lightly with a pestle to release the flavour.

3 Stir in the olive oil. Spread the mixture lightly over the cut sides of the pitta bread. Grill until they are golden brown and crisp. When completely cool, break into pieces and set aside.

---

1 Place the aubergines on the rack of a grill (broiler) pan. Grill the aubergines, turning them frequently, until the skin is blackened and blistered. Remove the skin, chop the flesh and leave to drain in a colander. Wait for 30 minutes, then squeeze out as much liquid from the aubergines as possible.

2 Process the flesh in a blender or food processor with the garlic, tahini, almonds, lemon juice and cumin. Season, chop half the mint and stir in.

3 Spoon into a bowl, scatter the remaining mint leaves on top and drizzle with olive oil.

Energy 129Kcal/535kJ; Protein 3.3g; Carbohydrate 1.9g, of which sugars 1.6g; Fat 12.2g, of which saturates 1.6g; Cholesterol 0mg; Calcium 85mg; Fibre 2.5g; Sodium 4mg.

Roasted peppers with sweet cicely

The sweet aniseed flavours of sweet cicely and fennel combine beautifully with the succulent tastes of the peppers and tomatoes and the piquancy of capers. Both sweet cicely and fennel are good herbal aids to digestion. This dish can be served as a light lunch or as an unusual appetizer for a dinner party during the warm summer months.

Serves 4

4 red or yellow (bell) peppers, halved and seeded
8 small or 4 medium tomatoes
15ml/1 tbsp semi-ripe sweet cicely seeds
15ml/1 tbsp fennel seeds
15ml/1 tbsp capers, rinsed
4 sweet cicely flowers, newly opened, stems removed
60ml/4 tbsp olive oil

For the garnish

a few small sweet cicely leaves
8 more flowers

1 Preheat the oven to 180°C/350°F/Gas 4. Place the red pepper halves in a large ovenproof dish and set aside.

2 To skin the tomatoes, cut a cross at the base, then put in a bowl and pour over boiling water. Leave them to stand for 1 minute. Cut in half if they are of medium size, or leave whole if small. Place a whole small or half a medium tomato in each half of a pepper cavity.

3 Cover with a scattering of sweet cicely seeds, fennel seeds and capers and about half the sweet cicely flowers. Drizzle the olive oil all over. Bake in for 1 hour. Serve hot, garnished with fresh sweet cicely leaves and flowers.

Variation
If sweet cicely is not available, this dish can be made with a range of different herbs, such as chervil or lovage, although they will all impart a distinctive flavour.

Energy 172Kcal/714kJ; Protein 2.5g; Carbohydrate 14.3g, of which sugars 13.8g; Fat 12g, of which saturates 1.9g; Cholesterol 0mg; Calcium 21mg; Fibre 3.8g; Sodium 16mg.

Griddled polenta with tangy pebre

Polenta is a good wheat-free starchy carbohydrate. Here it is flavoured with chillies and fresh herbs, then left to firm up before being cut into triangles to cook on a griddle. It's served with a tangy salsa from Chile called pebre, which combines onion, chilli, sweet cherry peppers and coriander. It makes an unusual and tasty appetizer.

Serves 6

10ml/2 tsp crushed dried chilli flakes
1.3 litres/2¼ pints/5⅔ cups water
250g/9oz/1¼ cups quick cook polenta
30ml/2 tbsp chopped fresh dill
30ml/2 tbsp chopped fresh coriander (cilantro)
45ml/3 tbsp olive oil

For the pebre

½ red onion, finely chopped
4 drained bottled sweet cherry peppers, finely chopped
1 fresh medium-hot red chilli, seeded and finely chopped
1 small red (bell) pepper, quartered and seeded
10ml/2 tsp cider vinegar
30ml/2 tbsp olive oil
4 tomatoes, halved, cored, seeded and roughly chopped
45ml/3 tbsp chopped fresh coriander (cilantro)

1 Put the chilli flakes in a pan with the water and bring to the boil. Pour the polenta into the water in a continuous stream, whisking all the time. Reduce the heat and continue to whisk for a few minutes.

2 When the polenta is thick and bubbling, whisk in half the olive oil and herbs. Pour into a greased 33 x 23cm/ 13 x 9in baking tray and leave to cool. Leave uncovered so that the surface firms up and chill overnight.

3 To make the pebre, place the onion, sweet cherry peppers and chilli in a mortar. Dice the red pepper finely and add it to the mortar with the cider vinegar and olive oil.

4 Pound the mixture with a pestle for about 1 minute, then tip into a serving dish. Stir in the tomatoes and coriander. Cover with clear film (plastic wrap) and leave in a cool place.

5 Remove the polenta from the refrigerator and leave it at room temperature for about 30 minutes.

6 Cut into 12 even triangles and brush the top with the remaining olive oil.

7 Heat a griddle until a few drops of water sprinkled on the surface evaporate instantly. Lower the heat to medium and grill the polenta triangles in batches oiled-side down for about 2 minutes, then turn through 180 degrees and cook for 1 minute more, to get a striking chequered effect. Serve immediately, with the pebre.

Variation

Any mixture of fresh herbs can be used in the polenta triangles, such as basil and chives, for a really distinctive flavour without adding any salt.

Energy 254Kcal/1060kJ; Protein 4.8g; Carbohydrate 33.7g, of which sugars 3g; Fat 10.9g, of which saturates 1.4g; Cholesterol 0mg; Calcium 25mg; Fibre 2.2g; Sodium 9mg.

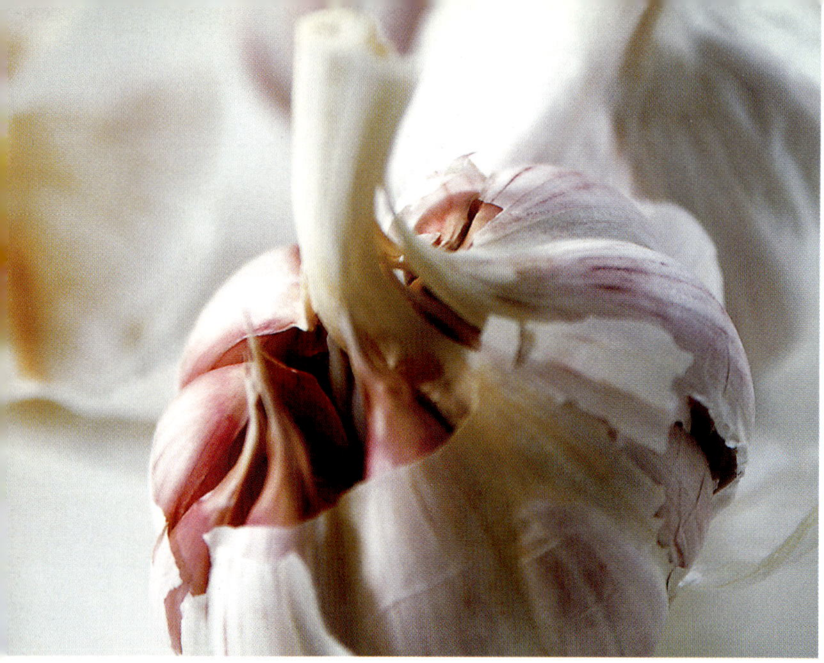
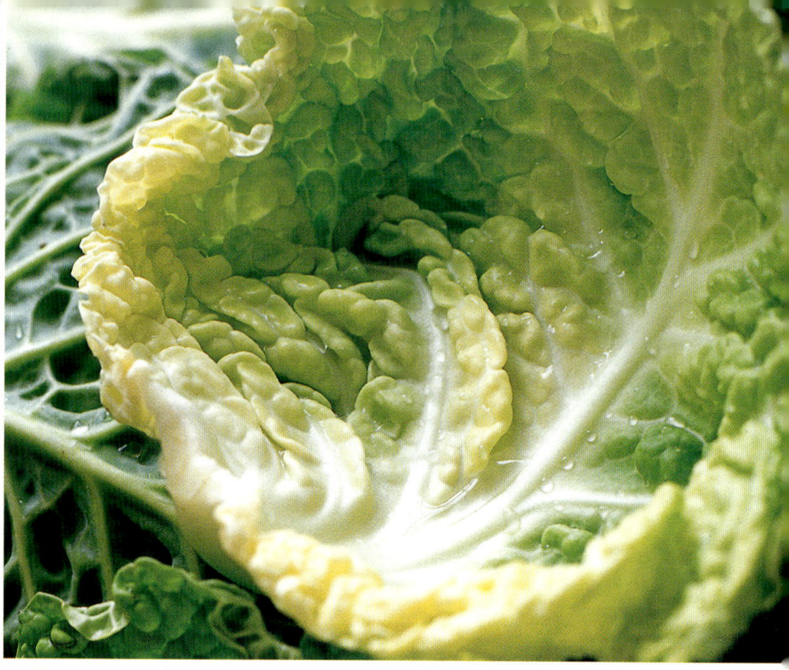
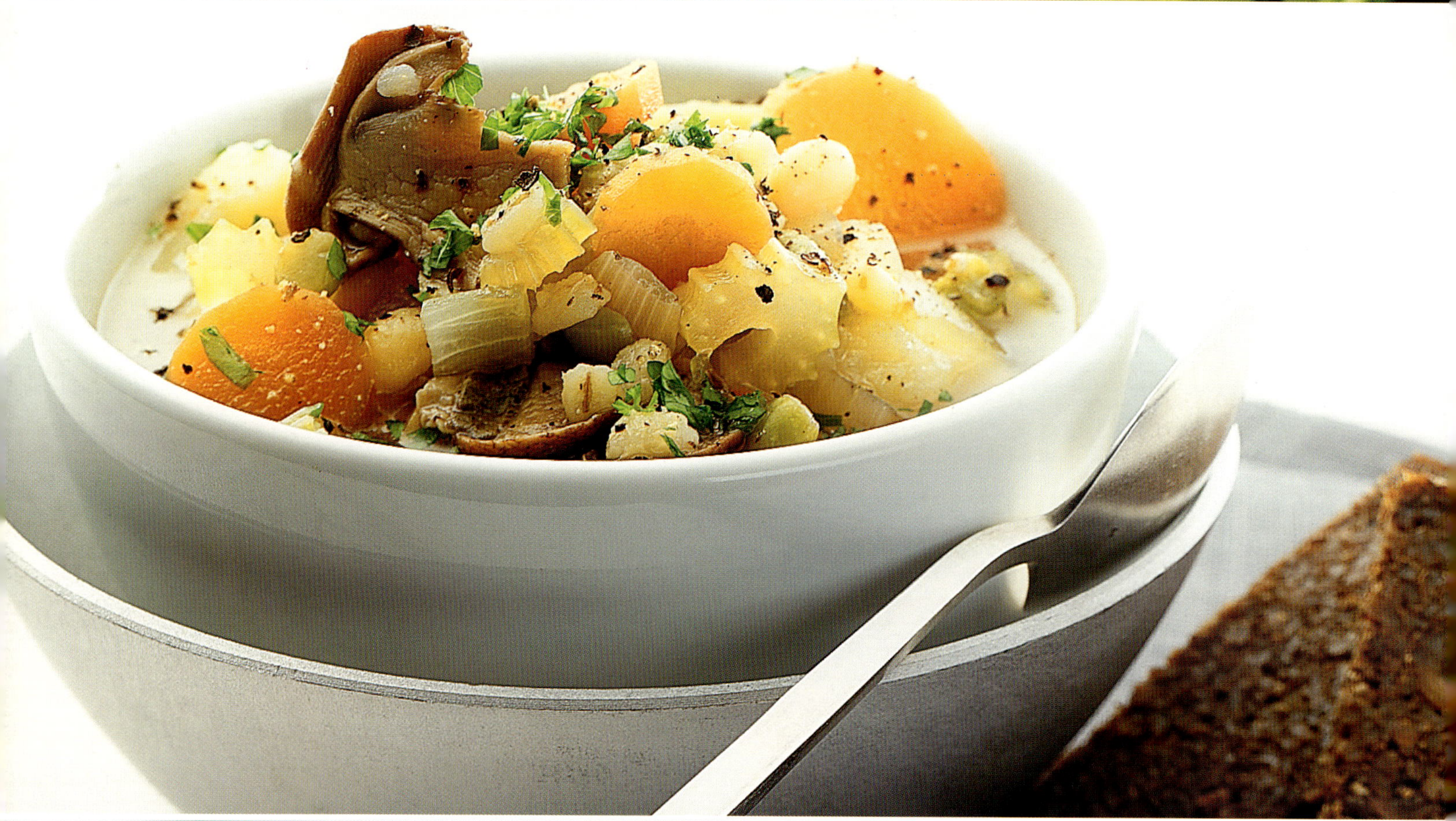
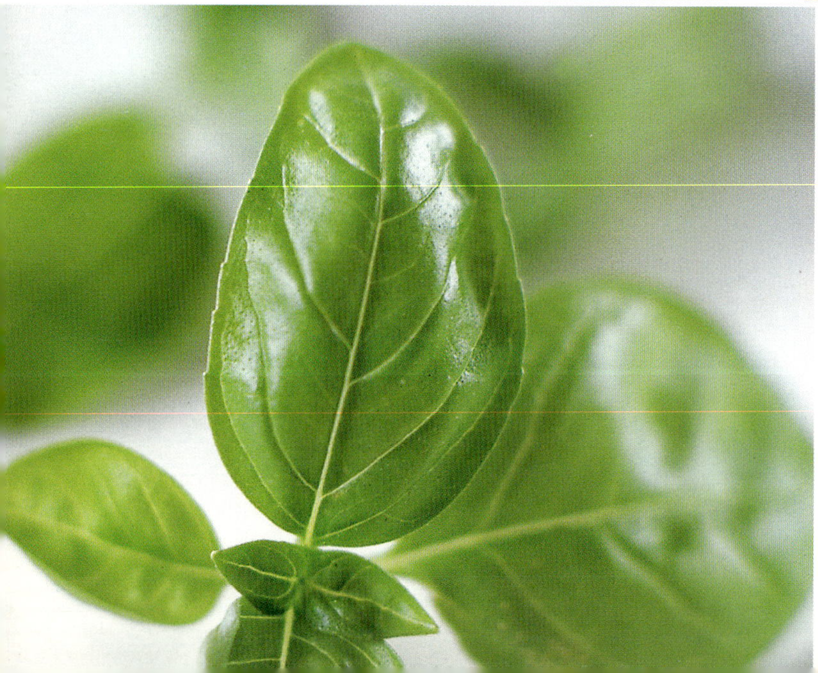
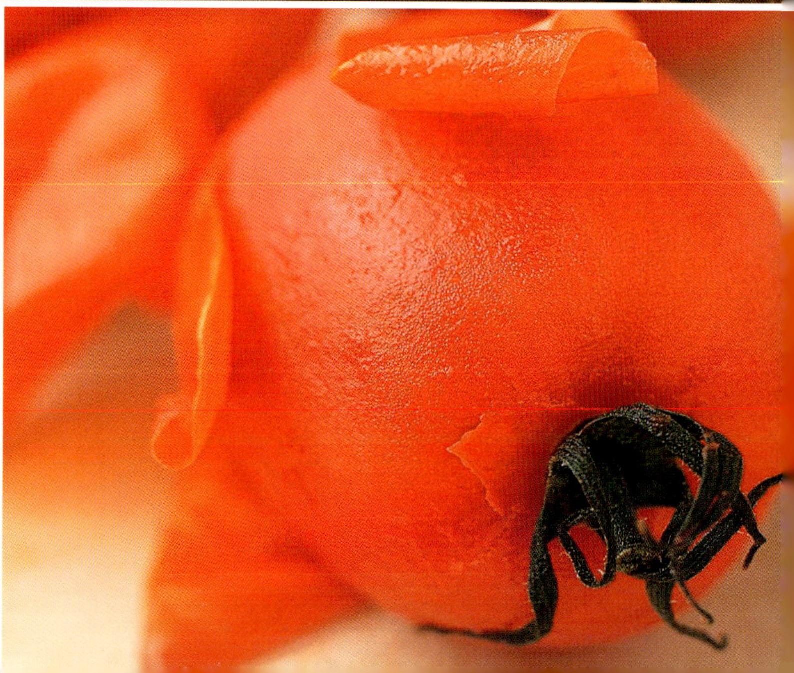

simply sensational soups

Soups are full of vegetable goodness and provide tempting and satisfying lunch or supper dishes all year round, whatever the weather. Tuck into classic favourites such as Fresh Cabbage Soup, or Chilled Tomato and Fresh Basil Soup, or treat your tastebuds to Fragrant Thai Fish Soup or American Red Bean Soup with Guacamole Salsa.

Chilled tomato and fresh basil soup

A refreshing chilled soup for late summer when fresh tomatoes are at their most flavoursome. Tomatoes provide valuable amounts of antioxidant vitamins as well as lypocene, which is thought to protect against certain types of cancer. Distinctively peppery basil, a classic partner to tomatoes, aids digestion and calms the nervous system.

Serves 4

45ml/3 tbsp olive oil
1 onion, finely chopped
900g/2lb ripe Italian plum tomatoes, roughly chopped
1 garlic clove, roughly chopped
about 1.5 litres/2½ pints/6¼ cups vegetable stock
30ml/2 tbsp sun-dried tomato paste
30ml/2 tbsp shredded fresh basil, plus a few whole leaves, to garnish
ground black pepper

1 Heat the oil in a large pan. Add the onion and cook gently for about 5 minutes, stirring frequently, until softened but not brown.

2 Stir in the chopped tomatoes and garlic, then add the vegetable stock, sun-dried tomato paste and ground black pepper to season.

3 Bring to the boil, then lower the heat, half cover the pan and simmer gently for 20 minutes, stirring occasionally.

4 Transfer the soup to a blender or food processor, add the shredded fresh basil and process. Press the blended soup through a sieve (strainer) into a clean pan. Gently heat through, stirring. Do not allow the soup to boil. Add more stock if necessary.

5 Leave to cool, then chill in the refrigerator for 2–3 hours. Serve in chilled bowls, garnished with basil.

Energy 107Kcal/448kJ; Protein 2.8g; Carbohydrate 10.3g, of which sugars 9.9g; Fat 6.4g, of which saturates 1g; Cholesterol 0mg; Calcium 49mg; Fibre 3.4g; Sodium 55mg.

Fresh cabbage soup

This hearty vegetable soup is good for the digestion. It's based on the popular diet recipe for cabbage soup, but includes a variety of vegetables, namely turnip, carrots, onion and celery as well as apple. You can use any variety of cabbage that's in season or another member of the same family, such as Brussels sprouts or broccoli, shredded or roughly chopped.

Serves 4

45ml/3 tbsp olive oil
1 small turnip, cut into matchstick strips
2 carrots, cut into matchstick strips
1 large onion, sliced
2 celery sticks, sliced
1 white or green cabbage, about 675g/1½lb, shredded
1.2 litres/2 pints/5 cups vegetable stock
1 sharp eating apple, cored, peeled and chopped
2 bay leaves
5ml/1 tsp chopped fresh parsley
10ml/2 tsp lemon juice
ground black pepper
fresh herbs, to garnish
low-fat probiotic yogurt and rye bread, to serve

1 Heat the oil in a large pan and gently fry the turnip, carrots, onion and celery for 10 minutes.

Health benefits
Cabbage is an excellent detoxifier and is reputed to aid the digestion, detoxify the stomach and upper bowels, cleanse the liver and reduce the risk of certain cancers. It is also rich in folate, vitamins C and E, potassium, iron, betacarotene and thiamin, and is well known for its potent antiviral and antibacterial qualities.

2 Coarsely shred the cabbage, and add to the pan. Pour in the vegetable stock, add the chopped apple, bay leaves and chopped parsley and bring to the boil. Cover and simmer for 40 minutes or until the vegetables are really tender.

3 Remove and discard the bay leaves, then stir in the lemon juice and season with freshly ground black pepper.

4 Serve hot, garnished with fresh herbs and accompanied by low-fat probiotic yogurt and rye bread.

Variation
Create a red, super-detox version of this cleansing soup by substituting the carrots with beetroot (beets) and the white or green cabbage with red cabbage.

Energy 167Kcal/694kJ; Protein 3.6g; Carbohydrate 19g, of which sugars 17.4g; Fat 8.9g, of which saturates 1.2g; Cholesterol 0mg; Calcium 121mg; Fibre 6.3g; Sodium 31mg.

Tomato and lentil soup

Lentils are a nourishing staple and make an excellent detox soup to serve as a satisfying lunch or supper dish. Unlike other dried beans and peas, lentils do not need soaking before cooking and therefore make an easy option for a quick meal. You can use brown or green lentils – both retain their shape after cooking, unlike the split variety.

Serves 4

275g/10oz/1¼ cups brown or green lentils, thoroughly rinsed
30ml/2 tbsp extra virgin olive oil
1 onion, thinly sliced
2 garlic cloves, sliced into thin matchsticks
1 carrot, thinly sliced
400g/14oz can chopped tomatoes
15ml/1 tbsp tomato purée (paste)
2.5ml/½ tsp dried oregano
1 litre/1¾ pints/4 cups hot water
ground black pepper
30ml/2 tbsp roughly chopped fresh herb leaves, to garnish

1 Put the lentils in a pan with cold water to cover. Bring the water to the boil and boil for 3–4 minutes. Strain, discarding the liquid, and set the lentils aside.

2 Wipe the pan clean and add the olive oil. Place it over a medium heat until hot and then add the thinly sliced onion and sauté until translucent.

3 Stir in the sliced garlic, then, as soon as it becomes aromatic, return the lentils to the pan. Add the carrot, tomatoes, tomato purée and oregano. Stir in the hot water and a little ground black pepper to taste.

4 Bring the soup to the boil, then lower the heat, cover the pan and cook gently for 20–30 minutes, or until the lentils are soft. Stir in the chopped herbs just before serving, and taste to check the seasoning.

Energy 298Kcal/1261kJ; Protein 17.6g; Carbohydrate 44.5g, of which sugars 7.3g; Fat 6.8g, of which saturates 1.1g; Cholesterol 0mg; Calcium 50mg; Fibre 5.1g; Sodium 59mg.

Black-eyed bean and tomato broth

This delicious bean soup is delicately flavoured with fragrant spices and tangy lemon, and has a mild chilli kick. It makes a hearty and warming lunch or light supper dish that is perfect for a cold winter day. Like all beans, peas and lentils, these pale, oval beans are an excellent source of fibre and vegetable protein, and they also provide valuable vitamins and minerals.

Serves 4

175g/6oz/1 cup dried black-eyed beans (peas)
15ml/1 tbsp olive oil
2 onions, chopped
4 garlic cloves, chopped
1 medium-hot or 2–3 mild fresh chillies, chopped
5ml/1 tsp ground cumin
5ml/1 tsp ground turmeric
250g/9oz fresh or canned tomatoes, diced
600ml/1 pint/2½ cups vegetable stock
25g/1oz fresh coriander (cilantro) leaves, roughly chopped
juice of ½ lemon

1 Put the beans in a pan, cover with cold water, bring to the boil and cook for 5 minutes. Remove from the heat, cover and leave to stand for 2 hours.

2 Drain the beans, return to the pan, cover with fresh cold water, then simmer for 35–40 minutes, or until the beans are tender. Drain and set aside.

3 Heat the oil in a pan, add the onions, garlic and chilli and cook for 5 minutes, or until the onion is soft.

4 Stir in the cumin, turmeric, tomatoes, stock, half the coriander and the beans and simmer for 20–30 minutes.

5 Stir in the lemon juice and the remaining coriander just before serving.

Cook's tip
Black-eyed beans have a creamy texture and distinctive flavour. They are characterized by a small black eye, and although they are often called beans, they are also known as black-eyed peas.

Energy 222Kcal/934kJ; Protein 14.3g; Carbohydrate 31.8g, of which sugars 10.9g; Fat 5.1g, of which saturates 0.6g; Cholesterol 0mg; Calcium 273mg; Fibre 13.9g; Sodium 50mg.

American red bean soup with guacamole salsa

This spicy soup is in Tex-Mex style, and it is served with a cooling avocado and lime salsa. It's packed with vitamins, minerals, protective compounds and fibre, all vital in a healthy diet.

2 Cool the soup slightly, then purée it in a food processor or blender until smooth. Return to the pan and season.

3 To make the guacamole salsa, halve, stone (pit) and peel the avocados, then dice them finely. Place in a small bowl and gently, but thoroughly, mix with the finely chopped red onion and chilli, and the coriander and lime juice.

4 Reheat the soup and ladle into bowls. Spoon a little guacamole salsa into the middle of each and serve, offering Tabasco sauce separately, if liked.

Serves 6

30ml/2 tbsp olive oil
2 onions, chopped
2 garlic cloves, chopped
10ml/2 tsp ground cumin
1.5ml/¼ tsp cayenne pepper
15ml/1 tbsp paprika
15ml/1 tbsp tomato purée (paste)
2.5ml/½ tsp dried oregano
400g/14oz can chopped tomatoes
2 x 400g/14oz cans red kidney beans, drained and rinsed
900ml/1½ pints/3¾ cups water
ground black pepper
Tabasco sauce, to serve (optional)

For the guacamole salsa
2 avocados
1 small red onion, finely chopped
1 green chilli, seeded and chopped
15ml/1 tbsp chopped fresh coriander (cilantro)
juice of 1 lime

1 Heat the oil in a pan, add the onions and garlic and cook for 4–5 minutes. Add the cumin, cayenne and paprika, and cook for 1 minute. Stir in the tomato purée and cook for a few seconds, then stir in the oregano. Add the chopped tomatoes, kidney beans and water. Bring to the boil and simmer for 15–20 minutes.

Energy 198Kcal/833kJ; Protein 10.4g; Carbohydrate 30.1g, of which sugars 10g; Fat 4.8g, of which saturates 0.7g; Cholesterol 0mg; Calcium 113mg; Fibre 9.7g; Sodium 534mg.

Country mushroom, bean and barley soup

This hearty main meal vegetable soup is perfect on a freezing cold day. Serve in warmed bowls, with plenty of rye or pumpernickel bread on the side.

Serves 6

30ml/2 tbsp haricot (navy) beans, soaked overnight
2 litres/4½ pints/8½ cups water
45ml/3 tbsp green split peas
45ml/3 tbsp yellow split peas
90ml/6 tbsp pearl barley
1 onion, chopped
3 celery sticks, diced or sliced
5 garlic cloves, sliced
2 carrots, sliced
1 large baking potato, peeled and cut into chunks
10g/¼oz mixed dried mushrooms
ground black pepper
chopped fresh parsley, to garnish

1 Put the beans in a large pan, cover with water and bring to the boil. Boil for 10 minutes, then skim any froth from the surface. Add the green and yellow split peas, pearl barley, onion, celery and garlic.

2 Bring the mixture to the boil, then reduce the heat, cover and simmer gently for about 1½ hours, or until the beans are tender.

Cook's tip
Dried beans should be soaked in a bowl of cold water overnight to reduce the cooking time.

3 Add the carrots, potato and dried mushrooms and cook for a further 30 minutes, or until the beans and vegetables are tender.

4 Season to taste, then ladle into bowls, garnish with parsley and serve with rye or pumpernickel bread.

Energy 162Kcal/689kJ; Protein 6.8g; Carbohydrate 34.1g, of which sugars 4.3g; Fat 0.8g, of which saturates 0.1g; Cholesterol 0mg; Calcium 34mg; Fibre 2.9g; Sodium 30mg.

Leek and potato soup

Also called vichyssoise, this less rich version of the popular soup makes a comforting, warming lunch, which can be taken to work in a flask. The chopped vegetables produce a chunky soup, but if you prefer a smooth texture, press the mixture through a sieve. Onion and related vegetables contain valuable phytochemicals that may help prevent disease.

Serves 4

30ml/2 tbsp vegetable oil
2 leeks, washed and chopped
1 small onion, peeled and finely chopped
350g/12oz potatoes, peeled and chopped
900ml/1½ pints/3¾ cups vegetable stock
ground black pepper
chopped fresh parsley or chives, to garnish

Health benefits
Members of the onion family are good decongestants.

1 Heat the oil in a large pan over a medium heat. Add the leeks and onion and cook gently, stirring occasionally, for about 7 minutes, until they are softened but not browned.

2 Add the potatoes to the pan and cook for about 2–3 minutes, then add the stock and bring to the boil. Cover and simmer for 30–35 minutes.

3 Season to taste with ground black pepper and remove the pan from the heat. Serve sprinkled with the chopped fresh parsley or chives.

Cook's tips
• Don't use a food processor to purée this soup as it can give the potatoes a gluey consistency if you are not careful. The potatoes should be left to crumble and disintegrate naturally as they boil, which means that the the longer you leave them, the thicker the consistency of the soup will be.
• If you have time, you should make your own chicken or vegetable stock by simmering bones and vegetables in water for 2 hours and straining the liquid.

Energy 138Kcal/580kJ; Protein 3.3g; Carbohydrate 18.2g, of which sugars 4.2g; Fat 6.3g, of which saturates 1g; Cholesterol 0mg; Calcium 33mg; Fibre 3.3g; Sodium 12mg.

Fragrant Thai fish soup

This light and aromatic soup is made with chunks of monkfish simmered in a light stock, flavoured with lime, lemon grass, ginger, fresh coriander and chillies. Packed with flavour, it makes a perfect dinner dish. It is an excellent source of low-fat protein and contains many vitamins and minerals that are essential for good health.

Serves 4

1 litre/1¾ pints/4 cups fish stock
4 lemon grass stalks
3 limes
2 small fresh hot red chillies, seeded and thinly sliced
2cm/¾in piece fresh root ginger, peeled and thinly sliced
6 coriander (cilantro) stalks, with leaves
2 kaffir lime leaves, coarsely chopped (optional)
350g/12oz monkfish fillet, skinned and cut into 2.5cm/1in pieces
15ml/1 tbsp rice vinegar
30ml/2 tbsp Thai fish sauce
30ml/2 tbsp chopped fresh coriander (cilantro) leaves, to garnish

1 Pour the stock into a large pan and bring to the boil. Slice the bulb ends of the lemon grass diagonally into 3mm/⅛in thick pieces. Peel off four wide strips of lime rind with a vegetable peeler, avoiding the white pith. Squeeze the limes and reserve the juice.

2 Add the lemon grass, lime rind, chillies, ginger, and coriander stalks to the stock, with the kaffir lime leaves, if using. Simmer for 1–2 minutes.

3 Add the monkfish, vinegar, Thai fish sauce and half the reserved lime juice. Simmer for 3 minutes, until the fish is just tender. Although cooked, it will still hold its shape.

4 Remove the coriander stalks from the pan and discard. Taste the broth and add more lime juice if necessary. Serve the soup very hot, sprinkled with the chopped coriander leaves.

Variation
Other fish or shellfish such as sole, prawns (shrimp), scallops or squid can be substituted for the monkfish, if you like.

Energy 65Kcal/278kJ; Protein 14.4g; Carbohydrate 1g, of which sugars 0.8g; Fat 0.5g, of which saturates 0.1g; Cholesterol 12mg; Calcium 33mg; Fibre 0.6g; Sodium 554mg.

Chicken, avocado and chickpea soup

Ideally choose organic chicken and use home-made stock to make this soup. It will taste far superior and be free of chemical additives. Turkey breast could be used in place of chicken. Avocado adds a delicious creaminess and chickpeas complete the nutritional balance, making this a tasty, satisfying and nourishing main course soup.

Serves 4–6

1.5 litres/2½ pints/6¼ cups chicken stock
½ fresh chilli, seeded and thinly sliced
2 skinless, boneless chicken breast fillets
1 avocado
4 spring onions (scallions), finely sliced
400g/14oz can chickpeas, drained and rinsed
freshly ground black pepper

1 Pour the chicken stock into a large pan and add the chilli. Bring to the boil, add the whole chicken breast fillets, then lower the heat and simmer gently for about 10 minutes, or until the chicken is cooked.

2 Remove the pan from the heat and lift out the chicken breasts with a slotted spoon. Leave to cool a little.

3 Once it has has cooled, shred the chicken into small pieces using two forks. Set the shredded chicken aside.

Cook's tip
Handle chillies with care as they can irritate the skin and eyes. It is advisable to wear rubber gloves when preparing them.

4 Cut the avocado in half, remove the skin and stone (pit), then slice the flesh into 2cm/¾in pieces.

5 Add the avocado to the stock, with the spring onions and chickpeas.

6 Return the shredded chicken to the pan, and season to taste. Heat gently, then spoon into warmed bowls and serve immediately.

Energy 163Kcal/686kJ; Protein 17.3g; Carbohydrate 11.3g, of which sugars 0.5g; Fat 5.7g, of which saturates 1g; Cholesterol 35mg; Calcium 36mg; Fibre 3.4g; Sodium 178mg.

Chicken and leek soup with prunes

This recipe is based on the traditional Scottish soup cock-a-leekie and makes a warming, tasty and satisfying main meal soup. The unusual sweet and savoury combination of chicken, leeks and prunes is not only delicious, but the prunes add useful fibre. Pearl barley adds further carbohydrate substance and makes a little go a long way.

Serves 6

1 chicken, weighing about 2kg/4½lb
900g/2lb leeks
1 fresh bay leaf
a few each of fresh parsley stalks and thyme sprigs
1 large carrot, thickly sliced
2.4 litres/5 pints/10 cups chicken or beef stock
115g/4oz/generous ½ cup pearl barley
400g/14oz prunes
ground black pepper
chopped fresh parsley, to garnish

1 Cut the breasts off the chicken and set aside. Place the remaining chicken carcass in a large pan. Cut half the leeks into 5cm/2in lengths and add them to the pan.

2 Tie the bay leaf, parsley and thyme into a bouquet garni and add to the pan with the carrot and the stock. Bring to the boil, then reduce the heat and cover. Simmer gently for 1 hour. Skim off any scum when the water first boils and occasionally during simmering.

3 Add the chicken breasts and cook for a further 30 minutes. Leave until cool enough to handle, then strain the stock. Reserve the chicken breasts and meat from the chicken carcass. Discard all the skin, bones, cooked vegetables and herbs. Skim as much fat as you can from the stock, then return it to the pan.

4 Meanwhile, rinse the pearl barley thoroughly in a sieve (strainer) under cold running water, then cook it in a large pan of boiling water for about 10 minutes. Drain, rinse well again and drain thoroughly.

5 Add the pearl barley to the stock. Bring to the boil over a medium heat, then lower the heat and cook very gently for 15–20 minutes, until the barley is just cooked and tender.

6 Season to taste with pepper, then add the prunes. Slice the remaining leeks and add them to the pan. Bring to the boil, then simmer for 10 minutes, or until the leeks are just cooked.

7 Slice the chicken breasts and add them to the soup with the chicken meat, sliced or cut into neat pieces.

8 Ladle the soup into deep plates and sprinkle with chopped parsley.

Energy 255Kcal/1083kJ; Protein 17.7g; Carbohydrate 44.4g, of which sugars 27.2g; Fat 2g, of which saturates 0.3g; Cholesterol 35mg; Calcium 69mg; Fibre 7.5g; Sodium 45mg.

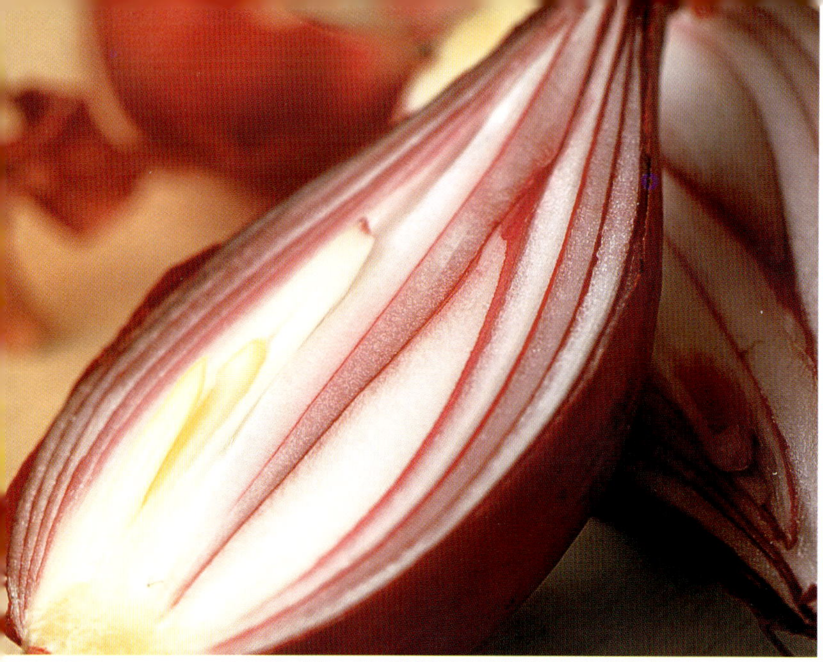
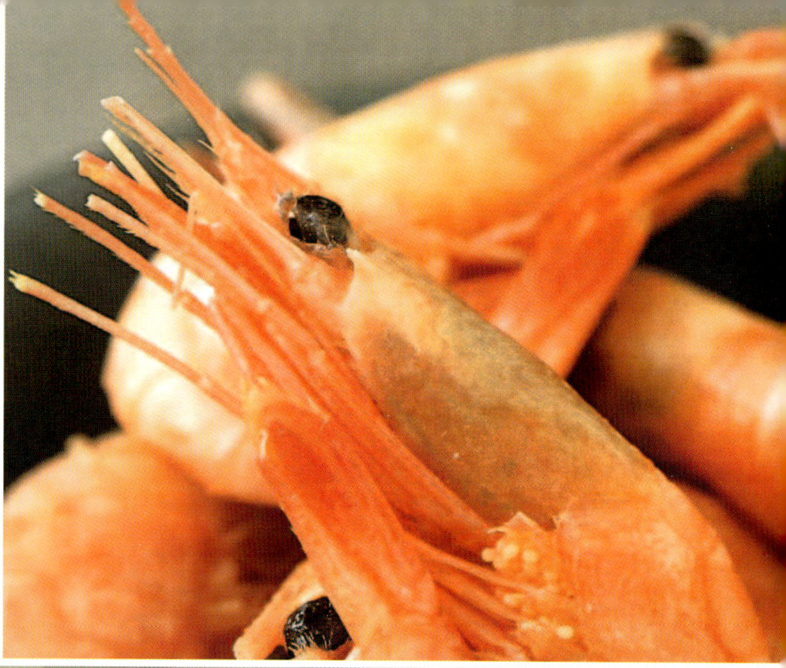
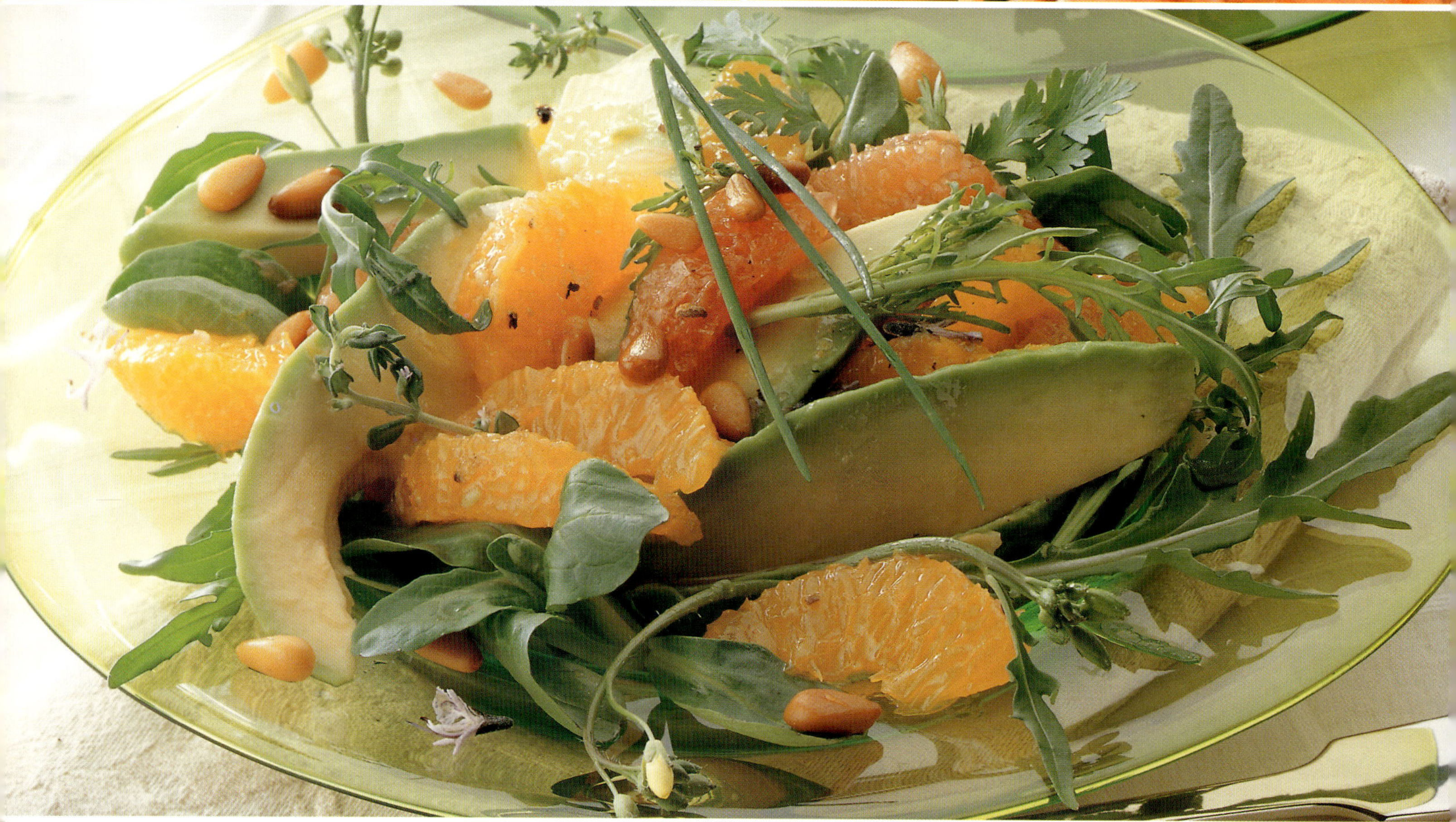
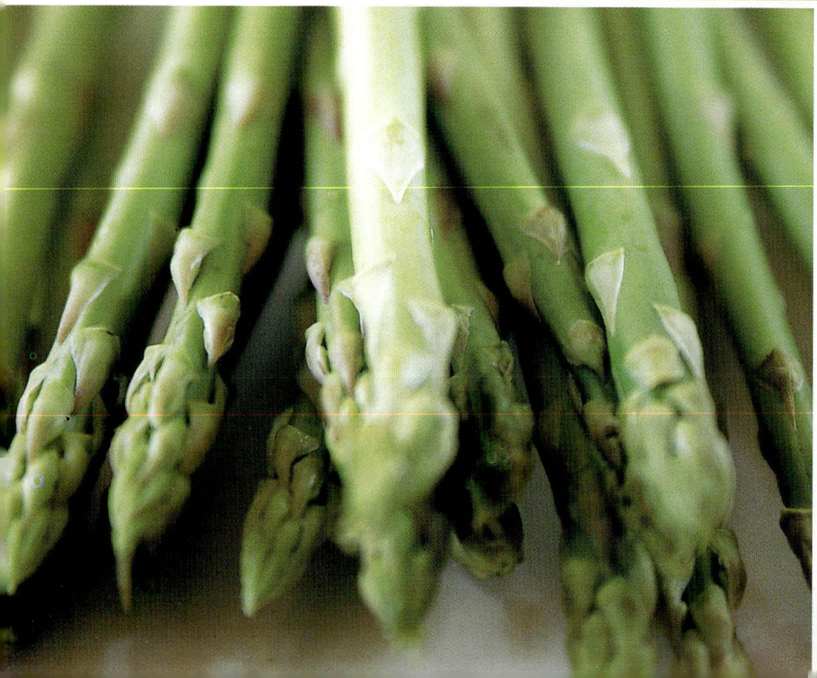
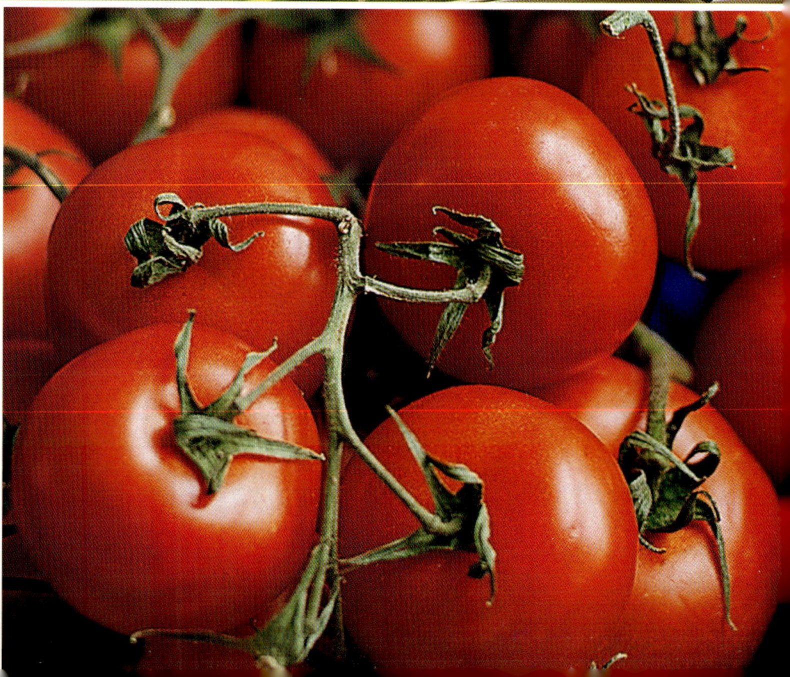

main dish salads

Tempting, nutritionally balanced salads can be made from an endless variety of ingredients, including vitamin-packed fruit and vegetables, lean poultry, oily fish, seafood, eggs, nuts or seeds for protein, and rice, pasta, potatoes, beans, peas, lentils, or grains. Many are ideal for packed lunches; others make quick weekday suppers.

New spring vegetable salad

This colourful, tempting salad makes a satisfying meal and is ideal for packing into a lunchbox container to take with you to work. It includes a delicious combination of tender new potatoes, young asparagus, baby spinach and cherry tomatoes, all of which are rich sources of vitamin C.

Serves 4

675g/1½lb small new potatoes, scrubbed
400g/14oz can haricot (navy) beans, drained
115g/4oz cherry tomatoes, halved
75g/3oz/½ cup walnut halves
30ml/2 tbsp cider vinegar
5ml/1 tsp wholegrain mustard
60ml/4 tbsp olive oil
pinch of sugar
225g/8oz young asparagus spears, trimmed
6 spring onions (scallions), trimmed
ground black pepper
baby spinach leaves, to serve

1 Put the potatoes in a pan, cover with water and bring to the boil. Cook for 15 minutes or until tender. Meanwhile, put the haricot beans in a large bowl, then add the tomatoes and walnuts.

2 Put the cider vinegar, mustard, olive oil and sugar into a jar and season with pepper. Screw the lid on the jar tightly and shake well.

3 Add the asparagus to the potatoes and cook for 3 minutes until just tender.

4 Drain the cooked vegetables well. Cool under cold running water and drain again. Thickly slice the potatoes and cut the spring onions in half.

5 Add the asparagus, potatoes and spring onions to the bowl containing the bean mixture.

6 Pour the dressing over the salad and toss well. Serve on a bed of baby spinach leaves.

Cook's tip
You can use any variety of canned beans for this salad, or you could try fresh, young, cooked broad (fava) beans, if you like.

Energy 469Kcal/1959kJ; Protein 14.7g; Carbohydrate 48.1g, of which sugars 8.7g; Fat 25.5g, of which saturates 3g; Cholesterol 0mg; Calcium 122mg; Fibre 10g; Sodium 414mg.

Bulgur wheat salad with walnuts

Bulgur wheat, often referred to as 'cracked wheat', makes a healthy salad with a nutty flavour. Bulgur contains all the wheat grain except the bran, so it is easy to digest. However, for a wheat-free salad during a strict detox or for a gluten-free alternative grain, substitute long-grain brown rice or quinoa, cooked following the packet instructions.

Serves 8

225g/8oz/1 generous cup bulgur wheat
350ml/12fl oz/1½ cups vegetable stock
1 cinnamon stick
generous pinch of ground cumin
pinch of cayenne pepper
pinch of ground cloves
10 mangetouts (snowpeas), topped and tailed
1 red and 1 yellow (bell) pepper, roasted, skinned, seeded and diced
2 plum tomatoes, peeled, seeded and diced
2 shallots, finely sliced
5 black olives, stoned and cut into quarters
30ml/2 tbsp each shredded fresh basil, mint and parsley
30ml/2 tbsp roughly chopped walnuts
30ml/2 tbsp lemon juice
30ml/1fl oz/2 tbsp olive oil
freshly ground black pepper
onion rings, to garnish

1 Place the bulgur wheat in a large bowl. Pour the vegetable stock into a pan, add the cinnamon, cumin, cayenne pepper and ground cloves and bring to the boil.

2 Heat the spices in the stock for 1 minute, then pour the flavoured stock over the bulgur wheat and leave to stand for 20–30 minutes.

3 In another bowl, combine the mangetouts, peppers, tomatoes, shallots, olives, herbs and walnuts.

4 Add the lemon juice, olive oil and a little freshly ground black pepper. Stir thoroughly to mix.

5 Strain the bulgur wheat, shaking to remove as much liquid as possible, and discard the cinnamon stick.

6 Place the bulgur wheat in a large serving bowl, stir in the fresh vegetable mixture and serve immediately, garnished with onion rings.

Energy 118Kcal/493kJ; Protein 2.7g; Carbohydrate 19g, of which sugars 4.2g; Fat 3.9g, of which saturates 0.5g; Cholesterol 0mg; Calcium 28mg; Fibre 1.5g; Sodium 6mg.

Citrus fruit salad with avocado

A refreshingly tangy combination – rocket and lamb's lettuce leaves are topped with fresh grapefruit, oranges and avocado in a light, fruity dressing for a vitamin-packed salad. Toasted pine nuts add a crunchy contrast and provide some protein. Almonds, hazelnuts or walnuts could be added as alternatives to the pine nuts, if you like.

Serves 4

1 pink grapefruit
2 large oranges
1 large avocado
50g/2oz/½ cup pine nuts
25ml/1½ tbsp olive oil
10ml/2 tsp cider vinegar
30ml/2 tbsp freshly squeezed orange juice
50g/2oz lamb's lettuce (corn salad)
50g/2oz rocket (arugula)
ground black pepper
15g/½oz fresh chives
fresh herb sprigs, to garnish

1 Halve and segment the grapefruit and oranges and place the segments in a mixing bowl. Prepare over the bowl to catch the juices.

2 Peel, stone (pit) and slice the avocado and add the slices to the bowl. Gently stir in the pine nuts, taking care not to break up the avocado.

3 Whisk together the olive oil, vinegar, orange juice and pepper in a small bowl or jug and stir into the fruit mixture.

4 Arrange the lamb's lettuce and rocket on four serving plates and divide the fruit and dressing evenly over each. Garnish with chives and herb sprigs and serve immediately.

Energy 237Kcal/983kJ; Protein 3.8g; Carbohydrate 10.8g, of which sugars 10.3g; Fat 20.1g, of which saturates 2.7g; Cholesterol 0mg; Calcium 58mg; Fibre 3.6g; Sodium 8mg.

Greek salad

A popular Mediterranean salad, that typifies the healthy diet found in the region. Traditionally it includes feta cheese, which adds protein and calcium to the salad. It may be made from ewe's milk, although usually it is made using cow's milk. For a dairy-free version while following a strict detox, or for those who are lactose intolerant, substitute a soya cheese.

Serves 4

1 small cos or romaine lettuce, sliced
450g/1lb well-flavoured tomatoes, cut into eighths
1 cucumber, seeded and chopped
200g/7oz feta cheese, crumbled
4 spring onions (scallions), sliced
50g/2oz/½ cup black olives, pitted and halved

For the dressing
45ml/3 tbsp olive oil
25ml/1½ tbsp lemon juice
ground black pepper

1 Put the lettuce, tomatoes, cucumber, crumbled feta cheese, spring onions and olives in a large salad bowl.

2 For the dressing, whisk together the olive oil and lemon juice, then season. Pour over the salad, toss well and serve immediately.

Energy 248Kcal/1026kJ; Protein 9.8g; Carbohydrate 6.2g, of which sugars 6.1g; Fat 20.6g, of which saturates 8.5g; Cholesterol 35mg; Calcium 242mg; Fibre 2.7g; Sodium 1017mg.

Warm mixed seafood and fresh herb salad

Quick and easy to prepare, this seafood salad makes a great light meal. Shellfish is rich in vitamins and minerals and is a good source of omega-3 fatty acids.

Serves 4

30ml/2 tbsp olive oil
15ml/1 tbsp flavoured oil, such as basil oil or chilli oil
finely grated rind of 1 lemon
15ml/1 tbsp lemon juice
1 garlic clove, crushed
30ml/2 tbsp chopped fresh basil
175g/6oz mixed salad leaves
225g/8oz sugar snap peas, sliced diagonally
400g/14oz packet frozen seafood mix, thawed and drained
ground black pepper

1 Place 15ml/1 tbsp of the olive oil, the flavoured oil, grated lemon rind, lemon juice, garlic and basil in a small bowl or jug (pitcher). Season with pepper and whisk together. Set aside.

2 Place the salad leaves and sugar snap peas in a serving bowl and toss lightly to mix.

3 Heat the remaining olive oil in a large frying pan or wok, add the seafood and stir-fry over a medium heat for about 5 minutes until cooked.

4 Scatter the seafood over the salad leaves, drizzle the dressing over the salad, toss together gently to combine and serve immediately.

Variation
If using cooked seafood, stir-fry for just 2 minutes to warm through, or toss in the dressing and add cold to the salad.

Energy 184Kcal/769kJ; Protein 18.2g; Carbohydrate 4.7g, of which sugars 3g; Fat 10.4g, of which saturates 1.6g; Cholesterol 225mg; Calcium 75mg; Fibre 2.3g; Sodium 117mg.

Buckwheat noodle salad with smoked salmon

Soba is the best known type of Japanese noodle. It is made from buckwheat flour and is satisfying to eat. It makes a nutrient-rich alternative to wheat pasta while following a detox diet.

Serves 4

225g/8oz soba (Japanese buckwheat) noodles
15ml/1 tbsp oyster sauce
juice of ½ lemon
30ml/2 tbsp olive oil
115g/4oz smoked salmon, cut into fine strips
115g/4oz watercress or rocket (arugula)
2 ripe tomatoes, peeled, seeded and cut into strips
15ml/1 tbsp chopped chives
ground black pepper

1 Cook the soba noodles in a large pan of boiling water for about 6 minutes or following the directions on the packet, until tender.

2 Drain, then rinse under cold running water and drain well.

3 Tip the noodles into a large bowl. Mix in the oyster sauce, lemon juice and olive oil, and season with pepper.

4 Add the smoked salmon, watercress or rocket, tomatoes and chives. Toss and serve immediately.

Energy 313Kcal/1307kJ; Protein 11.3g; Carbohydrate 48.9g, of which sugars 3g; Fat 7.2g, of which saturates 1.1g; Cholesterol 10mg; Calcium 65mg; Fibre 1.1g; Sodium 653mg.

Bean salad with tuna and red onion

This salad combines creamy haricot or cannellini beans, crunchy French beans, tuna, fresh tomatoes and a tangy tarragon dressing. It makes a nourishing main meal salad that is easy to pack up and take with you for lunch. Beans are high in fibre, so this salad is good for the digestion as well as filling to eat. It could be accompanied by a mixed green salad if you like.

Serves 4

250g/9oz/1½ cups dried haricot (navy) or cannellini beans, soaked overnight in cold water
½ onion
1 garlic clove
1 bay leaf
bunch of chopped fresh flat leaf parsley
250g/9oz French (green) beans, trimmed
1 large red onion, very thinly sliced
250g/9oz good-quality canned tuna in olive oil or spring water, drained
200g/7oz cherry tomatoes, halved
ground black pepper

For the dressing

90ml/6 tbsp extra virgin olive oil
15ml/1 tbsp tarragon vinegar
5ml/1 tsp herb mustard
1 garlic clove, finely chopped
5ml/1 tsp grated lemon rind
a little lemon juice (optional)
pinch of caster (superfine) sugar (optional)

1 Drain the haricot or cannellini beans and bring them to the boil in a pan of fresh water. Boil rapidly for about 10 minutes, then reduce the heat and add the ½ onion, garlic, bay leaf and half the parsley. Cook for 1–1½ hours, until tender (the cooking time will depend on the age of the dried beans).

2 When cooked, drain the beans well and discard the herbs, onion and garlic.

3 Meanwhile, place all the dressing ingredients, apart from the lemon juice and sugar, in a jug (pitcher) or bowl and whisk until mixed. Season to taste with pepper and add lemon juice and a pinch of sugar, if you like. Leave to stand.

4 Blanch the green beans in plenty of boiling water for 2–3 minutes. Drain, refresh under cold water and drain thoroughly again.

5 Place both types of beans in a large bowl. Add half the dressing and toss to mix. Chop half the remaining parsley and add to the beans with the onion. Flake the tuna into large chunks and add to the salad with the tomatoes.

6 Arrange the salad on four plates. Drizzle the remaining dressing over the salad. Chop the remaining parsley and sprinkle on top. Serve immediately, at room temperature.

Variation

For an alternative idea, add chickpeas in place of the haricot or cannellini beans. You can use canned instead of dried beans if you don't have time to soak the dried variety overnight.

Energy 336Kcal/1406kJ; Protein 15.2g; Carbohydrate 30.9g, of which sugars 4g; Fat 17.7g, of which saturates 2.6g; Cholesterol 0mg; Calcium 89mg; Fibre 11.5g; Sodium 12mg.

Salad niçoise

This classic French salad combines fresh tuna, hard-boiled eggs, salad leaves, tomato, cucumber, radish and a garlic-flavoured dressing to create a taste sensation. Using fresh tuna makes it all the more appetizing, as well as providing healthy omega-3 fatty acids. The salad ingredients could include sliced red or yellow peppers, and/or thinly sliced fennel.

Serves 2

115g/4oz French (green) beans, trimmed and halved
115g/4oz mixed salad leaves
½ small cucumber, sliced
4 ripe tomatoes, quartered
1 tuna steak, weighing about 175g/6oz
olive oil, for brushing
50g/2oz can anchovies, drained, rinsed and halved lengthways (optional)
2 eggs, hard-boiled, shelled and quartered
4 small radishes, trimmed
50g/2oz/½ cup black olives, pitted
ground black pepper

For the dressing
45ml/3 tbsp extra virgin olive oil
2 garlic cloves, crushed
15ml/1 tbsp white wine vinegar

1 To make the dressing, whisk all the ingredients together in a bowl and season to taste.

2 Cook the beans in boiling water for 2–3 minutes, until just tender, then drain. In a large shallow bowl, combine the salad leaves, sliced cucumber, tomatoes and beans.

3 Preheat the grill (broiler). Brush the tuna lightly with olive oil and season with pepper. Grill (broil) for 3–4 minutes on each side until cooked through. Leave to cool, then flake.

4 Sprinkle the flaked tuna, anchovies, if using, quartered eggs, radishes and olives over the salad. Pour over the dressing and toss lightly to combine, then serve.

> **Variation**
> For a more substantial salad, or to serve more people, add thickly sliced, boiled new potatoes.

Energy 466Kcal/1941kJ; Protein 36.4g; Carbohydrate 8.2g, of which sugars 7.6g; Fat 32.4g, of which saturates 6.1g; Cholesterol 231mg; Calcium 188mg; Fibre 4.3g; Sodium 1674mg.

Warm chicken and tomato salad with hazelnut dressing

This simple, warm salad combines pan-fried chicken, fresh baby spinach leaves and cherry tomatoes with a light hazelnut and fresh herb dressing.

Serves 4

45ml/3 tbsp olive oil
15ml/1 tbsp hazelnut oil
15ml/1 tbsp white wine vinegar or cider vinegar
1 garlic clove, crushed
30ml/2 tbsp chopped fresh mixed herbs
225g/8oz baby spinach leaves
250g/9oz cherry tomatoes, halved
1 bunch of spring onions (scallions), chopped
400g/14oz skinless chicken breast fillets, cut into strips
ground black pepper

Variations
Turkey, textured vegetable protein or salmon fillet could all be used as alternatives to chicken.

1 First make the dressing: place 30ml/2 tbsp of the olive oil, the hazelnut oil, vinegar, garlic and chopped herbs in a small bowl or jug (pitcher) and whisk together until mixed. Set aside.

2 Trim any long stalks from the spinach leaves, then place in a large serving bowl with the tomatoes and spring onions, and toss together to mix.

3 Heat the remaining olive oil in a frying pan, and stir-fry the chicken over a high heat for 7–10 minutes, until it is cooked, tender and lightly browned.

4 Arrange the cooked chicken pieces over the salad. Give the dressing a quick whisk to blend, then drizzle it over the salad. Add pepper to taste, toss lightly and serve immediately.

Energy 235Kcal/984kJ; Protein 26.5g; Carbohydrate 3.6g, of which sugars 3.5g; Fat 12.9g, of which saturates 2g; Cholesterol 70mg; Calcium 115mg; Fibre 2.2g; Sodium 146mg.

Warm Oriental chicken and rice stir-fry salad

Succulent chicken pieces are combined with a vibrant selection of vegetables and brown rice in a light chilli dressing, making an exciting salad packed with fibre and nutrients.

Serves 4

50g/2oz mixed salad leaves
50g/2oz baby spinach leaves
50g/2oz watercress or rocket (arugula)
30ml/2 tbsp sweet chilli sauce
30ml/2 tbsp dry sherry
15ml/1 tbsp light soy sauce
15ml/1 tbsp tomato ketchup
10ml/2 tsp olive oil
8 shallots, finely chopped
1 garlic clove, crushed
350g/12oz skinless chicken breast fillets, cut into thin strips
1 red (bell) pepper, seeded and sliced
175g/6oz mangetouts (snowpeas), trimmed
400g/14oz can baby corn, drained and halved lengthways
275g/10oz brown rice, cooked
ground black pepper
fresh flat leaf parsley, to garnish

1 If any of the mixed salad leaves are large, tear them into smaller pieces and arrange them with the spinach leaves on a serving dish. Add the watercress or rocket, if using and toss together lightly to mix.

2 In a small bowl, mix together the chilli sauce, sherry, soy sauce and tomato ketchup. Set the sauce mixture aside.

3 Heat the olive oil in a large, non-stick frying pan or wok. Add the shallots and garlic and stir-fry over a medium heat for 1 minute.

4 Add the chicken to the pan and stir-fry for a further 3–4 minutes, until cooked through and tender.

5 Add the pepper, mangetouts, baby corn and cooked brown rice, and stir-fry for a further 2–3 minutes, until the vegetables are just tender.

6 Pour in the chilli sauce mixture and stir-fry for 2–3 minutes, until hot and bubbling. Season to taste.

7 Spoon the chicken mixture over the salad leaves, toss together to mix and serve immediately, garnished with a sprig of fresh parsley.

Energy 278Kcal/1173kJ; Protein 29.1g; Carbohydrate 32.8g, of which sugars 9.8g; Fat 4.2g, of which saturates 0.8g; Cholesterol 61mg; Calcium 104mg; Fibre 4.7g; Sodium 1699mg.

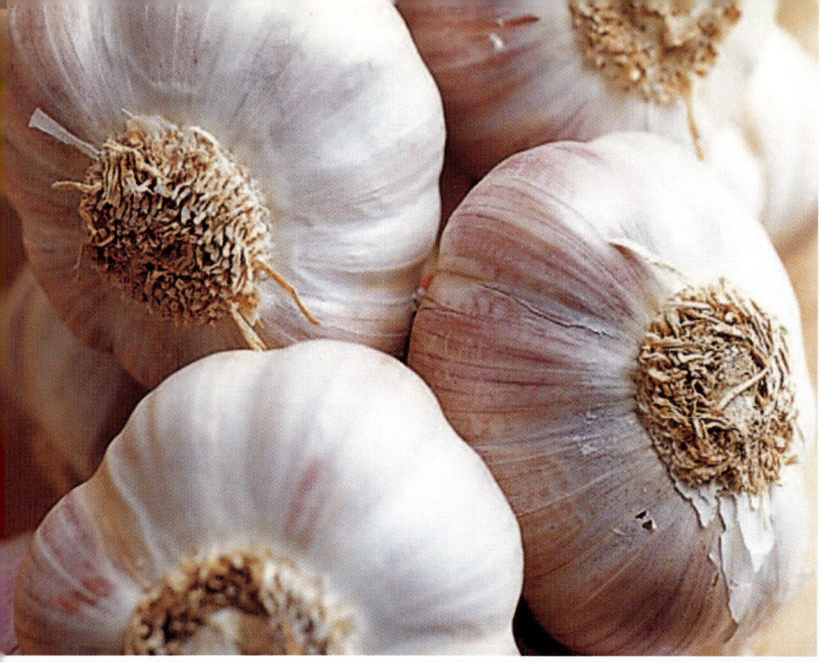
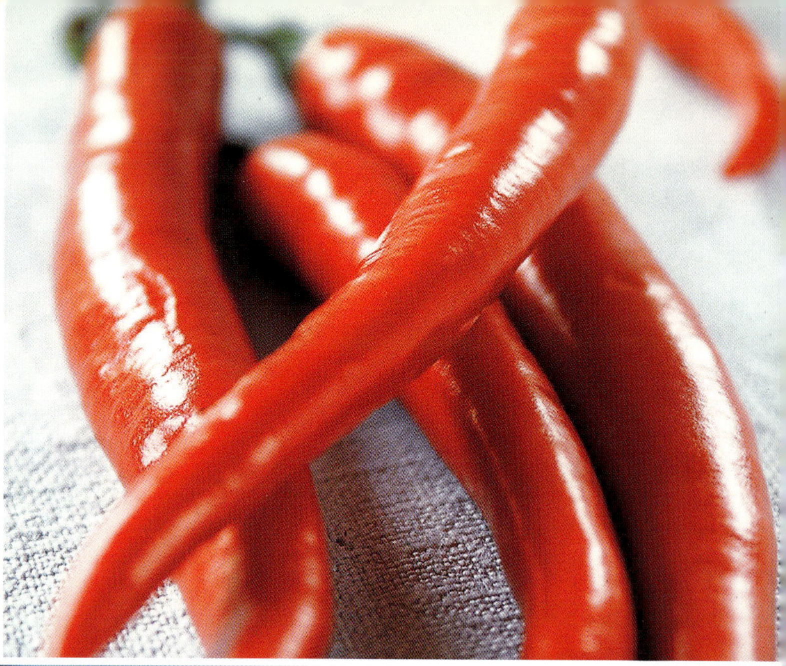
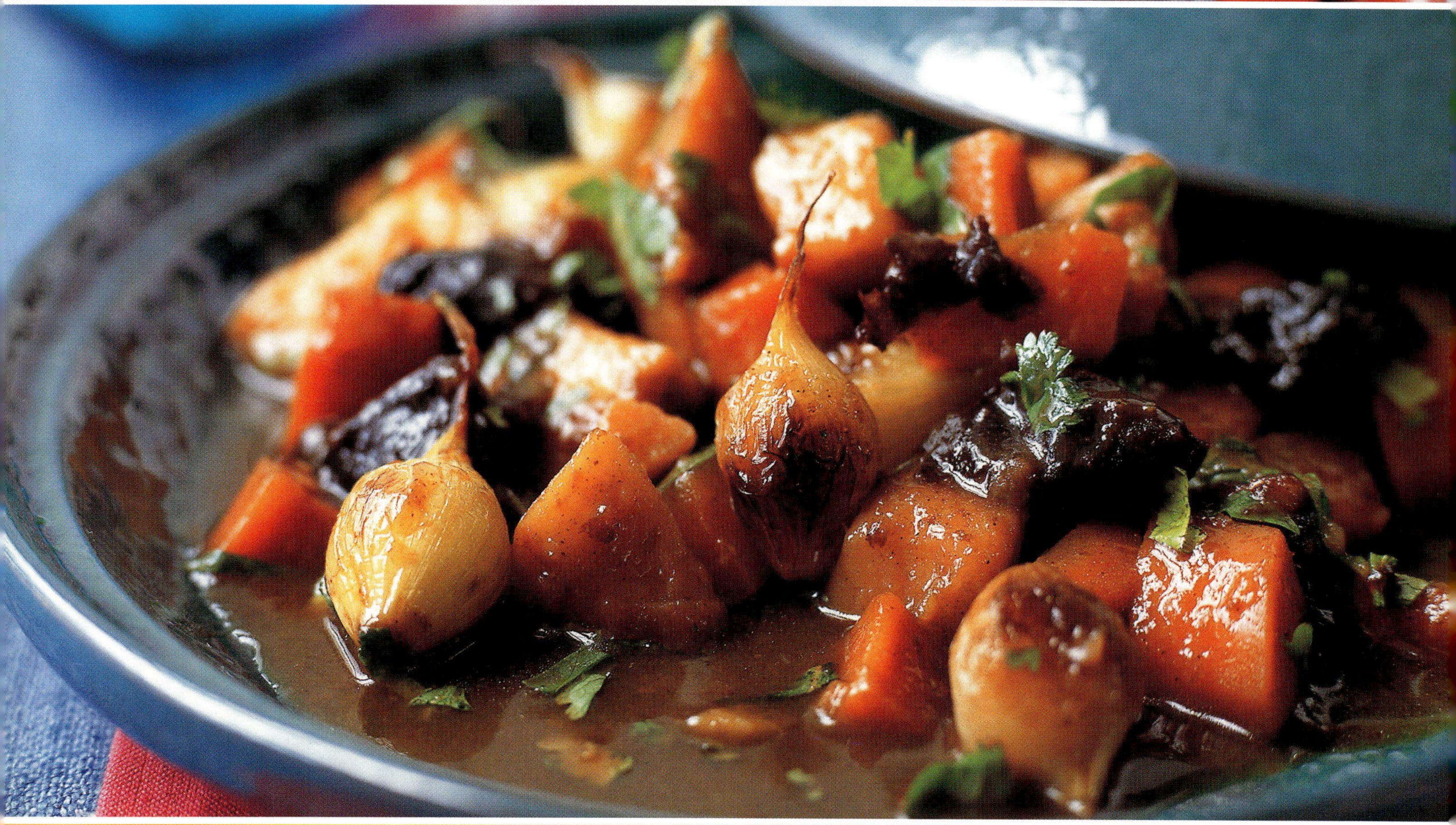
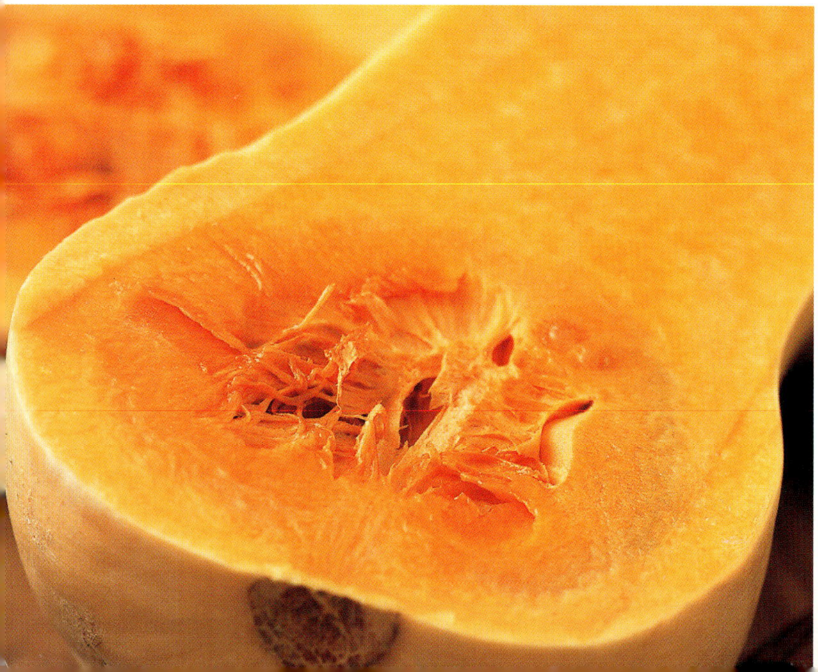
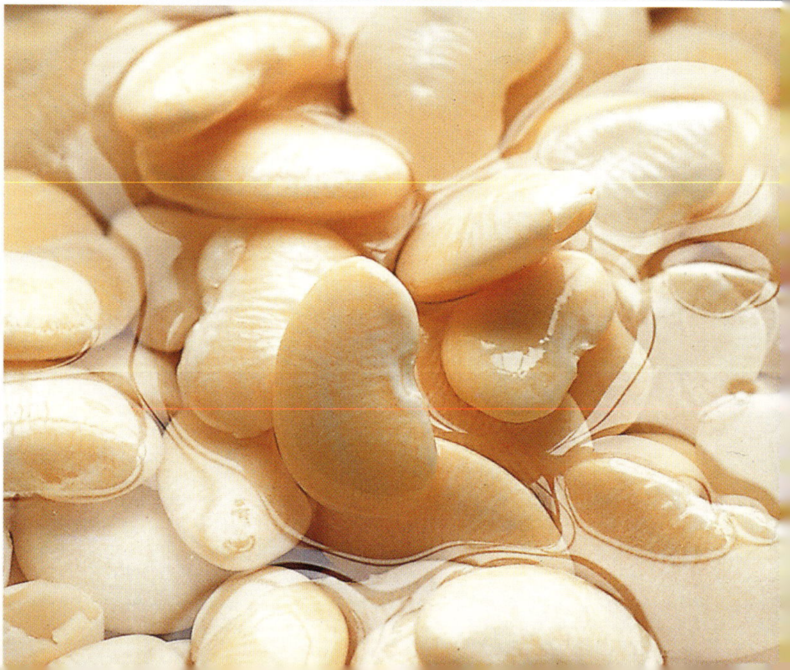

vegetable main dishes

Take advantage of the wide variety of cereal grains, dried beans, peas and lentils, and vegetables to make wholesome and satisfying meals, such as Butter Bean, Tomato and Olive Stew, Stir-fried Vegetables and Seeds or Brown Rice Risotto with Mushrooms. These are ideal for a detox diet as they are packed with nutrients, easily digested and filling to eat, and they are suitable for vegetarians. They also lend themselves to flavouring with fresh herbs and spices, which aid the digestion.

Turkish-style new potato casserole

This delicious casserole combines aubergines, courgettes, peppers, onion, peas, beans, tomatoes and potatoes for a really colourful and nutritious hot pot. Together, the many vegetables provide fantastic nutrient value, with plenty of fibre, vitamins, minerals and long-term energy. It is great served on its own or could be an accompaniment to grilled fish or chicken.

Serves 4

60ml/4 tbsp olive oil
1 large onion, chopped
2 small to medium aubergines (eggplants), cut into small cubes
4 courgettes (zucchini), cut into small chunks
1 green (bell) pepper, and 1 red or yellow (bell) pepper, seeded and chopped
115g/4oz/1 cup fresh or frozen peas
115g/4oz French (green) beans
450g/1lb new potatoes, cubed
2.5ml/½ tsp ground cinnamon
2.5ml/½ tsp paprika
ground black pepper
4–5 tomatoes, skinned
400g/14oz can chopped tomatoes
15g/½oz/2 tbsp chopped fresh parsley
3–4 garlic cloves, crushed
350ml/12fl oz/1½ cups vegetable stock
pitted black olives and fresh parsley, to garnish

1 Heat the oven to 190°C/375°F/Gas 5. Heat 45ml/3 tbsp of the oil in a heavy pan, then add the onion and fry until golden. Add the cubed aubergines to the pan and sauté for 3 minutes.

2 Add the courgettes, peppers, peas, beans and potatoes to the pan, together with the spices and freshly ground black pepper, to taste. Stir to mix thoroughly.

3 Continue to cook the vegetables over a high heat for about 3 minutes, stirring continuously. Transfer them to a large, shallow ovenproof dish.

4 Halve the fresh tomatoes and remove their seeds, using a teaspoon. Chop the flesh and place in a bowl.

5 Mix in the canned tomatoes with their juice, the parsley, crushed garlic and the remaining olive oil.

6 Pour the vegetable stock over the aubergine mixture, then spoon the prepared tomato mixture over the top.

7 Cover with foil and bake in the oven for 30–45 minutes until the vegetables are tender. Serve garnished with olives and parsley.

Variation
You could add extra black olives to the mixture in step 2.

Energy 307Kcal/1282kJ; Protein 9.4g; Carbohydrate 39.9g, of which sugars 17.8g; Fat 13.3g, of which saturates 2.1g; Cholesterol 0mg; Calcium 92mg; Fibre 8.7g; Sodium 30mg.

Tagliatelle with vegetable ribbons

Narrow strips of lightly cooked courgette and carrot mingle well with tagliatelle to resemble coloured pasta. You can use a non-wheat, gluten-free spaghetti or other pasta, or buckwheat noodles, during a strict detox. Garlic-flavoured olive oil is used in this dish – flavoured oils such as rosemary, chilli or basil are a quick way of adding flavour to pasta.

Serves 4

2 large courgettes (zucchini)
2 large carrots
250g/9oz fresh egg tagliatelle or non-wheat pasta
60ml/4 tbsp garlic-flavoured olive oil
ground black pepper

Cook's tip
If you can't find or don't have a garlic- or herb-flavoured oil, you can use plain olive oil and simply add crushed garlic, chopped fresh herbs or chilli to it.

1 Using a vegetable peeler, peel the courgettes and carrots into long thin ribbons. Bring a large pan of water to the boil, then add the courgette and carrot ribbons. Bring the water back to the boil and cook the ribbons for 30 seconds, then drain and set aside.

2 Cook the tagliatelle according to the instructions on the packet. Drain and return it to the pan. Add the vegetable ribbons, garlic flavoured oil and pepper and toss over a medium to high heat until the pasta and vegetables are flavoured through. Serve immediately.

Energy 348Kcal/1464kJ; Protein 9.6g; Carbohydrate 52.1g, of which sugars 7.5g; Fat 12.7g, of which saturates 1.9g; Cholesterol 0mg; Calcium 53mg; Fibre 3.9g; Sodium 16mg.

Penne with green vegetable sauce

Lightly cooked fresh green vegetables are tossed with pasta quills to create this low-fat Italian-style dish, ideal for a light lunch or supper. A wide range of non-wheat, gluten-free pastas, made from buckwheat, corn or rice, are readily available in many health food stores and large supermarkets as alternatives to wheat pasta. Choose any shape or variety you like.

Serves 4

2 carrots
1 courgette (zucchini)
75g/3oz French (green) beans
1 leek, washed
2 ripe Italian plum tomatoes
handful of fresh flat leaf parsley
15ml/1 tbsp extra virgin olive oil
2.5ml/½ tsp sugar
115g/4oz/1 cup frozen peas
350g/12oz/3 cups dried penne
ground black pepper

1 Dice the carrots and the courgette finely. Top and tail the French beans, then cut them into 2cm/¾in lengths. Slice the leek thinly. Skin and dice the tomatoes. Finely chop the parsley.

2 Heat the oil in a medium frying pan. Add the carrots and leek. Sprinkle the sugar over and cook, stirring frequently, for about 5 minutes.

3 Stir in the courgette, French beans and peas and season with black pepper.

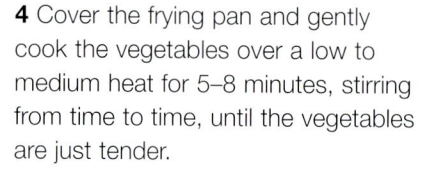

4 Cover the frying pan and gently cook the vegetables over a low to medium heat for 5–8 minutes, stirring from time to time, until the vegetables are just tender.

5 Meanwhile, cook the pasta in a large pan of rapidly boiling water for 10–12 minutes or according to the packet instructions, until it is tender but not soggy.

6 Drain the pasta well, return to the pan and cover to keep warm.

7 Stir in the chopped parsley and the diced chopped plum tomatoes and adjust the seasoning to taste. Toss with the pasta and serve immediately.

Energy 401Kcal/1698kJ; Protein 15.5g; Carbohydrate 76.7g, of which sugars 11.3g; Fat 5.7g, of which saturates 0.9g; Cholesterol 0mg; Calcium 99mg; Fibre 8.1g; Sodium 26mg.

Rice noodles with vegetable chilli sauce

Rice noodles are very fine, string-like noodles, sometimes called rice vermicelli. They are made from rice flour, so they are wheat- and gluten-free. They are also very quick to prepare and just require a short soaking in boiling water. Here they are served with a colourful vegetable sauce, flavoured with fresh chilli and coriander to give the dish an aromatic, hot and spicy flavour kick.

Serves 4

15ml/1 tbsp vegetable oil
1 onion, chopped
2 garlic cloves, crushed
1 fresh red chilli, seeded and finely chopped
1 red (bell) pepper, seeded and diced
2 carrots, finely chopped
175g/6oz baby corn, halved
225g/8oz can sliced bamboo shoots, rinsed and drained
400g/14oz can red kidney beans, rinsed and drained
300ml/½ pint/1¼ cups passata (bottled strained tomatoes)
15ml/1 tbsp soy sauce
5ml/1 tsp ground coriander
250g/9oz rice noodles
30ml/2 tbsp chopped fresh coriander (cilantro)
ground black pepper
fresh coriander, to garnish

1 Heat the oil in a deep frying pan, add the onion, garlic, chilli and red pepper and cook gently for 5 minutes, stirring.

2 Add the carrots, baby corn, bamboo shoots, kidney beans, passata, soy sauce and ground coriander and stir everything together to combine.

3 Bring the mixture to the boil, then reduce the heat, cover and simmer for 30 minutes, stirring occasionally, until the vegetables are tender. Season with pepper.

4 Meanwhile, place the noodles in a bowl and cover with boiling water. Stir with a fork and leave to stand for 3–4 minutes or according to the packet instructions. Rinse and drain.

5 Stir the chopped fresh coriander into the sauce. Spoon the noodles in to warmed serving bowls, top with the sauce, then garnish with coriander sprigs and serve immediately.

Energy 221Kcal/932kJ; Protein 11.7g; Carbohydrate 35.9g, of which sugars 14.6g; Fat 4.2g, of which saturates 0.6g; Cholesterol 0mg; Calcium 113mg; Fibre 10.1g; Sodium 1345mg.

Stir-fried vegetables with cashew nuts

Stir-frying is the perfect way to make a speedy meal that retains the nutrient value of the vegetables. This is also a very flexible dish as you can use any combination of vegetables, according to what's available and your own personal preference. Simply add the firmer vegetables that require longer cooking to the pan first, then finish with leafy or tender varieties.

Serves 4

900g/2lb mixed vegetables (see Cook's Tip)
30ml/2 tbsp vegetable oil
2 garlic cloves, crushed
15ml/1 tbsp grated fresh root ginger
50g/2oz/½ cup unsalted cashew nuts
soy sauce, to taste
ground black pepper

Variation
Substitute a squeeze of lemon juice for the soy sauce, if you prefer.

1 Prepare the vegetables according to which type you are using. Carrots, celery and cucumber should be cut into very fine matchsticks to ensure that they cook quickly.

2 Heat a wok or frying pan, then trickle the oil around the rim so that it runs down to coat the surface. When the oil is hot, add the garlic and ginger and cook for 1–2 minutes, stirring. Add the harder vegetables and toss over the heat for 5 minutes, until they soften.

3 Add the softer vegetables and stir-fry over a high heat for 3–4 minutes.

4 Stir in the cashew nuts and stir-fry for 1–2 minutes until golden. Sprinkle with soy sauce and black pepper to taste. Serve immediately.

Cook's tip
Use a pack of stir-fry vegetables or make up your own mixture. Choose from carrots, baby corn, mangetouts (snowpeas), peppers, beansprouts, mushrooms, and spring onions (scallions). Drained, canned bamboo shoots and water chestnuts are delicious additions.

Energy 205Kcal/849kJ; Protein 3.9g; Carbohydrate 20.1g, of which sugars 17.4g; Fat 12.5g, of which saturates 2.1g; Cholesterol 0mg; Calcium 61mg; Fibre 5.8g; Sodium 93mg.

Stir-fried vegetables and seeds

The contrast between the crunchy seeds and vegetables and the rich, savoury sauce is what makes this dish so delicious. Seeds are nutritional powerhouses, packed with vitamins and minerals, as well as beneficial oils and protein. Oyster mushrooms are included for their delicate texture and in keeping with the Oriental style of this dish. Serve it solo, or with rice or noodles.

Serves 4

30ml/2 tbsp vegetable oil
30ml/2 tbsp sesame seeds
30ml/2 tbsp sunflower seeds
30ml/2 tbsp pumpkin seeds
2 garlic cloves, finely chopped
2.5cm/1in piece fresh root ginger, peeled and finely chopped
2 large carrots, cut into matchsticks
2 large courgettes (zucchini), cut into matchsticks
90g/3½oz/1½ cups oyster mushrooms, torn into pieces
150g/5oz watercress or baby spinach leaves, coarsely chopped
small bunch fresh mint or coriander (cilantro), leaves and stems chopped
60ml/4 tbsp black bean sauce
30ml/2 tbsp light soy sauce
15ml/1 tbsp light muscovado (brown) sugar
30ml/2 tbsp rice vinegar

1 Heat the oil in a wok or large frying pan. Add the seeds. Toss over a medium heat for 1 minute, then add the garlic and ginger and continue to stir-fry for a further minute. Do not let the garlic burn or it will taste bitter.

2 Add the carrot and courgette matchsticks and the sliced mushrooms to the wok and stir-fry for a further 5 minutes, or until all the vegetables are crisp-tender and golden at the edges.

3 Add the watercress or spinach with the fresh herbs. Toss over the heat for 1 minute, then stir in the black bean sauce, soy sauce, sugar and vinegar. Stir-fry for 1–2 minutes, until combined and hot. Serve immediately.

Cook's tip
Oyster mushrooms are delicate so should be torn rather than cut.

Energy 245Kcal/1015kJ; Protein 7.7g; Carbohydrate 14.2g, of which sugars 11g; Fat 17.7g, of which saturates 2.1g; Cholesterol 0mg; Calcium 163mg; Fibre 4.2g; Sodium 1671mg.

Indian rice with tomatoes and spinach

This tasty rice dish is good solo or can be served as part of an Indian meal with other curries and side dishes. It's based on brown basmati rice, flavoured with onion, garlic and spices, cooked with tomatoes and carrots. Baby spinach is added at the end of the cooking time, then it is attractively served with toasted cashew nuts sprinkled over the top.

Serves 4

30ml/2 tbsp vegetable oil
1 onion, chopped
2 garlic cloves, crushed
3 tomatoes, peeled, seeded and chopped
225g/8oz/generous 1 cup brown basmati rice, rinsed and drained
5ml/1 tsp ground coriander
5ml/1 tsp ground cumin
2 carrots, coarsely grated
900ml/1½ pints/3¾ cups vegetable stock
275g/10oz baby spinach leaves, washed
50g/2oz/½ cup unsalted cashew nuts, toasted
ground black pepper

1 Heat the vegetable oil in a large flameproof casserole and gently fry the chopped onion and garlic for 4–5 minutes until softened. Add the chopped tomatoes and cook for a further 3–4 minutes, stirring until slightly thickened.

2 Add the drained rice to the casserole and cook gently for 1–2 minutes, stirring, until the rice is coated with the tomato and onion mixture.

3 Stir in the coriander and cumin, then add the grated carrots and season with pepper. Pour in the stock and stir well to mix.

4 Bring to the boil, then cover tightly and simmer over a very gentle heat for 20–25 minutes until the rice is tender.

5 Lay the spinach on the surface of the rice, cover again and cook for 2–3 minutes until the spinach has wilted. Fold the spinach into the rest of the rice and check the seasoning. Sprinkle with cashew nuts and serve.

Cook's tip
If you are using large fresh spinach leaves, remove any tough stalks and chop the leaves roughly.

Energy 381Kcal/1586kJ; Protein 9.7g; Carbohydrate 55.8g, of which sugars 8.6g; Fat 13.1g, of which saturates 2.1g; Cholesterol 0mg; Calcium 154mg; Fibre 4g; Sodium 152mg.

Brown rice risotto with mushrooms

This twist on the classic risotto includes health-giving herbs and brown long grain rice. Both fresh and dried porcini mushrooms are included for a really powerful mushroom flavour. This risotto makes a satisfying and hearty main dish that could be accompanied with a leafy green side salad for extra vitamin nourishment, if you like.

Serves 4

15g/½oz/2 tbsp dried porcini mushrooms
15ml/1 tbsp olive oil
4 shallots, finely chopped
2 garlic cloves, crushed
250g/9oz/1⅓ cups brown long grain rice
900ml/1½ pints/3¾ cups vegetable stock
450g/1lb/6 cups mixed mushrooms, wiped clean and quartered
45ml/3 tbsp chopped fresh flat leaf parsley
ground black pepper

1 Place the dried porcini mushrooms in a bowl and cover with 150ml/¼ pint/⅔ cup hot water. Leave to soak for at least 20 minutes, until the mushrooms are rehydrated.

2 Heat the olive oil in a large pan, add the shallots and garlic and cook gently for 5 minutes, stirring. Drain the porcini, reserving their soaking liquid, and chop roughly. Add the brown rice to the shallot mixture and stir to coat the grains in the oil.

3 Stir the vegetable stock and the porcini soaking liquid into the rice mixture in the pan. Bring to the boil, lower the heat and simmer, uncovered, for about 20 minutes or until most of the liquid has been absorbed, stirring frequently to prevent it from sticking.

Health benefits
Brown rice is a good source of most B vitamins, essential for the release of energy from food. It also contains a good range of minerals and provides fibre, which helps to speed the passage of waste through the body and helps to protect against bowel cancer.

4 Add all the mushrooms, stir well to combine, and cook the risotto for a further 10–15 minutes more until the liquid has been absorbed.

5 Season to taste with freshly ground black pepper. Stir in the chopped fresh parsley, toss through to combine and serve immediately.

Energy 269Kcal/1125kJ; Protein 6.8g; Carbohydrate 51.5g, of which sugars 1.1g; Fat 3.7g, of which saturates 0.5g; Cholesterol 0mg; Calcium 23mg; Fibre 1.5g; Sodium 6mg.

Tagine of yam, carrots and prunes

This comforting stew has a Moroccan influence. The yam (or sweet potatoes), carrots and prunes give it a delicious sweet flavour, enhanced with honey and warm cinnamon and ginger spices. Chopped fresh herbs add to the tempting combination. Serve it with rice or couscous and a mixed, leafy green salad that includes some bitter leaves.

Serves 4

45ml/3 tbsp olive oil
25–30 baby (pearl) onions, blanched and peeled
900g/2lb yam or sweet potatoes, peeled and cut into bitesize chunks
2–3 carrots, cut into bitesize chunks
150g/5oz/generous ½ cup ready-to-eat pitted prunes
5ml/1 tsp ground cinnamon
2.5ml/½ tsp ground ginger
10ml/2 tsp clear honey
450ml/¾ pint/scant 2 cups vegetable stock
small bunch of fresh coriander (cilantro), finely chopped
small bunch of fresh mint, finely chopped
ground black pepper

1 Preheat the oven to 200°C/400°F/Gas 6. Heat the olive oil in a flameproof casserole and stir in the onions. Cook for about 5 minutes until the onions are tender, then remove half of the onions from the pan and set aside.

2 Add the yam or sweet potatoes and carrots to the pan and cook until lightly browned. Stir in the prunes with the cinnamon, ginger and honey, then pour in the stock. Season well, cover the casserole and transfer to the oven for about 45 minutes.

3 Stir in the reserved onions and bake for a further 10 minutes. Gently stir in the chopped coriander and mint, and serve the tagine immediately.

Energy 431Kcal/1825kJ; Protein 5.6g; Carbohydrate 86.4g, of which sugars 23g; Fat 9.5g, of which saturates 1.5g; Cholesterol 0mg; Calcium 97mg; Fibre 7.6g; Sodium 27mg.

Butter bean, tomato and olive stew

This hearty vegetarian stew is based on creamy butter beans. They offer plenty of dietary fibre, essential for a healthy digestive system. Little cherry tomatoes provide vitamin C and lycopene, both valuable antioxidants, and onions, garlic and ginger all contribute beneficial compounds. Serve on its own or with rice and a side salad.

Serves 4

115g/4oz/⅔ cup butter (lima) beans, soaked overnight
30–45ml/2–3 tbsp olive oil
1 onion, chopped
2–3 garlic cloves, crushed
25g/1oz fresh root ginger, peeled and finely chopped
pinch of saffron threads
16 cherry tomatoes
pinch of sugar
handful of fleshy black olives, pitted
5ml/1 tsp ground cinnamon
5ml/1 tsp paprika
small bunch of fresh flat leaf parsley
ground black pepper

1 Rinse the beans and place them in a large pan with plenty of water. Bring to the boil and boil for about 10 minutes, and then reduce the heat and simmer gently for 1–1½ hours until tender. Drain the beans and refresh under cold running water, then drain again.

2 Heat the olive oil in a heavy pan. Add the onion, garlic and ginger, and cook for about 10 minutes until softened but not browned. Stir in the saffron threads, followed by the cherry tomatoes and a sprinkling of sugar.

3 As the tomatoes begin to soften, stir in the butter beans. When the tomatoes have heated through, stir in the olives, ground cinnamon and paprika. Season to taste and sprinkle over the chopped parsley. Serve immediately.

Cook's tip
If you are in a hurry, you could use two 400g/14oz cans of butter (lima) beans for this tagine. Make sure you rinse them well before adding, as canned beans are salty if packed in brine.

Energy 138Kcal/578kJ; Protein 5.5g; Carbohydrate 12.8g, of which sugars 3.5g; Fat 7.6g, of which saturates 1.1g; Cholesterol 0mg; Calcium 51mg; Fibre 5.2g; Sodium 605mg.

Aromatic chickpea and spinach curry

High in fibre, this hearty, warming curry tastes great and boosts vitality with essential vitamins. Despite its name, the chickpea is not really a pea, but a seed. It is richer in vitamin E than most dried beans, peas and lentils, and like them it is an important source of vegetable protein. Serve it with rice or couscous, if liked, mango chutney and a cooling mint raita.

Serves 4

15ml/1 tbsp vegetable oil
1 large onion, finely chopped
2 garlic cloves, crushed
2.5cm/1in fresh root ginger, finely chopped
1 green chilli, seeded and finely chopped
30ml/2 tbsp medium curry paste
10ml/2 tsp ground cumin
5ml/1 tsp ground turmeric
225g/8oz can chopped tomatoes
1 green or red (bell) pepper, seeded and chopped
300ml/½ pint/1¼ cups vegetable stock
15ml/1 tbsp tomato purée (paste)
450g/1lb fresh spinach
400g/14oz can chickpeas, drained
45ml/3 tbsp chopped fresh coriander (cilantro)
5ml/1 tsp garam masala (optional)

1 Heat the vegetable oil in a large, heavy pan and cook the chopped onion, crushed garlic, root ginger and chilli over a gentle heat for about 5 minutes, or until the onion has softened, but not browned. Stir in the curry paste, mix thoroughly and cook for 1 minute, then stir in the ground cumin and turmeric. Stir over a low heat for 1 minute more.

2 Add the tomatoes and pepper and stir to coat with the spice mixture. Pour in the stock and stir in the tomato purée. Bring to the boil, lower the heat, cover and simmer for 15 minutes.

3 Remove any coarse stalks from the spinach, then rinse the leaves thoroughly, drain them and tear into large pieces. Add them to the pan, in batches, adding a handful more as each batch cooks down and wilts.

4 Stir in the chickpeas, cover and cook gently for 5 minutes more. Add the fresh chopped coriander, season to taste and stir well. Spoon into a warmed serving bowl and sprinkle with the garam masala, if using. Serve immediately.

Energy 221Kcal/925kJ; Protein 12.3g; Carbohydrate 28.7g, of which sugars 11.1g; Fat 7.1g, of which saturates 0.8g; Cholesterol 0mg; Calcium 262mg; Fibre 8.8g; Sodium 396mg.

Vegetable main dishes 113

Tomato and lentil dhal with almonds

Spices have long been recognized for their medicinal qualities, from relieving flatulence to warding off colds and flu. Dhal, made with lentils, is one of the staples of Indian cooking. It can be served either as an accompaniment or as a filling and tasty main dish. Lentils are bland in flavour and are therefore a good carrier of spicy flavours.

Serves 4

30ml/2 tbsp vegetable oil
1 large onion, finely chopped
3 garlic cloves, chopped
1 carrot, diced
10ml/2 tsp cumin seeds
10ml/2 tsp mustard seeds
2.5cm/1in fresh root ginger, grated
10ml/2 tsp ground turmeric
5ml/1 tsp mild chilli powder
5ml/1 tsp garam masala
225g/8oz/1 cup split red lentils
800ml/1½ pints/3¼ cups vegetable stock or water
5 tomatoes, peeled, seeded and chopped
juice of 2 limes
60ml/4 tbsp chopped fresh coriander (cilantro)
ground black pepper
25g/1oz/¼ cup flaked (sliced) almonds, toasted, to serve

1 Heat the oil in a heavy pan. Sauté the onion for 5 minutes until softened, stirring occasionally. Add the garlic, carrot, cumin and mustard seeds, and ginger. Cook for 5 minutes, stirring, until the seeds pop and the carrot softens slightly.

2 Stir in the ground turmeric, chilli powder and garam masala, and cook the mixture on a low heat for 1 minute or until the flavours begin to mingle, stirring continuously to prevent the spices from burning.

3 Add the lentils, stock or water and chopped tomatoes, and season well with freshly ground black pepper. Bring to the boil, then reduce the heat and simmer, covered, for about 45 minutes, stirring occasionally.

4 Stir in the lime juice and 45ml/3 tbsp of the coriander. Cook for a further 15 minutes until the lentils are tender. Sprinkle with the remaining coriander and the flaked almonds.

Health benefits
• Limes are rich in vitamin C, which can aid the absorption of iron.
• Lentils are a useful source of low-fat protein, providing sustained, long-term energy. They contain significant amounts of B vitamins and are rich in zinc and iron.

Energy 326Kcal/1372kJ; Protein 16.9g; Carbohydrate 43.8g, of which sugars 11.5g; Fat 10.5g, of which saturates 1.2g; Cholesterol 0mg; Calcium 102mg; Fibre 6.6g; Sodium 44mg.

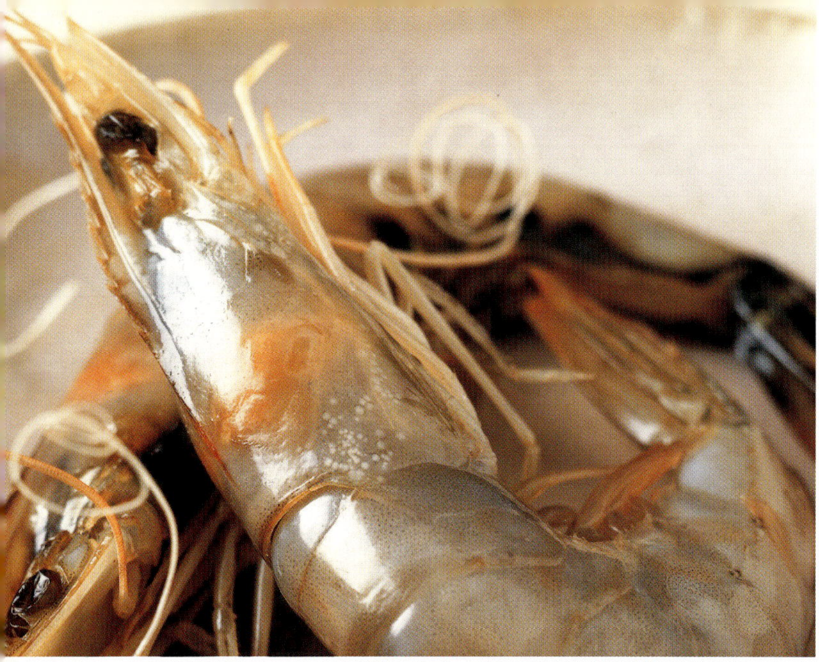
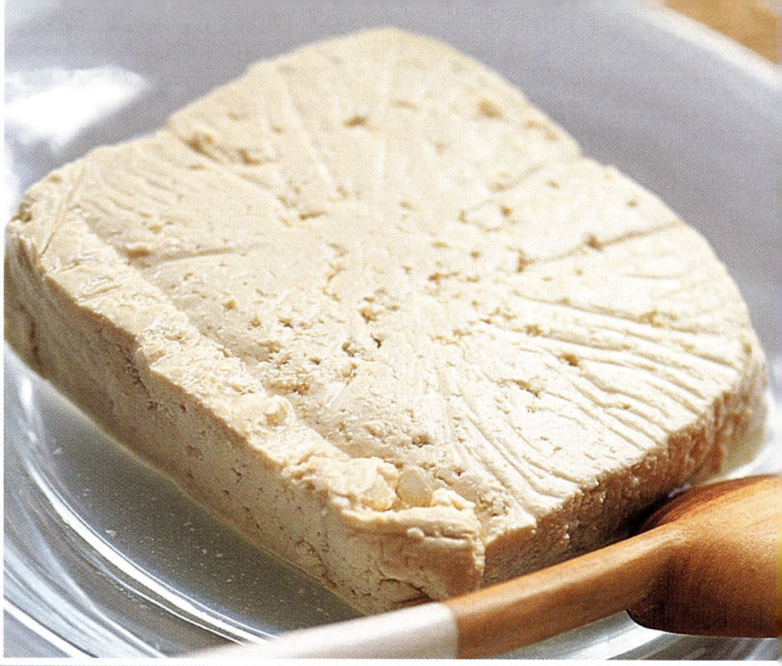
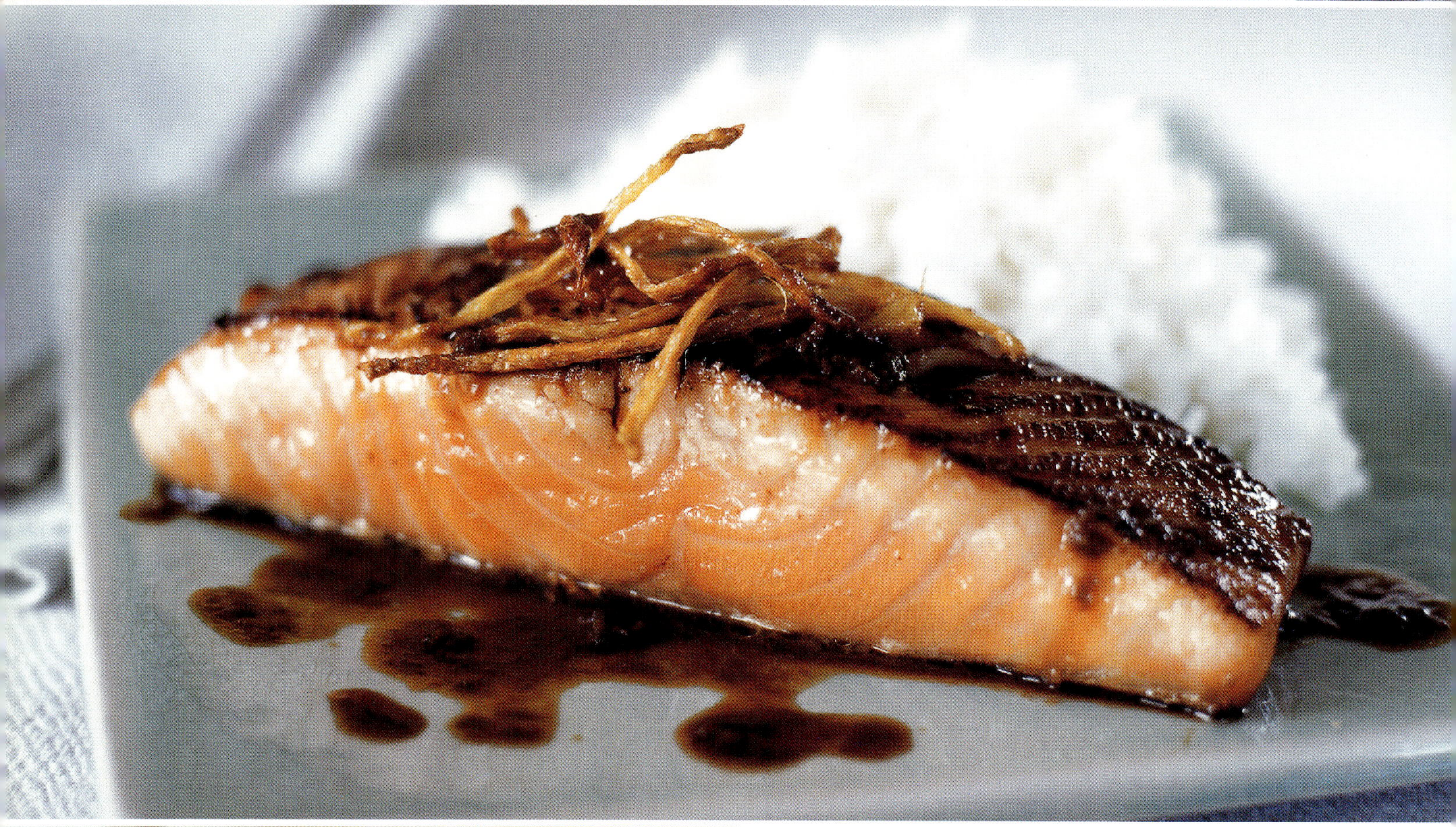
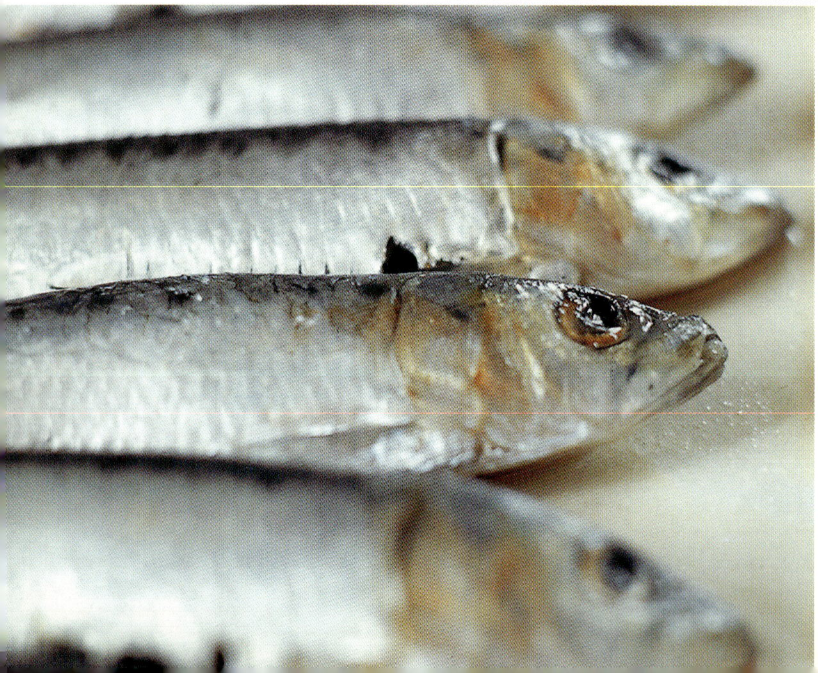
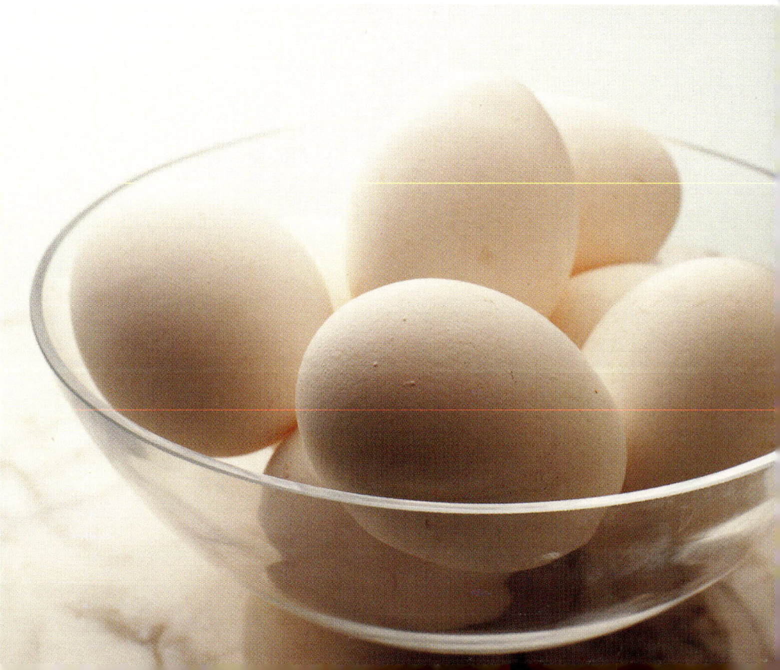

tofu, egg, fish, shellfish and chicken dishes

This selection of main course dishes made from tofu, eggs, fish, shellfish and chicken adds variety to your diet, especially if you plan to follow a detox regime for two weeks. There are simple ideas for midweek meals, like Spring Vegetable Omelette, as well as delicious "healthy eating" suggestions for casual entertaining, such as Spicy Paella, or Moroccan Fish Tagine. Some ingredients are optional and you can serve your own choice of accompaniments to suit your diet.

Tofu and pepper kebabs

A simple coating of ground peanuts pressed on to cubed tofu provides plenty of protein and additional flavour along with the colourful red and green peppers. Use metal or bamboo skewers for the kebabs – if you use bamboo, then soak them in cold water for 30 minutes before using to prevent them from scorching during cooking. Serve with rice and a side salad.

2 If you are making the kebabs in advance, cover them with clear film (plastic wrap) and store them in the fridge until they are needed.

3 Preheat the grill (broiler) to moderate. Halve and seed the peppers, and cut them into large, even chunks. Thread the chunks of pepper on to four large skewers, alternating with the coated tofu cubes, and place on a foil-lined grill rack.

4 Grill (broil) the kebabs, turning frequently, for 10–12 minutes, or until the peppers and peanuts are beginning to brown. (The kebabs can also be cooked on a barbecue, if you prefer.) Transfer the kebabs to plates and serve with the sweet chilli dipping sauce.

Serves 4

250g/9oz firm tofu, rinsed and drained
50g/2oz/½ cup unsalted peanuts
2 red and 2 green (bell) peppers
60ml/4 tbsp sweet chilli dipping sauce

1 Pat the tofu dry on kitchen paper and then cut it into bitesize cubes. Put the peanuts in a blender or food processor and process until coarsely ground, then transfer to a plate. Turn the tofu in the ground nuts to coat.

Variation
For an alternative version if you don't like peanuts, toss the tofu cubes in sesame seeds to coat, before threading them on to the skewers with the large chunks of red and green pepper.

Energy 187Kcal/778kJ; Protein 10.2g; Carbohydrate 16.8g, of which sugars 15.1g; Fat 9.1g, of which saturates 1.6g; Cholesterol 0mg; Calcium 342mg; Fibre 3.7g; Sodium 214mg.

Tofu, egg, fish, shellfish and chicken dishes **117**

Provençal stuffed peppers

Peppers make a perfect container for a tasty vegetable filling, including onions, courgettes, mushrooms and tomatoes, flavoured with fresh basil. This dish is bursting with valuable vitamins and the addition of pine nuts supplies useful protein. The vegetable sauce could be used to stuff other vegetables, such as large courgettes or baby aubergines.

Serves 4

15ml/1 tbsp olive oil
1 red onion, sliced
1 courgette (zucchini), diced
115g/4oz mushrooms, sliced
1 garlic clove, crushed
400g/14oz can chopped tomatoes
15ml/1 tbsp tomato purée (paste)
40g/1½oz/scant ⅓ cup pine nuts
30ml/2 tbsp chopped fresh basil
2 red and 2 yellow (bell) peppers
ground black pepper
fresh basil leaves, to garnish

1 Preheat the oven to 180°C/350°F/Gas 4. Heat the olive oil in a large pan, add the onion, courgette, mushrooms and garlic and cook gently over a medium heat for 3 minutes, stirring from time to time.

2 Stir in the chopped tomatoes and the tomato purée. Bring to the boil, then reduce the heat and simmer, uncovered, for 10–15 minutes, stirring, until thickened slightly.

3 Remove from the heat and stir in the pine nuts, basil and seasoning.

4 Cut the peppers in half lengthways and seed them. Blanch in a pan of boiling water for 3 minutes. Drain.

5 Place the peppers in a shallow, ovenproof dish and fill each one with the vegetable mixture. Cover the dish with foil and bake for 20 minutes.

6 Remove the foil and bake for a further 5–10 minutes until bubbling. Garnish with basil leaves and serve immediately.

Variation

If not following a strict detox, sprinkle the peppers with a little grated hard cheese for the final 5–10 minutes of the cooking time.

Energy 185Kcal/769kJ; Protein 5.5g; Carbohydrate 16.9g, of which sugars 15.9g; Fat 11g, of which saturates 1.2g; Cholesterol 0mg; Calcium 40mg; Fibre 5g; Sodium 19mg.

Spring vegetable omelette

An omelette makes a quick and easy, nourishing meal. Omelettes are very versatile and can be filled with all kinds of ingredients, but this one, packed with seasonal spring vegetables, is particularly healthy. It includes tender asparagus tips, spring greens, onion, baby new potatoes, and tomatoes, and is flavoured with fresh mixed herbs.

Serves 4

50g/2oz asparagus tips
50g/2oz spring greens (collards), shredded
15ml/1 tbsp vegetable oil
1 onion, sliced
175g/6oz cooked baby new potatoes, halved or diced
2 tomatoes, chopped
6 eggs
30ml/2 tbsp chopped fresh mixed herbs
ground black pepper
cherry tomatoes and leafy salad, to serve

1 Steam the asparagus tips and spring greens over a pan of boiling water for 5–10 minutes until tender. Drain the vegetables and keep warm.

2 Heat the vegetable oil in a large frying pan, add the onion and cook gently for 5–10 minutes until softened, stirring.

3 Add the cooked baby potatoes and cook for 3 minutes, stirring. Stir in the chopped tomatoes, asparagus and spring greens.

4 Lightly beat the eggs in a small bowl with the herbs, and season with ground black pepper.

5 Pour the beaten eggs over the vegetables, then cook over a gentle heat until the bottom of the omelette is golden brown.

6 Preheat the grill to hot and cook the omelette under the grill for 2–3 minutes until the top is golden brown. Serve with cherry tomatoes and a salad.

Energy 187Kcal/780kJ; Protein 11.4g; Carbohydrate 10.4g, of which sugars 3.5g; Fat 11.6g, of which saturates 2.8g; Cholesterol 285mg; Calcium 82mg; Fibre 1.8g; Sodium 118mg.

Egg and lentil curry

Eggs are an excellent addition to vegetarian curries and, combined with lentils, make a substantial and extremely tasty vegetarian curry. Serve with fluffy basmati rice and mango chutney. Follow this main dish with a vitamin C-rich fruit, such as sliced mango or orange, to ensure maximum absorption of iron from the eggs.

Serves four

75g/3oz/½ cup green lentils
750ml/1¼ pints/3 cups stock
6 eggs
30ml/2 tbsp vegetable oil
3 cloves
1.5ml/¼ tsp black peppercorns
1 onion, finely chopped
2 fresh green chillies, finely chopped
2 garlic cloves, crushed
2.5cm/1in piece of fresh root ginger, peeled and chopped
30ml/2 tbsp curry paste
400g/14oz can chopped tomatoes
2.5ml/½ tsp sugar
2.5ml/½ tsp garam masala

1 Wash the lentils thoroughly under cold running water, checking for small stones. Put the lentils in a large, heavy pan with the vegetable stock. Cover and simmer gently for about 15 minutes, or until the lentils are soft. Drain and set aside.

2 Put the eggs in a pan and cover with tepid water. Slowly bring the water to the boil, then reduce the heat and simmer for 7–8 minutes.

3 Remove the eggs from the pan of boiling water with a slotted spoon and place them in a bowl of cold water to cool. When they are cool enough to handle, peel the eggs and cut them in half lengthways.

4 Heat the oil in a large frying pan and fry the cloves and peppercorns for about 2 minutes. Add the onion, chillies, garlic and ginger and fry the mixture for a further 5–6 minutes, stirring frequently.

5 Stir in the curry paste and fry for a further 2 minutes, stirring constantly. Add the chopped tomatoes and sugar and stir in 175ml/6fl oz/¾ cup water. Simmer for about 5 minutes until the sauce thickens, stirring occasionally. Add the boiled eggs, drained lentils and garam masala. Cover and simmer gently for 5 minutes, then serve.

Cook's tip
You can substitute red lentils for the green if liked. Red lentils tend to disintegrate more when cooked.

Energy 238Kcal/997kJ; Protein 14.6g; Carbohydrate 14.2g, of which sugars 4.1g; Fat 14.4g, of which saturates 3.1g; Cholesterol 285mg; Calcium 60mg; Fibre 1.9g; Sodium 121mg.

Roasted cod with fresh tomato sauce

Really fresh cod fillets have a sweet, delicate flavour and pure white flaky flesh. Served with an aromatic fresh tomato sauce on a bed of steamed French beans, they make a delicious and nutritious meal that's quick to prepare. Accompany this simple yet delicious dish with some boiled baby new potatoes for a more substantial meal, if liked.

Serves 4

60ml/4 tbsp olive oil
350g/12oz ripe tomatoes
pinch of sugar
2 strips of pared orange rind
1 fresh thyme sprig
6 fresh basil leaves
900g/2lb fresh cod fillet, skin on
ground black pepper
steamed French (green) beans, to serve

1 Preheat the oven to 230°C/450°F/Gas 8. Using a small, sharp knife, roughly chop the tomatoes, leaving their skins on, and set aside.

2 Heat 15ml/1 tbsp of the olive oil in a heavy pan, add the tomatoes, sugar, orange rind, thyme and basil, and simmer for 5 minutes, until the tomatoes are soft and juicy. Remove the pan from the heat.

3 Press the tomato mixture through a fine sieve (strainer), discarding the solids that remain in the sieve. Pour into a small pan and heat gently.

4 Scale the cod fillet and cut on the diagonal into 4 pieces. Season well.

5 Heat the remaining oil in a heavy frying pan and fry the cod, skin side down, until the skin is crisp. Place the fish on a greased baking sheet, skin side up, and roast in the oven for 8–10 minutes, until cooked through. Serve on top of the steamed French beans with the fresh tomato sauce.

Variation
Try haddock, hake, monkfish or any other firm white fish fillet instead of the cod, if you like.

Energy 294Kcal/1229kJ; Protein 41.8g; Carbohydrate 2.7g, of which sugars 2.7g; Fat 12.8g, of which saturates 1.9g; Cholesterol 104mg; Calcium 27mg; Fibre 0.9g; Sodium 143mg.

Seared tuna steaks with tomato salsa

Fresh and fruity tomato salsa provides a delicious boost of vitamins to accompany the health-promoting omega-3 fatty acids that can be found in abundance in fresh tuna fish. Take care not to cook the tuna for too long, as the flesh can become dry if it is overcooked. It should remain pinky-red in the centre and be moist and succulent in texture.

Serves 4

4 tuna steaks, each weighing about 175–200g/6–7oz
30ml/2 tbsp olive oil
5ml/1 tsp cumin seeds, toasted
grated rind and juice of 1 lime
pinch of dried red chilli flakes
1 small red onion, finely chopped
200g/7oz cherry tomatoes, chopped
1 avocado, peeled, stoned (pitted) and chopped
2 kiwi fruit, peeled and chopped
1 fresh red chilli, seeded and chopped
15g/½oz fresh coriander (cilantro), chopped
6 fresh mint sprigs, leaves only, chopped
5–10ml/1–2 tsp Thai fish sauce (*nam pla*)
ground black pepper
lime wedges and fresh coriander (cilantro) sprigs, to garnish

1 Place the tuna steaks on a glass or ceramic plate and drizzle over the olive oil. Sprinkle the steaks with half the toasted cumin seeds, ground black pepper, half the lime rind and the dried chilli flakes. Set aside and leave to stand for about 30 minutes.

2 Meanwhile, make the salsa. Combine the onion, tomatoes, avocado, kiwi fruit, chilli, coriander and mint in a bowl. Add the remaining cumin seeds and lime rind and half the lime juice. Stir in Thai fish sauce to taste. Cover with clear film (plastic wrap) and set aside for about 20 minutes.

3 Heat a ridged, cast-iron griddle pan until it is very hot. Carefully lay the tuna steaks in the pan and cook for 2 minutes on each side for rare tuna or a little longer for a medium result.

4 Transfer the tuna steaks to four warmed serving plates and garnish with lime wedges and fresh coriander sprigs. Spoon on the tomato salsa, or transfer it to a serving bowl and offer it separately.

Cook's tip
Do not move the tuna around in the pan while it is cooking. The steak needs to stay in one position to be seared with neat and attractive chargrill lines.

Energy 397Kcal/1662kJ; Protein 48.9g; Carbohydrate 5.6g, of which sugars 5.1g; Fat 20g, of which saturates 4.3g; Cholesterol 56mg; Calcium 71mg; Fibre 2.6g; Sodium 105mg.

Barbecued sardines with orange

Sardines are another healthy oil-rich fish and they taste delicious in combination with juicy oranges and fresh parsley. They are ideal for cooking on a barbecue – the meaty flesh holds together, the skin crisps nicely and there are no lingering indoor cooking smells. However, they cook just as well under a grill indoors. Serve them with a selection of salads.

Serves 6

6 whole large sardines, gutted
1 orange, sliced
small bunch of fresh flat leaf parsley, chopped
60ml/4 tbsp olive oil
ground black pepper

1 Arrange the sardines and orange slices in a single layer in a large, shallow, non-metallic dish.

2 Sprinkle over half of the chopped fresh parsley and season with ground black pepper.

3 Drizzle the oil over the sardines and orange slices and brush to coat well.

4 Cover the dish with clear film (plastic wrap) and keep chilled in the refrigerator until ready to cook.

5 Meanwhile, prepare the barbecue. Remove the sardines and orange slices from the marinade and cook the fish for 7–8 minutes on each side, until cooked through. Sprinkle with the remaining parsley and serve immediately.

Energy 175Kcal/729kJ; Protein 13.3g; Carbohydrate 1.9g, of which sugars 1.9g; Fat 12.7g, of which saturates 2.6g; Cholesterol 0mg; Calcium 89mg; Fibre 0.8g; Sodium 75mg.

Grilled mackerel with spicy dhal

Mackerel is a well-flavoured, highly nutritious oily fish and it tastes good simply grilled. It is often served with a sharp, fruity sauce, but for a more satisfying dish, these delicious tamarind-flavoured lentils or split peas make an appealing accompaniment. Serve with a tomato and onion salad. If not following a strict detox, flat bread would also be a good accompaniment.

Serves 4

250g/9oz/generous 1 cup red lentils, or yellow split peas rinsed
1 litre/1¾ pints/4 cups water
30ml/2 tbsp vegetable oil
2.5ml/½ tsp each mustard seeds, cumin seeds, fennel seeds and fenugreek or cardamom seeds
5ml/1 tsp ground turmeric
3–4 dried red chillies, crumbled
30ml/2 tbsp tamarind paste
30ml/2 tbsp chopped fresh coriander (cilantro)
4 mackerel
ground black pepper
fresh red chilli slices and finely chopped coriander, to garnish

1 Put the lentils or split peas in a pan. Pour in the water and bring to the boil. Lower the heat, partially cover the pan and simmer the lentils or split peas for 30–40 minutes, stirring occasionally, until they are tender and mushy.

2 Heat the oil in a wok or shallow pan. Add the mustard seeds, then cover and cook for a few seconds until they pop. Remove the lid, add the rest of the seeds, with the turmeric and chillies and fry for a few more seconds.

3 Stir in the lentils or split peas and the tamarind paste and mix well. Bring to the boil, then simmer for 10 minutes until thick. Stir in the coriander.

4 Clean the fish then heat a ridged griddle or the grill (broiler) until very hot. Make six diagonal slashes on either side of each fish and remove the head. Season, then grill for 5–7 minutes on each side. Serve, garnished with sliced red chilli and chopped coriander, accompanied by the dhal.

Energy 578Kcal/2420kJ; Protein 43.5g; Carbohydrate 35.2g, of which sugars 1.5g; Fat 30.2g, of which saturates 5.7g; Cholesterol 80mg; Calcium 49mg; Fibre 3.1g; Sodium 110mg.

Teriyaki salmon

Teriyaki is a popular cooking style in Japan, and is frequently used to flavour fish, poultry and meat. Teriyaki marinade is usually made with soy sauce, rice wine and sugar and although it is easy to make, you can also buy it in bottles from supermarkets and Asian stores. It is a great way of perking up the flavour of salmon fillets for a light and healthy meal.

Serves 4

4 salmon fillets, about 150g/5oz each
75ml/5 tbsp teriyaki marinade
5cm/2in piece of fresh root ginger, peeled and cut into matchsticks
150ml/¼ pint/⅔ cup sunflower oil

1 Put the salmon fillets in a shallow, non-metallic dish and pour over the teriyaki marinade. Turn the fish in the marinade a few times to coat thoroughly. Cover with clear film (plastic wrap), then keep chilled in the refrigerator for 2 hours.

2 Meanwhile, heat the sunflower oil in a small pan and add the ginger. Fry for 1–2 minutes, or until golden and crisp. Remove with a slotted spoon and drain on kitchen paper.

3 Heat a griddle pan until smoking hot. Remove the salmon from the marinade and add, skin side down, to the pan. Cook for 2–3 minutes, then turn over and cook for a further 1–2 minutes, or until cooked through. Remove from the pan and divide among four serving plates. Top the salmon fillets with the crispy fried ginger.

4 Pour the teriyaki marinade into the pan and cook for 1–2 minutes, to heat through and reduce slightly. Pour the marinade over the salmon and serve immediately.

Energy 290Kcal/1208kJ; Protein 30.4g; Carbohydrate 2.2g, of which sugars 2.1g; Fat 17.8g, of which saturates 3g; Cholesterol 75mg; Calcium 33mg; Fibre 0.1g; Sodium 190mg.

Chinese-style steamed trout

Trout is another oily fish that is rich in essential fatty acids, which are vital for good health. Serve this simple Oriental dish with plain boiled rice and a vegetable dish, such as stir-fried spring greens, for a satisfying meal. This would be a great meal for entertaining as it looks impressive, as well as tasting delicious and being super-healthy.

Serves 6

2 trout, each weighing about 675–800g/1½–1¾lb
25ml/1½ tbsp salted black beans, rinsed
pinch of sugar
30ml/2 tbsp finely shredded fresh root ginger
4 garlic cloves, thinly sliced
30ml/2 tbsp Chinese rice wine or dry sherry
30ml/2 tbsp light soy sauce
4–6 spring onions (scallions), finely shredded or sliced diagonally
15ml/1 tbsp sesame oil

1 Wash the trout inside and out under cold running water, then pat the fish dry on a sheet of kitchen paper. Using a sharp knife, carefully slash 3–4 deep crosses on each side of each fish.

2 Place half the black beans and the sugar in a small bowl and mash together with the back of a fork. Stir in the remaining whole beans.

3 Place a little ginger and garlic inside the cavity of each fish, then lay them on a plate or dish that will fit inside a large steamer. Rub the bean mixture into the fish, working it into the slashes, then sprinkle the remaining ginger and garlic over the top. Cover with clear film (plastic wrap) and place the fish in the refrigerator for at least 30 minutes.

4 Remove the fish from the refrigerator and place the steamer over a pan of boiling water. Sprinkle the rice wine or sherry and half the soy sauce over the fish and place the plate of fish inside the steamer. Steam for 15–20 minutes, or until the fish is just cooked and the flesh flakes easily when tested with the tip of a knife.

5 Using a fish slice (metal spatula), carefully lift the cooked fish on to a warmed serving dish. Sprinkle the fish with the remaining soy sauce and then sprinkle with the shredded or sliced spring onions.

6 Lightly sprinkle the sesame oil over the cooked fish and spring onions, then serve immediately.

Cook's tip
Black beans and soy sauce are both high in salt, so use reduced-salt soy sauce if available and rinse the black beans under cold running water to remove the excess salt. Salted black beans can often be bought from Chinese restaurants if there is not an Asian grocery store near to where you live.

Energy 235Kcal/990kJ; Protein 36.6g; Carbohydrate 1g, of which sugars 0.9g; Fat 8.9g, of which saturates 1.9g; Cholesterol 149mg; Calcium 61mg; Fibre 0.1g; Sodium 789mg.

Moroccan fish tagine

Firm-fleshed fish, such as monkfish, makes a good low-fat choice for this North African-style dish. It is cooked with onions, aubergines, courgettes and tomatoes with a spicy harissa paste to make a healthy dish that's a bit special. Serve in traditional style with couscous, or for a wheat-free accompaniment, serve with rice, pearl barley or quinoa.

4 Heat the remaining oil in a separate pan. Add the aubergine cubes and fry for 10 minutes. Add the cubed courgettes and fry the vegetables for a further 2 minutes, stirring occasionally.

5 Tip the aubergine mixture into the pan and combine with the onions, then stir in the chopped tomatoes, the passata and fish stock. Bring to the boil, then lower the heat and simmer

6 Stir the fish cubes and preserved lemon into the pan. Add the olives and stir gently. Cover and simmer over a low heat for about 15–20 minutes until the fish is just cooked through. Season to taste. Stir in the chopped coriander. Garnish with coriander sprigs.

Serves 6–8

1.3kg/3lb firm fish fillets such as monkfish or hoki, skinned and cut into 5cm/2in cubes
60ml/4 tbsp olive oil
4 onions, chopped
1 large aubergine (eggplant), cut into 1cm/½in cubes
2 courgettes (zucchini), cut into 1cm/½in cubes
400g/14oz can chopped tomatoes
400ml/14fl oz/1⅔ cups passata (bottled strained tomatoes)
200ml/7fl oz/scant 1 cup fish stock
1 preserved lemon, chopped
90g/3½oz/scant 1 cup olives
60ml/4 tbsp chopped fresh coriander (cilantro)
ground black pepper
coriander sprigs, to garnish

For the harissa

3 large fresh red chillies, seeded and chopped
3 garlic cloves, peeled
15ml/1 tbsp ground coriander
30ml/2 tbsp ground cumin
5ml/1 tsp ground cinnamon
grated rind of 1 lemon
30ml/2 tbsp vegetable oil

1 To make the harissa, whizz everything in a food processor to a smooth paste.

2 Put the fish in a wide bowl and add 30ml/2 tbsp of the harissa. Toss to coat, cover and chill for at least 1 hour.

3 Heat half the oil in a shallow pan. Add the onions and cook for 10 minutes. Stir in the remaining harissa; cook for 5 minutes, stirring occasionally.

Cook's tip
To boost the fibre value, you could add 225g/8oz/1¼ cups cooked chickpeas to the tagine.

Energy 230Kcal/968kJ; Protein 28.5g; Carbohydrate 11.7g, of which sugars 9.6g; Fat 8.1g, of which saturates 1.3g; Cholesterol 23mg; Calcium 65mg; Fibre 3.7g; Sodium 406mg.

Spicy paella

Recipes vary from region to region for this famous Spanish rice dish, but this version uses lean chicken breast fillets, white fish and shellfish with plenty of vegetables for a healthy combination. Note that the fish and chicken are marinated, so you need to start preparing this dish a couple of hours before cooking. It's ideal for casual entertaining.

Serves 6

2 large boneless chicken breast fillets
about 150g/5oz prepared squid
8–10 raw king prawns (jumbo shrimp)
325g/11oz cod or haddock fillets
8 scallops, trimmed and halved
350g/12oz raw mussels in shells
30ml/2 tbsp vegetable oil
bunch of spring onions (scallions), cut into strips
2 small courgettes (zucchini), cut into strips
1 red (bell) pepper, cut into strips
250g/9oz/1⅓ cups long grain rice, rinsed
400ml/14fl oz/1⅔ cups chicken stock
250ml/8fl oz/1 cup passata (bottled strained tomatoes)
ground black pepper
coriander (cilantro), lemon wedges, to garnish

For the marinade

2 fresh red chillies, seeded
good handful of fresh coriander (cilantro)
10ml/2 tsp ground cumin
15ml/1 tbsp paprika
2 garlic cloves
90ml/6 tbsp olive oil
juice of 1 lemon

1 First blend all the ingredients for the marinade in a food processor.

2 Skin the chicken and cut into bitesize pieces. Place in a glass bowl. Slice the squid into rings and shell the prawns. Skin the fish and cut into bitesize chunks. Place the fish and shellfish (apart from the mussels) in a separate bowl. Divide the marinade between the fish and chicken and mix well. Cover and marinate for 2 hours.

3 Scrub the mussels, discarding any that do not close when tapped. Drain the chicken and fish, and reserve the marinade. Heat the oil in a pan and fry the chicken until lightly browned.

4 Add the spring onions to the wok or pan, fry for 1 minute and then add the courgettes and red pepper strips and fry for a further 3–4 minutes until slightly softened. Remove the chicken and then the vegetables with a slotted spoon to separate plates.

5 Scrape the marinade into the pan and cook for 1 minute. Add the rice to the pan and stir-fry for 1 minute. Add the chicken stock, passata and reserved chicken and stir well. Bring to the boil, then reduce the heat, cover and simmer gently for 15–20 minutes until the rice is almost tender.

6 Add the reserved vegetables to the pan and place all the fish and mussels on top. Cover and cook gently for 10–12 minutes until the fish is cooked and the mussels have opened. Discard any mussels that have not opened during cooking. Serve garnished with coriander and lemon wedges.

Energy 352Kcal/1479kJ; Protein 36.4g; Carbohydrate 37.8g, of which sugars 4.1g; Fat 6g, of which saturates 0.9g; Cholesterol 156mg; Calcium 88mg; Fibre 1.3g; Sodium 257mg.

Griddled chicken with tomato salsa

This aromatic dish is a great way to enjoy the flavour, colour and health benefits of good quality fresh ingredients. Plum tomatoes are richly flavoured, less watery and have less seeds than regular tomatoes. If unavailable, use ripe, flavoursome salad tomatoes – sun-ripened would be ideal. For the best result, marinate the chicken overnight.

Serves 4

4 skinless chicken breast fillets, about 175g/6oz each
30ml/2 tbsp fresh lemon juice
30ml/2 tbsp olive oil
10ml/2 tsp ground cumin
10ml/2 tsp dried oregano
15ml/1 tbsp coarsely ground black pepper

For the salsa

1 fresh green chilli
450g/1lb plum tomatoes, skinned (optional), seeded and chopped
3 spring onions (scallions), chopped
15ml/1 tbsp chopped fresh parsley
30ml/2 tbsp chopped fresh coriander (cilantro)
30ml/2 tbsp fresh lemon juice
45ml/3 tbsp olive oil

1 With a meat mallet, pound the chicken between two sheets of clear film (plastic wrap) until thin.

2 In a shallow dish, combine the lemon juice, oil, cumin, oregano and pepper. Add the chicken, cover and leave to marinate for at least 2 hours.

3 To make the salsa, char the chilli over a gas flame or under the grill (broiler). Leave to cool, then carefully rub off the charred skin.

4 Chop the chilli very finely and place in a bowl. Add the seeded and chopped tomatoes, the chopped spring onions, chopped fresh parsley and coriander, lemon juice and olive oil and mix well. Set aside until ready to serve.

5 Remove the chicken from the marinade. Heat a ridged griddle pan. Add the chicken fillets and cook on one side until browned, for about 3 minutes. Turn over and cook for 4 minutes more. Serve with the tomato salsa.

Energy 260Kcal/1096kJ; Protein 43.3g; Carbohydrate 4.1g, of which sugars 4g; Fat 8g, of which saturates 1.4g; Cholesterol 123mg; Calcium 45mg; Fibre 1.9g; Sodium 120mg.

Pan-fried chicken with pesto

Pan-fried chicken, served with warm home-made basil pesto, makes a deliciously quick main course. Make this simple dish in the summer, when basil leaves are plentiful. Omit the Parmesan cheese for a dairy-free pesto. Walnuts make a good alternative to pine nuts. Serve with braised baby carrots and celery, and rice, noodles or potatoes.

Serves 4

15ml/1 tbsp olive oil
4 skinless, chicken breast fillets
fresh basil leaves, to garnish

For the pesto
90ml/6 tbsp olive oil
50g/2oz/½ cup pine nuts
50g/2oz/⅔ cup freshly grated
    Parmesan cheese (optional)
50g/2oz/1 cup fresh basil leaves
15g/½oz/¼ cup fresh parsley
2 garlic cloves, crushed
ground black pepper

1 Heat the 15ml/1 tbsp oil in a frying pan. Add the chicken breasts and cook gently for 15–20 minutes, turning several times until the chicken breasts are tender, lightly browned and thoroughly cooked.

2 Meanwhile, make the pesto. Place the olive oil, pine nuts, Parmesan cheese, if using, basil leaves, parsley, garlic and pepper in a blender or food processor and process until smooth.

3 Remove the chicken from the pan, cover and keep hot. Reduce the heat slightly, then add the pesto to the pan and cook gently, stirring constantly, for a few minutes until the pesto has warmed through.

4 Pour the warm pesto over the chicken, garnish with basil leaves, and serve immediately.

Energy 419Kcal/1745kJ; Protein 37.9g; Carbohydrate 0.6g, of which sugars 0.6g; Fat 29.5g, of which saturates 3.8g; Cholesterol 105mg; Calcium 17mg; Fibre 0.4g; Sodium 91mg.

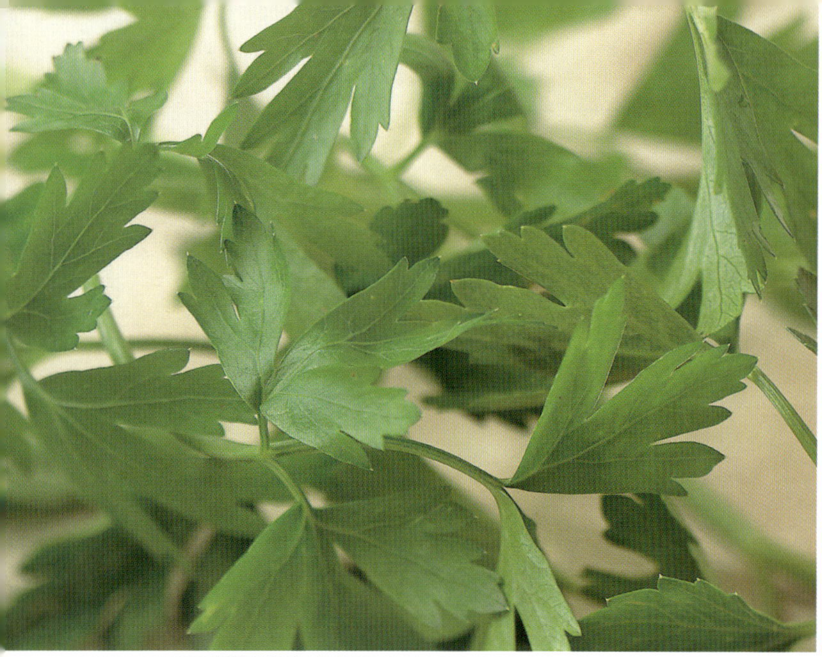
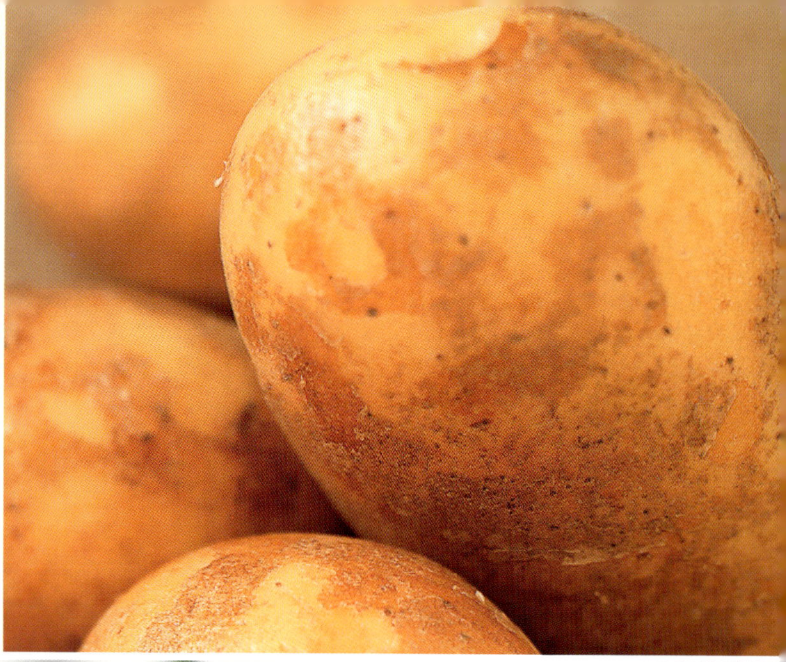
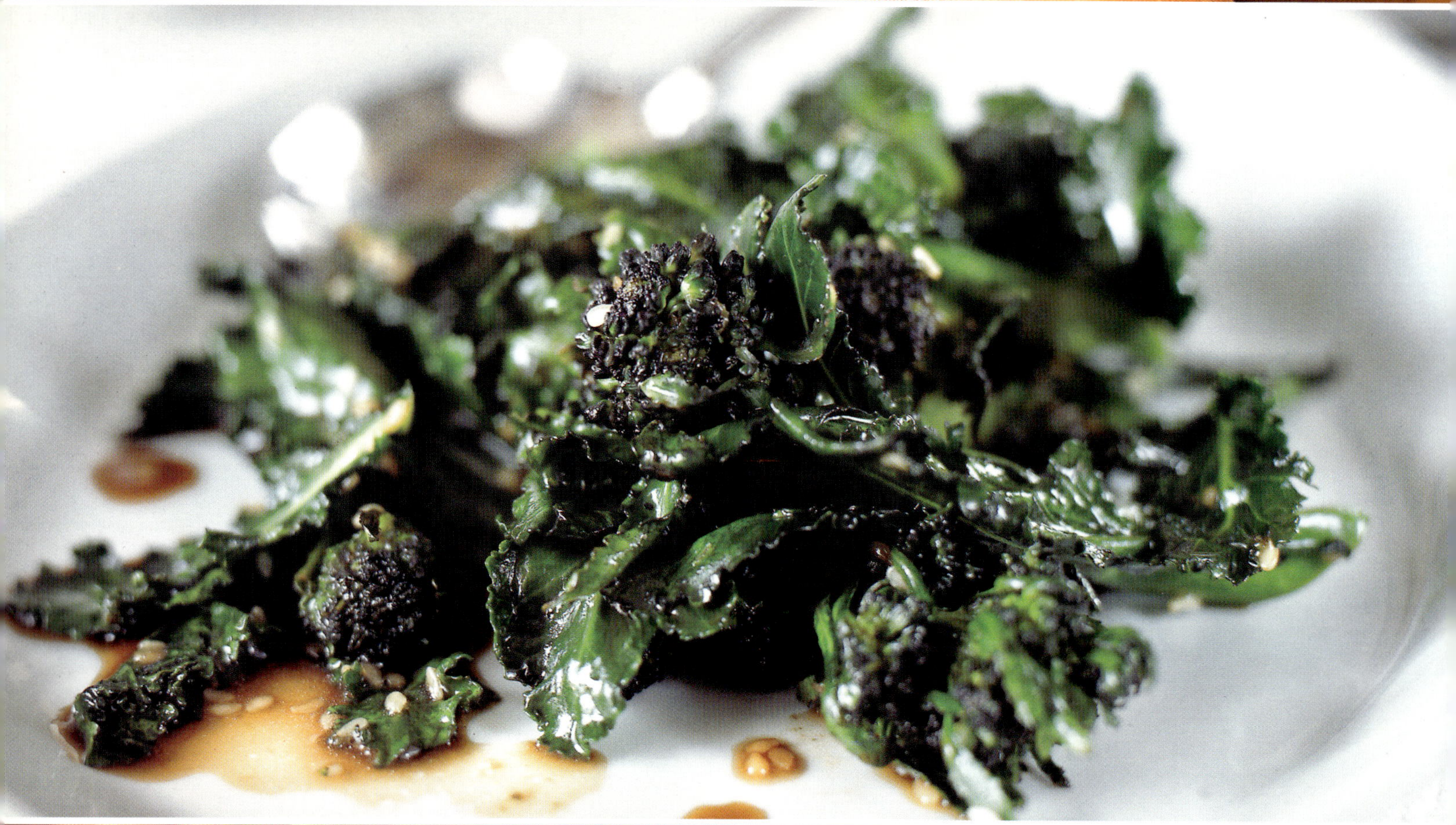
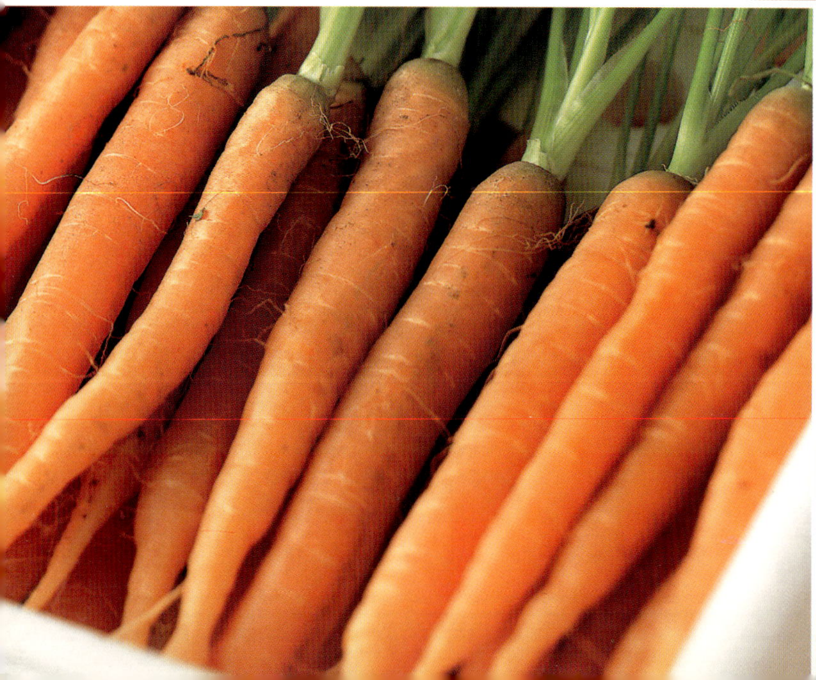
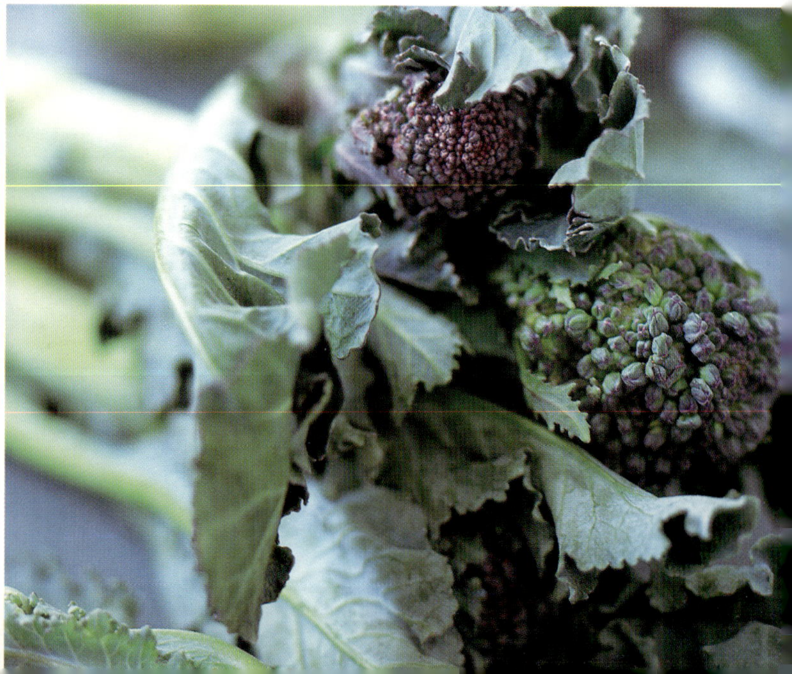

simple salads and side dishes

Eating plenty of vegetables is an essential part of any healthy diet, and having a good proportion of them raw, as salads, ensures that they retain the maximum nutritional value. The recipes in this chapter include a wide selection of hot and cold vegetable, potato, bean and rice ideas to serve as accompaniments. Alternatively, several dishes could be combined to make up a vitamin-packed meal, ideal for a detox regime and providing a healthy option for the entire family.

Spinach and roast garlic salad

Do not worry about the large amount of garlic in this salad. Roasting garlic significantly sweetens and subdues its flavour. It will lose its pungent taste, becoming succulent and subtle and will provide all of the health benefits without the after-effects. Toasted pine nuts are also included in this salad, adding a nutritious crunch and added flavour.

Serves 4
12 garlic cloves, unpeeled
60ml/4 tbsp olive oil
450g/1lb baby spinach leaves
50g/2oz/½ cup pine nuts, lightly toasted
juice of ½ lemon
ground black pepper

Cook's tip
If spinach is to be served raw in a salad, the leaves should be young and tender. Wash well, then drain and pat dry with kitchen paper.

1 Preheat the oven to 190°C/375°F/Gas 5. Place the unpeeled garlic cloves in a small roasting dish, drizzle over 30ml/2 tbsp of the olive oil and toss to coat evenly.

2 Bake for about 15 minutes until the garlic cloves become slightly charred around the edges.

3 While still warm, tip the garlic cloves, still in their skins, into a salad bowl. Add the spinach, pine nuts, lemon juice and remaining olive oil. Toss well and season with pepper to taste.

4 Serve immediately, squeezing the softened garlic out of the skins to eat.

Health benefits
Spinach is a superb source of nutrients, providing a rich supply of antioxidant betacarotene, vitamin C, calcium, folate and iron. Spinach offers the greatest health benefits when eaten raw. Garlic is believed to aid circulation and help fight infections.

Energy 238Kcal/980kJ; Protein 6.9g; Carbohydrate 6.4g, of which sugars 2.6g; Fat 20.6g, of which saturates 2.3g; Cholesterol 0mg; Calcium 198mg; Fibre 3.6g; Sodium 159mg.

Mixed green leaf and herb salad

This cleansing salad makes an ideal light side salad. You can use any combination of soft salad leaves and a variety of delicate herbs, depending on availability and personal preference. The herbs are a good aid to digestion as well as tasting wonderfully aromatic. You could turn it into a more substantial main salad dish by making one of the variations.

Serves 4

15g/½oz/½ cup mixed fresh herbs, such as chervil, dill, basil, marjoram (use sparingly), flat leaf parsley, mint, sorrel, fennel or coriander (cilantro)
350g/12oz mixed salad leaves, such as rocket (arugula), radicchio, chicory (Belgian endive), watercress, baby spinach, oakleaf lettuce and dandelion

For the dressing
50ml/2fl oz/¼ cup extra virgin olive oil
15ml/1 tbsp lemon juice
ground black pepper

1 Wash the herbs and salad leaves under running water and dry them in a salad spinner, or use two clean, dry dish towels to pat them dry.

Variations
If you are making this salad to serve as a light meal, you will need to give it a little more substance. Try adding some of the following combinations of ingredients:
• Tiny new potatoes in their jackets, crumbled hard-boiled egg yolks and beansprouts.
• Cooked baby broad (fava) beans, sliced artichoke hearts and whole cherry tomatoes.
• Cooked chickpeas, asparagus tips and pitted green olives.

2 In a small bowl, blend together the olive oil and lemon juice and season with ground black pepper to taste.

3 Place the mixed salad leaves and herbs in a large serving bowl. Pour over the dressing and mix well, using your hands to toss the leaves.

4 Serve immediately after adding the dressing to prevent the leaves wilting.

Cook's tip
This salad makes the perfect foundation for a detox salad. You can add any number of other ingredients to it, as suggested in the variations, or your own choice of extra ingredients.

Energy 92Kcal/377kJ; Protein 0.7g; Carbohydrate 1.6g, of which sugars 1.6g; Fat 9.2g, of which saturates 1.4g; Cholesterol 0mg; Calcium 26mg; Fibre 0.8g; Sodium 3mg.

Wild rocket and cos lettuce salad with fresh herbs

Rocket makes a delicious addition to a salad. The wild variety has a particularly robust, peppery flavour. Parsley and dill add to the appeal and the digestive qualities of this clean-tasting salad.

Serves 4

a large handful of rocket (arugula) leaves
2 cos or romaine lettuce hearts
3 or 4 fresh flat leaf parsley sprigs, roughly chopped
30–45ml/2–3 tbsp finely chopped fresh dill
60ml/4 tbsp extra virgin olive oil
15–30ml/1–2 tbsp lemon juice
ground black pepper

Cook's tip
It is important to balance the bitterness of the rocket (arugula) and the sweetness of the cos or romaine lettuce, and the best way to do so is by taste.

1 If the rocket leaves are young and tender they can be left whole, but older ones should be trimmed of thick stalks and then sliced coarsely. Discard any tough stalks.

2 Slice the cos or romaine lettuce hearts into thin ribbons and place these in a bowl, then add the rocket and the chopped fresh parsley and dill.

3 Make a dressing by whisking the extra virgin olive oil and lemon juice with ground black pepper to taste in a bowl until the mixture emulsifies and thickens. Just before serving, pour the dressing over the salad and toss lightly to coat the leaves in the sharp and fruity dressing.

Energy 111Kcal/458kJ; Protein 0.7g; Carbohydrate 1.5g, of which sugars 1.5g; Fat 11.4g, of which saturates 1.7g; Cholesterol 0mg; Calcium 25mg; Fibre 0.8g; Sodium 3mg.

Cabbage salad with lemon dressing and black olives

An unusual salad with a crisp and refreshing texture. Usually white cabbage is dressed with a rich mayonnaise, so this recipe provides a lighter, healthier alternative idea for a detox regime.

Serves 4

1 white cabbage
12 black olives

For the dressing
75ml/5 tbsp extra virgin olive oil
30ml/2 tbsp lemon juice
1 garlic clove, crushed
30ml/2 tbsp finely chopped fresh flat leaf parsley
ground black pepper

1 Cut the cabbage in quarters, discard the outer leaves and trim off any thick, hard stems as well as the hard base. Stone (pit) the olives, if you prefer.

2 Lay each quarter in turn on its side and cut long, very thin slices until you reach the central core, which should be discarded. Shred the cabbage as finely as possible. Place the shredded cabbage in a large bowl and stir in the black olives.

3 Make the dressing by whisking the extra virgin olive oil, lemon juice, garlic, chopped parsley and pepper together in a small bowl until well blended. Pour the dressing over the cabbage and olives, and toss the salad until everything is evenly coated.

Energy 211Kcal/871kJ; Protein 2.9g; Carbohydrate 8.8g, of which sugars 8.6g; Fat 18.4g, of which saturates 2.6g; Cholesterol 0mg; Calcium 115mg; Fibre 4.5g; Sodium 297mg.

Grilled fennel salad with Niçoise olives

Fennel is particularly high in beneficial phytoestrogens, which are believed to help to protect against hormone-related cancers, such as breast or prostate cancer. In this Italian-style recipe, it is cooked on a piping hot griddle with sweet-tasting baby orange peppers, then served with torn savory leaves, juicy olives and sprinkled with a simple vinaigrette.

Serves 6

3 sweet baby orange (bell) peppers
5 fennel bulbs with green tops, total weight about 900g/2lb
30ml/2 tbsp olive oil
15ml/1 tbsp cider vinegar or white wine vinegar
45ml/3 tbsp extra virgin olive oil
24 small Niçoise olives
2 sprigs of fresh savory, leaves removed
ground black pepper

1 Heat a griddle pan until a few drops of water sprinkled on to the surface evaporate instantly.

2 Put the baby peppers on the pan and roast, turning them every few minutes, until charred all over.

3 Remove the pan from the heat, place the peppers in a bowl and cover with clear film (plastic wrap).

4 Remove the green fronds from the fennel and reserve. Slice the fennel lengthways into five roughly equal pieces. Place the fennel pieces in a flat dish, coat with the olive oil and season. Rub off the charred skin from the grilled peppers, remove the seeds and cut the flesh into small dice.

5 Reheat the griddle, then lower the heat slightly and grill the fennel slices in batches for about 8–10 minutes, turning frequently, until they are branded with golden grill marks. As each batch cooks, transfer it to a flat serving dish.

6 Whisk the vinegar and olive oil together, then pour over the fennel. Fold in the baby orange peppers and the olives. Tear the savory leaves and fennel fronds and scatter them over the salad. Serve warm or cold.

Cook's tip
If cooking directly on the barbecue, char the peppers when the coals are hot, then cool ready for peeling. Grill the fennel over medium-hot coals and turn frequently once stripes have formed.

Energy 137Kcal/567kJ; Protein 2.2g; Carbohydrate 7.5g, of which sugars 7.1g; Fat 11.1g, of which saturates 1.6g; Cholesterol 0mg; Calcium 50mg; Fibre 5.2g; Sodium 301mg.

Potato, caraway seed and parsley salad

Potatoes provide a good steady release of energy. They are high in fibre and especially nutritious when freshly harvested and if eaten in their skins, as here. The caraway seeds and parsley both add a wonderful flavour and help to stimulate the digestion. This recipe would also be delicious made with peeled and chopped, cooked sweet potatoes.

Serves 4–6

675g/1½lb new potatoes, scrubbed
15ml/1 tbsp caraway seeds, lightly crushed
45ml/3 tbsp chopped fresh parsley
45ml/3 tbsp garlic-infused olive oil
ground black pepper

1 Cook the potatoes in salted, boiling water for about 10 minutes, or until they are just tender.

2 Put the potatoes in a colander and drain, then transfer to a large bowl.

3 Stir the garlic-infused oil, caraway seeds and some pepper into the hot potatoes, set aside to cool, then stir in the parsley and serve.

Energy 131Kcal/549kJ; Protein 2.1g; Carbohydrate 18.3g, of which sugars 1.6g; Fat 5.9g, of which saturates 0.9g; Cholesterol 0mg; Calcium 22mg; Fibre 1.5g; Sodium 15mg.

Minty broad beans with lemon

Young, tender broad beans have a sweet, mild taste and are delicious served in a simple salad. Take advantage of them when they're in season and make them into this fresh, zesty dish. Green peas – either fresh or frozen – are also delicious served in the same way. All peas and beans are a good souce of fibre, essential for healthy digestion.

Serves 4

450g/1lb broad (fava) beans, thawed if frozen
30ml/2 tbsp garlic-infused olive oil
grated rind and juice of 1 lemon
1 small bunch of fresh mint, roughly chopped
ground black pepper

1 Using your fingers, slip the grey skins off the broad beans and discard – this takes a little time, but the result is well worthwhile for the attractive appearance of the bright green skinned beans.

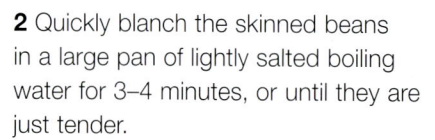

2 Quickly blanch the skinned beans in a large pan of lightly salted boiling water for 3–4 minutes, or until they are just tender.

3 Drain the beans well and toss with the oil, lemon rind and juice, and mint in a large bowl. Season with pepper, and serve immediately.

Variation
If broad beans are unavailable, you can use drained and rinsed canned flageolet or cannellini beans.

Gingered carrot salad

This fresh and zesty salad is ideal served as an accompaniment to simple grilled chicken or fish. Some food processors have an attachment that can be used to cut the carrots into matchsticks, which makes quick work of the preparation. Root ginger goes perfectly with sweet carrots, and the tiny black poppy seeds not only add taste and texture, but also look stunning.

Serves 4

350g/12oz carrots, peeled and cut into
   fine matchsticks
30ml/2 tbsp garlic-infused olive oil
2.5cm/1in piece of fresh root ginger,
   peeled and grated
15ml/1 tbsp poppy seeds
ground black pepper

1 Put the carrots in a bowl and stir in the oil and grated ginger.

2 Cover with clear film (plastic wrap) and chill for at least 30 minutes, to allow the flavours to develop.

3 Season the salad with pepper to taste. Sprinkle the poppy seeds over the salad just before serving. The black seeds make a stunning contrast against the bright orange of the carrots and also add a pleasing crunch.

Variations
• To make a parsnip and sesame seed salad, replace the carrots with parsnips that have been cut into matchsticks. Blanch the parsnips in lightly salted boiling water for 1 minute before combining with the olive oil and ginger.
• Replace the poppy seeds with the same quantity of lightly toasted sesame seeds. Sesame seeds provide a useful source of calcium and vitamin E and have a distincitve flavour that works well in this salad.

Top: Energy 145Kcal/608kJ; Protein 9.3g; Carbohydrate 13.5g, of which sugars 1.8g; Fat 6.3g, of which saturates 0.9g; Cholesterol 0mg; Calcium 88mg; Fibre 8g; Sodium 13mg.
Above: Energy 103Kcal/424kJ; Protein 1.2g; Carbohydrate 7g, of which sugars 6.5g; Fat 7.9g, of which saturates 1.2g; Cholesterol 0mg; Calcium 47mg; Fibre 2.4g; Sodium 23mg.

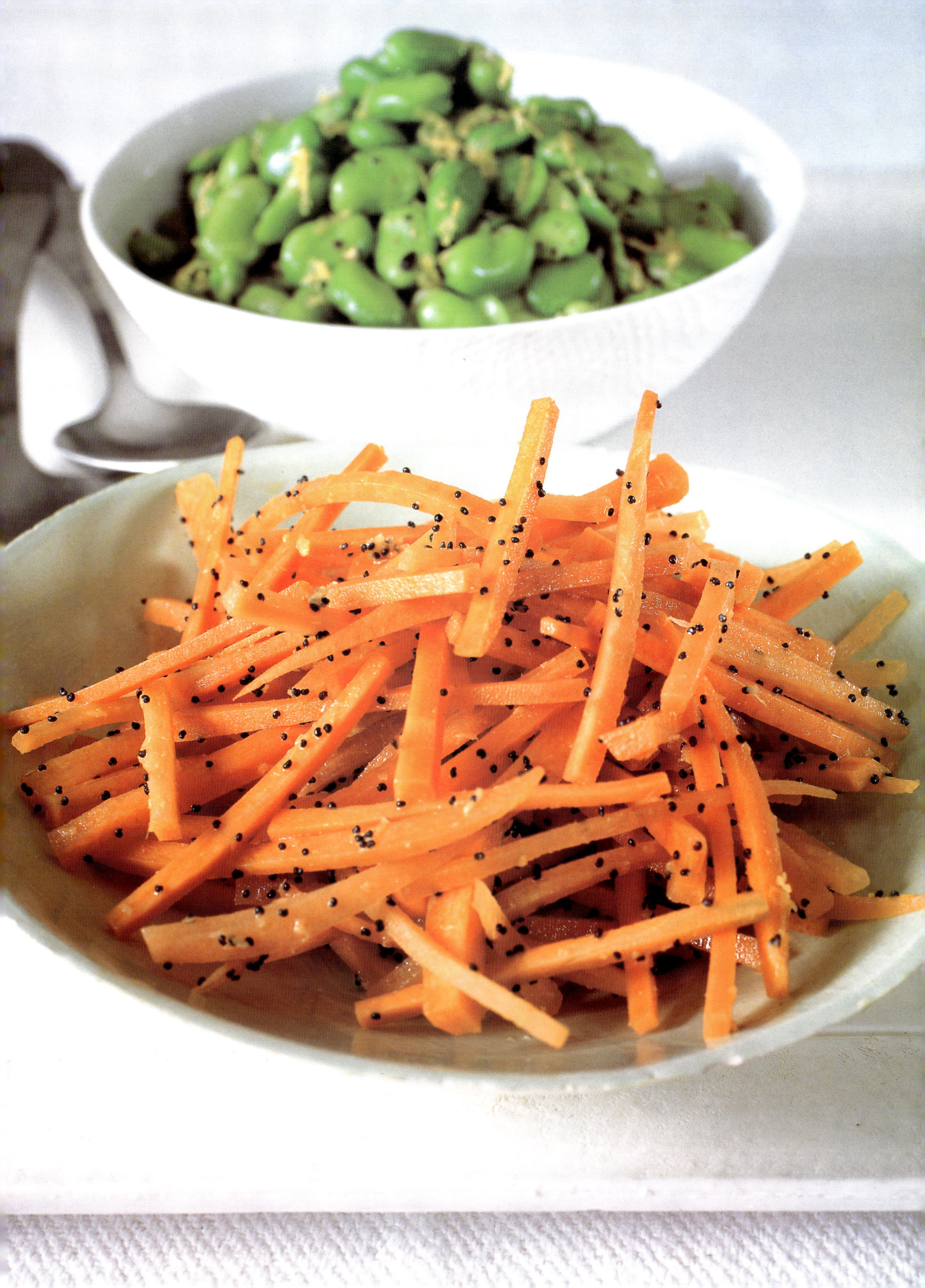

Date, orange and carrot salad

A colourful and unusual salad made with an assortment of exotic ingredients – fresh dates and orange flower water – combined with crisp leaves, carrots, oranges and toasted almonds. This delicious combination of detoxifying fruit and vegetables will not only stimulate the body's cleansing processes but will provide an energy boost as well.

2 Arrange the lettuce leaves in a large salad bowl or on individual serving plates. Place the grated carrot in a mound on top.

3 Peel the oranges and cut them into segments. Arrange them around the mound of grated carrot.

4 Pile the dates on top, then sprinkle with the toasted almonds. Mix together the lemon juice and orange flower water and sprinkle over the salad.

5 Serve the salad chilled with freshly ground black pepper, if you like.

Variation
You can vary the taste of this delicious salad without affecting its cleansing properties by substituting the oranges with another citrus fruit, such as pink grapefruit, clementines or Ugli fruit.

Serves 4

1 Little Gem (Bibb) lettuce
2 carrots, finely grated
2 oranges
150g/5oz fresh dates, stoned (pitted) and cut into eighths, lengthways
25g/1oz/¼ cup toasted whole almonds, chopped
30ml/2 tbsp lemon juice
15ml/1 tbsp orange flower water
ground black pepper (optional)

1 Separate the lettuce leaves, then wash and pat dry with a dish towel.

Energy 137Kcal/578kJ; Protein 3.4g; Carbohydrate 23.4g, of which sugars 22.9g; Fat 4g, of which saturates 0.4g; Cholesterol 0mg; Calcium 86mg; Fibre 4.1g; Sodium 21mg.

Herby rice pilaff

A quick and easy recipe to make, this simple pilaff makes a delicious accompaniment or could be served just with a selection of fresh seasonal vegetables, such as broccoli florets, baby corn and carrots, for a light detox meal. Rice provides a good source of starchy carbohydrate, and it is suitable for those with a gluten or wheat sensitivity.

Serves 4

225g/8oz/1 cup mixed brown basmati and wild rice
15ml/1 tbsp olive oil
1 onion, chopped
1 garlic clove, crushed
5ml/1 tsp ground cumin
5ml/1 tsp ground turmeric
50g/2oz/½ cup sultanas
750ml/1¼ pints/3 cups vegetable stock
30–45ml/2–3 tbsp chopped fresh herbs
ground black pepper
sprigs of fresh herbs
25g/1oz/¼ cup unsalted pistachio nuts, chopped, to garnish

1 Wash the rice under cold running water, then drain well.

2 Heat the oil in a large pan, add the onion and garlic and cook gently for 5 minutes, stirring occasionally.

3 Add the spices and rice and cook gently for 1 minute, stirring. Stir in the sultanas and stock, bring to the boil, cover and simmer gently for 20–25 minutes, stirring occasionally.

4 Stir in the chopped mixed fresh herbs and season to taste with pepper.

5 Spoon the pilaff into a warmed serving dish and garnish with fresh herb sprigs and a scattering of chopped pistachio nuts. Serve immediately, or cool, then cover and keep chilled to serve as a cold rice salad.

Energy 304Kcal/1271kJ; Protein 5.8g; Carbohydrate 55.3g, of which sugars 9.9g; Fat 6.6g, of which saturates 0.9g; Cholesterol 0mg; Calcium 29mg; Fibre 0.9g; Sodium 36mg.

Stir-fried broccoli with sesame seeds

Purple sprouting broccoli has been used for this recipe, but when it is not available an ordinary variety of broccoli, such as calabrese, will also work very well. Broccoli should form a regular part of your everyday diet, even when you are not on a detox diet. It is exceptionally rich in antioxidant vitamins and minerals, and it is believed to reduce the risk of certain cancers.

Serves 2

225g/8oz purple sprouting broccoli
15ml/1 tbsp olive oil
15ml/1 tbsp soy sauce
15ml/1 tbsp sesame seeds, toasted
ground black pepper

Cook's tip
To toast sesame seeds, put them on a large baking sheet and brown under a medium-hot grill (broiler).

1 Using a sharp knife, cut off and discard any thick stems from the broccoli, then cut the remainder into long, slender florets.

2 Heat the olive oil in a wok or large frying pan and add the broccoli.

3 Stir-fry for 3–4 minutes, or until tender, adding a splash of water if the pan becomes too dry.

4 Add the soy sauce, then season with ground black pepper to taste.

5 Add the lightly toasted sesame seeds to the pan and toss well to combine thoroughly. Transfer to a large dish and serve immediately.

Energy 135Kcal/558kJ; Protein 6.6g; Carbohydrate 2.7g, of which sugars 2.3g; Fat 10.9g, of which saturates 1.7g; Cholesterol 0mg; Calcium 115mg; Fibre 3.5g; Sodium 545mg.

Roasted plum tomatoes with garlic

These roast tomatoes flavoured with garlic and bay leaves are so simple to prepare, yet taste absolutely wonderful. Cooking the tomatoes in a shallow earthenware dish will allow them to char slightly around the edges, adding colour, texture and flavour. Plum tomatoes are used here, but the dish would be equally good with halved beefsteak tomatoes.

Serves 4

8 plum tomatoes
12 garlic cloves, unpeeled
20ml/4 tsp extra virgin olive oil
3 bay leaves
ground black pepper
45ml/3 tbsp fresh oregano leaves, to garnish

1 Preheat the oven to 230°C/450°F/Gas 8. Cut the plum tomatoes in half lengthways with a sharp knife, leaving a small part of the green stem intact for the final decoration.

2 Select an ovenproof dish that will hold all the tomatoes snugly together in a single layer. Place them in the dish with the cut side facing upwards, and push each of the whole, unpeeled garlic cloves among them.

3 Lightly brush the tomatoes with the oil, add the bay leaves and sprinkle black pepper over the top.

4 Bake for about 35–45 minutes until the tomatoes have softened and are sizzling in the dish, and slightly charred around the edges. Season with a little black pepper. Garnish with the fresh oregano leaves and serve immediately.

Variation
For a sweet alternative, use halved and seeded red or yellow (bell) peppers instead of the tomatoes.

Energy 114Kcal/474kJ; Protein 2g; Carbohydrate 7.1g, of which sugars 5.6g; Fat 8.8g, of which saturates 1.4g; Cholesterol 0mg; Calcium 14mg; Fibre 2.2g; Sodium 16mg.

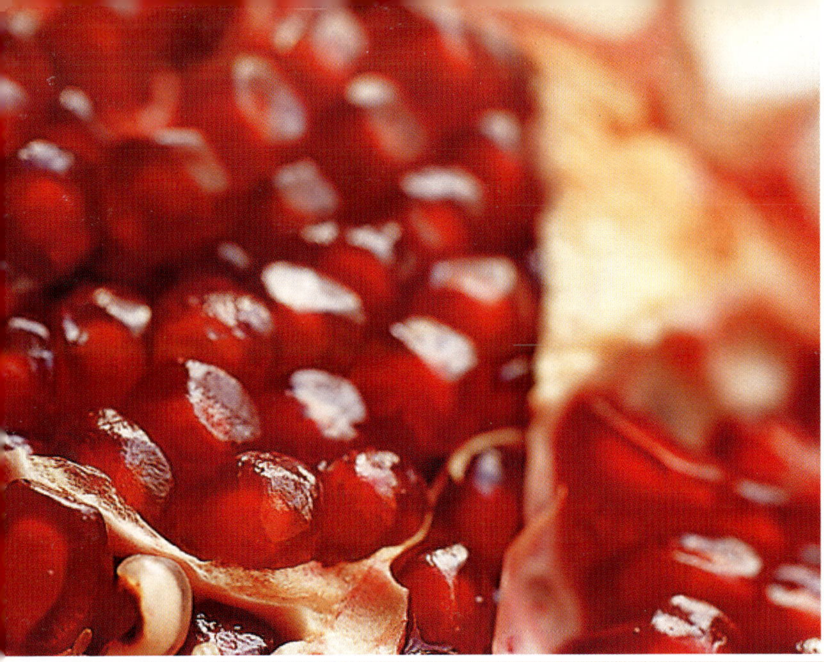
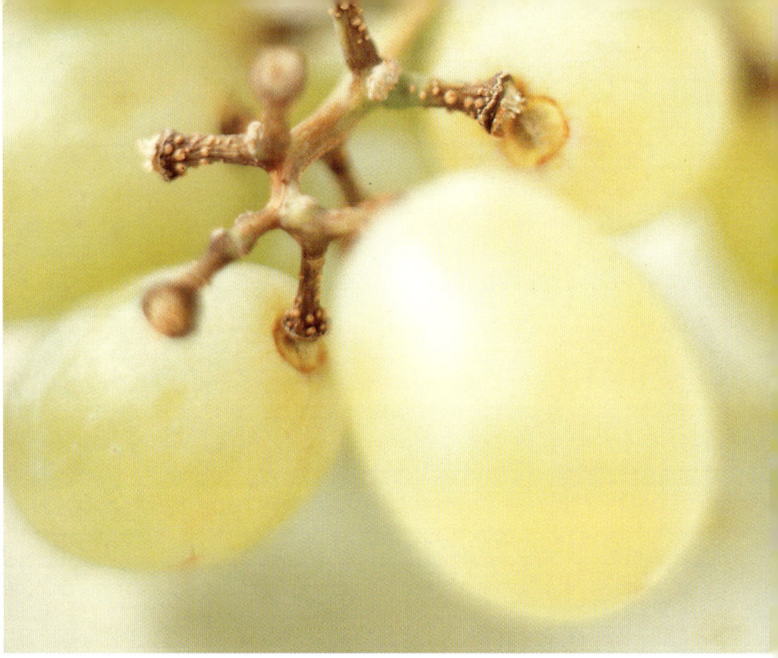
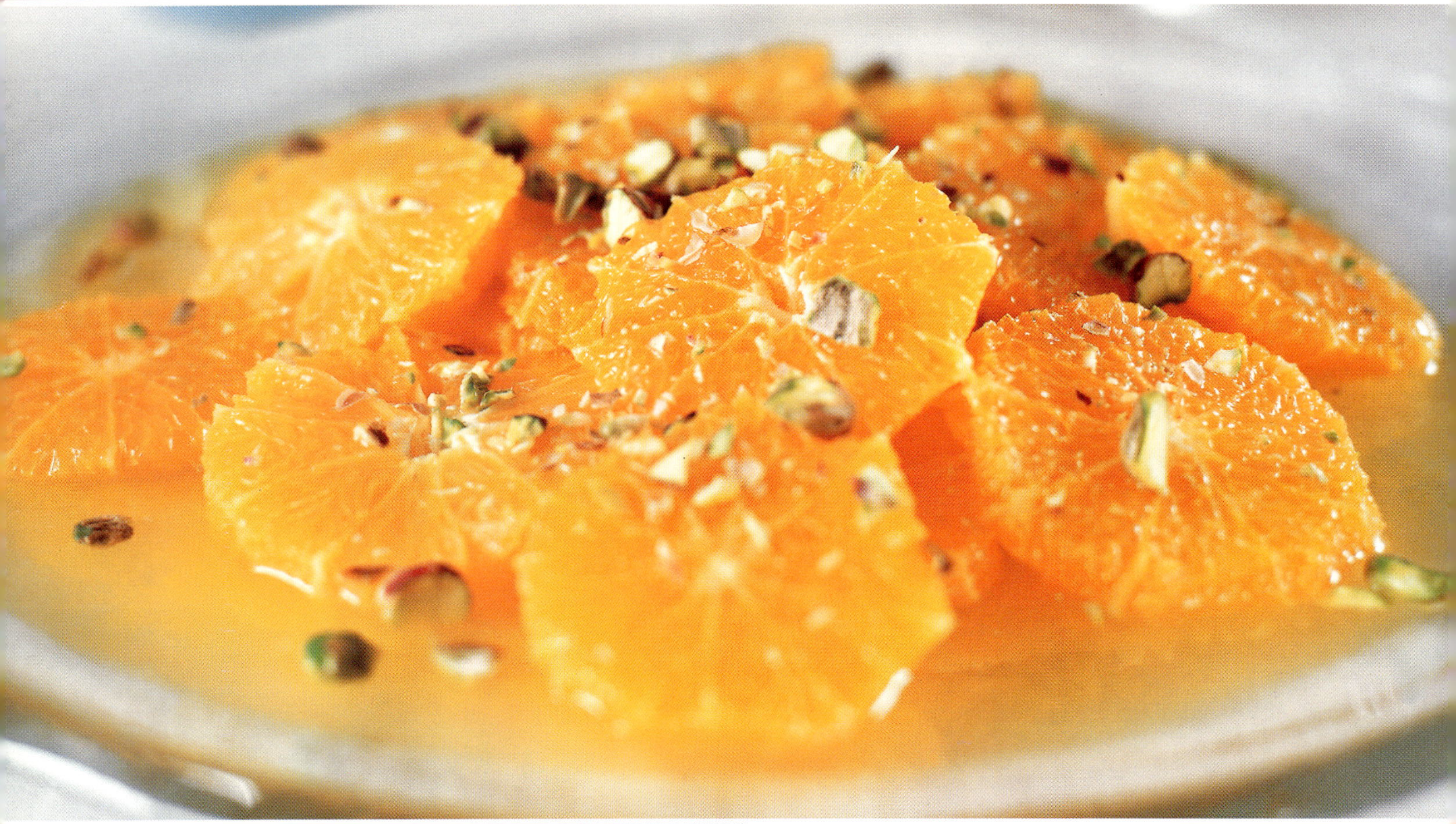
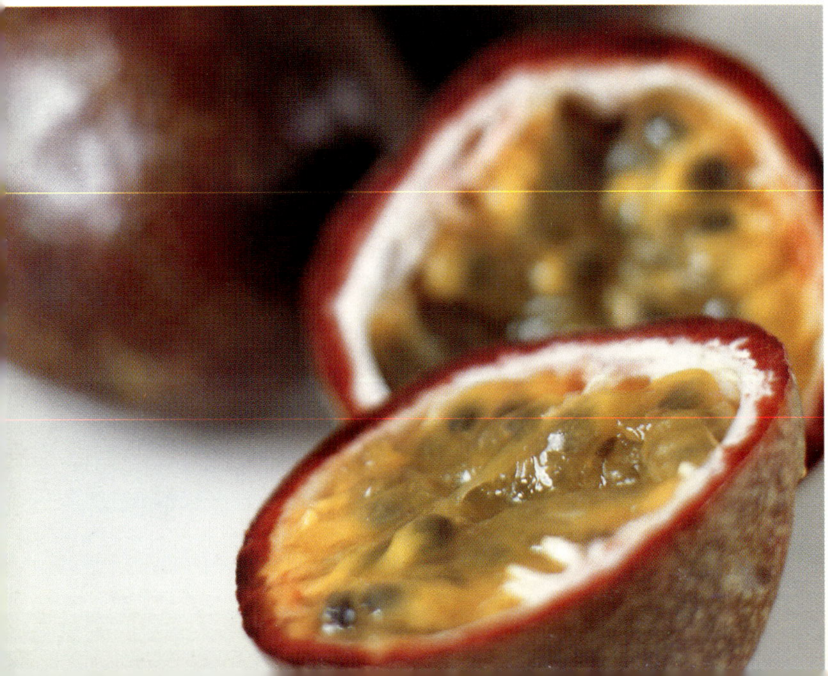
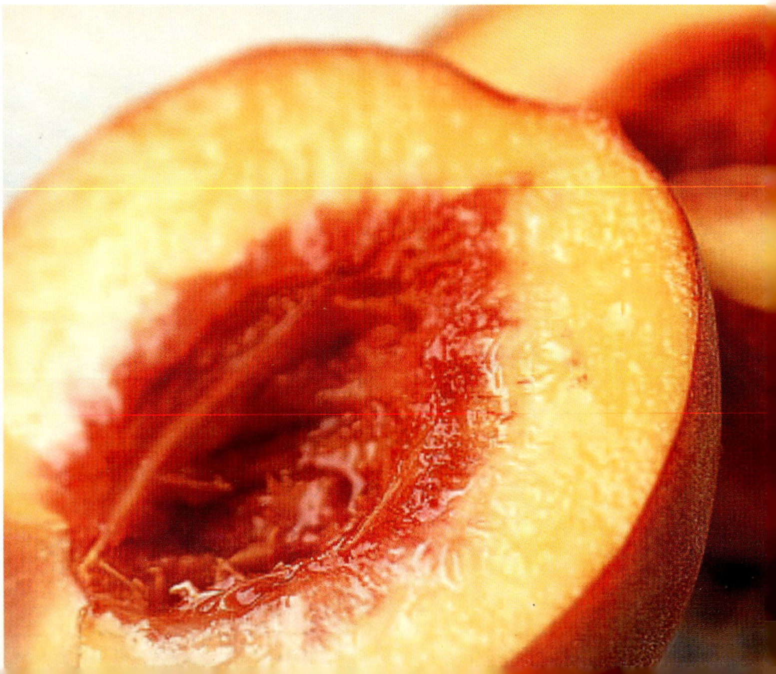

delicious healthy desserts

A range of desserts can be enjoyed while following a detox diet and provide a great opportunity to include plenty of vitamin-packed fruit in your diet. All fruit is good for you, whether fresh, frozen, dried or canned (ideally in natural juice), so go ahead and tuck into fruit salads, baked stuffed fruits and frozen yogurt, sorbet or granita.

Strawberries with passion fruit sauce

Fragrant strawberries are always a treat, but they are full of nutrients too. They are rich in antioxidants, including betacarotene and vitamin C, which help to neutralize harmful free radicals in the body. Berry fruits taste best when they are served at room temperature, so remove strawberries from the refrigerator at least one hour before serving.

Serves 4

350g/12oz/2 cups raspberries, fresh or frozen
30ml/2 tbsp clear honey
1 passion fruit
700g/1½lb/6 cups small strawberries

1 Place the raspberries and honey in a pan and warm over a very gentle heat to release the juices. When the juices start to run, simmer for 5 minutes, stirring occasionally. Set aside and allow the mixture to cool.

2 Halve the passion fruit and, using a teaspoon, carefully scoop out the seeds and juice into a small bowl.

3 Put the raspberries into a food processor or blender, add the passion fruit and blend until smooth.

4 Place the raspberry and passion fruit sauce in a fine nylon sieve and press the purée through to remove the gritty seeds.

5 Divide the strawberries among serving bowls, spoon over some of the sauce and serve. Offer extra sauce separately, in a small jug (pitcher).

Energy 92Kcal/391kJ; Protein 2.8g; Carbohydrate 20.5g, of which sugars 20.5g; Fat 0.5g, of which saturates 0.1g; Cholesterol 0mg; Calcium 51mg; Fibre 4.2g; Sodium 15mg.

Lemon grass skewers

Grilled fruits make a delicious end to a cleansing meal. The lemon grass skewers give the fruit a subtle lemon tang. The fruits used here make an ideal exotic mix, but almost any soft fruit that will thread easily on to skewers can be substituted as preferred. If lemon grass is unavailable, use bamboo skewers that have been pre-soaked, to prevent them from burning.

Serves 4

4 long fresh lemon grass stalks
1 mango, peeled, stoned (pitted) and cut into chunks
1 papaya, peeled, seeded and cut into chunks
1 star fruit, cut into thick slices and halved
8 fresh bay leaves
a little nutmeg
60ml/4 tbsp clear honey
low-fat probiotic yogurt, to serve

1 Preheat the grill (broiler). Cut the top of each lemon grass stalk into a point. Bruise each with the back of a knife.

2 Thread each lemon grass stalk with the prepared fruit and bay leaves.

3 Cover a large baking sheet in kitchen foil, raising the edges slightly, and lay the skewers on top.

Cook's tip
Only fresh lemon grass will work as skewers for this recipe. It is now possible to buy lemon grass stalks in jars, but they are too soft to use as skewers.

4 Grate nutmeg over each of the fruit skewers and drizzle with honey. Grill for 5 minutes, until they are lightly browned. Serve immediately with probiotic yogurt.

Energy 92Kcal/393kJ; Protein 0.9g; Carbohydrate 23.2g, of which sugars 23.1g; Fat 0.2g, of which saturates 0g; Cholesterol 0mg; Calcium 29mg; Fibre 3.5g; Sodium 7mg.

Minted pomegranate yogurt with grapefruit salad

The vitamin-rich jewel-like seeds of the pomegranate make any dessert look beautiful. Here they are stirred into yogurt to make a stunning sauce for a refreshing grapefruit salad.

Serves 3–4

300ml/½ pint/1¼ cups low-fat probiotic yogurt
2–3 ripe pomegranates
small bunch of fresh mint, finely chopped
clear honey or caster (superfine) sugar, to taste (optional)

For the grapefruit salad
2 red grapefruits
2 pink grapefruits
1 white grapefruit
15–30ml/1–2 tbsp orange flower water

To decorate
handful of pomegranate seeds
fresh mint leaves

1 Put the yogurt in a bowl and beat well. Cut open the pomegranates and scoop out the seeds, removing and discarding all the bitter pith. Fold the pomegranate seeds and chopped mint into the yogurt. Sweeten with a little honey or sugar, if using, then chill until ready to serve.

2 To make the salad, peel the red, pink and white grapefruits, cutting off and discarding all the pith.

3 Holding each fruit in the palm of your hand, cut between the membranes to remove the segments. Prepare the fruit over a bowl to catch the juices.

4 Discard the membranes and mix the fruit segments with the reserved fruit juices. Sprinkle the segments with the orange flower water and add a little honey or sugar, if using. Stir gently to mix, then decorate with a few pomegranate seeds.

5 Just before serving, decorate the chilled yogurt with a sprinkling of pomegranate seeds and mint leaves.

6 Serve the minted pomegranate yogurt with the grapefruit salad.

Variation
Alternatively, you can use a mixture of oranges and blood oranges, interspersed with thin segments of lemon. Lime segments work well with the grapefruit and mandarins or tangerines could be used too. As the idea is to create a refreshing, scented salad, juicy melons and kiwi fruit would also make an ideal combination.

Energy 115Kcal/482kJ; Protein 6g; Carbohydrate 21.7g, of which sugars 21.7g; Fat 1.1g, of which saturates 0.4g; Cholesterol 1mg; Calcium 210mg; Fibre 3.4g; Sodium 73mg.

Rose water-scented oranges with pistachio nuts

This delightfully fragrant and refreshing dessert combines three favourite Middle Eastern ingredients. If you don't have pistachio nuts, use hazelnuts instead.

Serves 4

4 large oranges
30ml/2 tbsp rose water
30ml/2 tbsp unsalted shelled pistachio nuts, roughly chopped

Cook's tip
Rose-scented sugar is delicious lightly sprinkled over fresh fruit salads. To make, wash and dry a handful of rose petals and place them in a sealed container filled with caster (superfine) sugar for 2–3 days. Remove the petals before using the sugar.

1 Slice the top and bottom off one of the oranges to expose the flesh. Using a small serrated knife, slice down between the pith and the flesh, working around the orange, to remove all the peel and pith. Slice the orange into six rounds, reserving any juice. Repeat with the remaining oranges.

2 Arrange the orange rounds on a serving dish. Mix the reserved juice with the rose water and drizzle over the oranges. Cover the dish with clear film (plastic wrap) and chill for about 30 minutes. Sprinkle the chopped pistachio nuts over the oranges just before serving.

Energy 91Kcal/384kJ; Protein 2.7g; Carbohydrate 11.3g, of which sugars 11.1g; Fat 4.3g, of which saturates 0.6g; Cholesterol 0mg; Calcium 67mg; Fibre 2.6g; Sodium 46mg.

Papaya and green grapes with mint sauce

Papaya is rich in vitamin C and betacarotene, and provides a useful amount of dietary fibre. It is easy to digest and has a tonic effect on the stomach.

Serves 4

2 large papayas
225g/8oz/2 cups seedless green grapes
juice of 3 limes
2.5cm/1in fresh root ginger, peeled and finely grated
15ml/1 tbsp clear honey
5 fresh mint leaves, cut into thin strips, plus extra whole leaves, to decorate

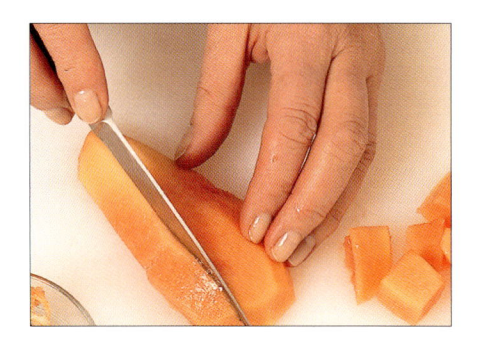

1 Peel the papayas and cut into small cubes, discarding the seeds. Cut the grapes in half.

2 In a large mixing bowl, thoroughly combine the lime juice, ginger, honey and shredded mint leaves.

3 Add the papaya and grapes to the bowl and toss together gently. Cover with clear film (plastic wrap) and leave in a cool place to allow the flavours to mingle for 1 hour.

4 Serve in a large glass dish or individual stemmed glasses, decorated with whole fresh mint leaves, if liked.

Orange granita with strawberries

A granita is a refreshing alternative to ice cream, and makes the ideal dessert after a spicy main dish such as a curry. It's made with just frozen freshly-squeezed fruit juice and is therefore dairy-free. The combination of orange juice in the granita and the accompanying portion of fresh, ripe strawberries provides a generous amount of vitamin C.

Serves 4

6 large juicy oranges
350g/12oz ripe strawberries
finely pared strips of orange rind, to decorate

1 Juice the oranges and pour into a shallow freezerproof bowl.

Cook's tips
• Granita will keep for up to 3 weeks in the freezer. If you prefer a more tart ice, use sweet pink grapefruits or blood oranges or, alternatively, add a little fresh lemon or lime juice.
• Look out for Valencia oranges. They are the best variety for juicing.

2 Place the bowl in the freezer. Remove after 30 minutes and beat the semi-frozen juice thoroughly with a wooden spoon. Repeat this process at 30-minute intervals over a 4-hour period. This will break the ice crystals down into small particles and prevent the granita from freezing solid.

3 Halve the strawberries and arrange them on a serving plate. Scoop the granita into serving glasses, decorate with strips of orange rind and serve immediately with the strawberries.

Top: Energy 90Kcal/382kJ; Protein 0.9g; Carbohydrate 22.5g, of which sugars 22.5g; Fat 0.2g, of which saturates 0g; Cholesterol 0mg; Calcium 36mg; Fibre 3.2g; Sodium 8mg.
Above: Energy 79Kcal/336kJ; Protein 2.4g; Carbohydrate 18g, of which sugars 18g; Fat 0.2g, of which saturates 0g; Cholesterol 0mg; Calcium 85mg; Fibre 3.5g; Sodium 13mg.

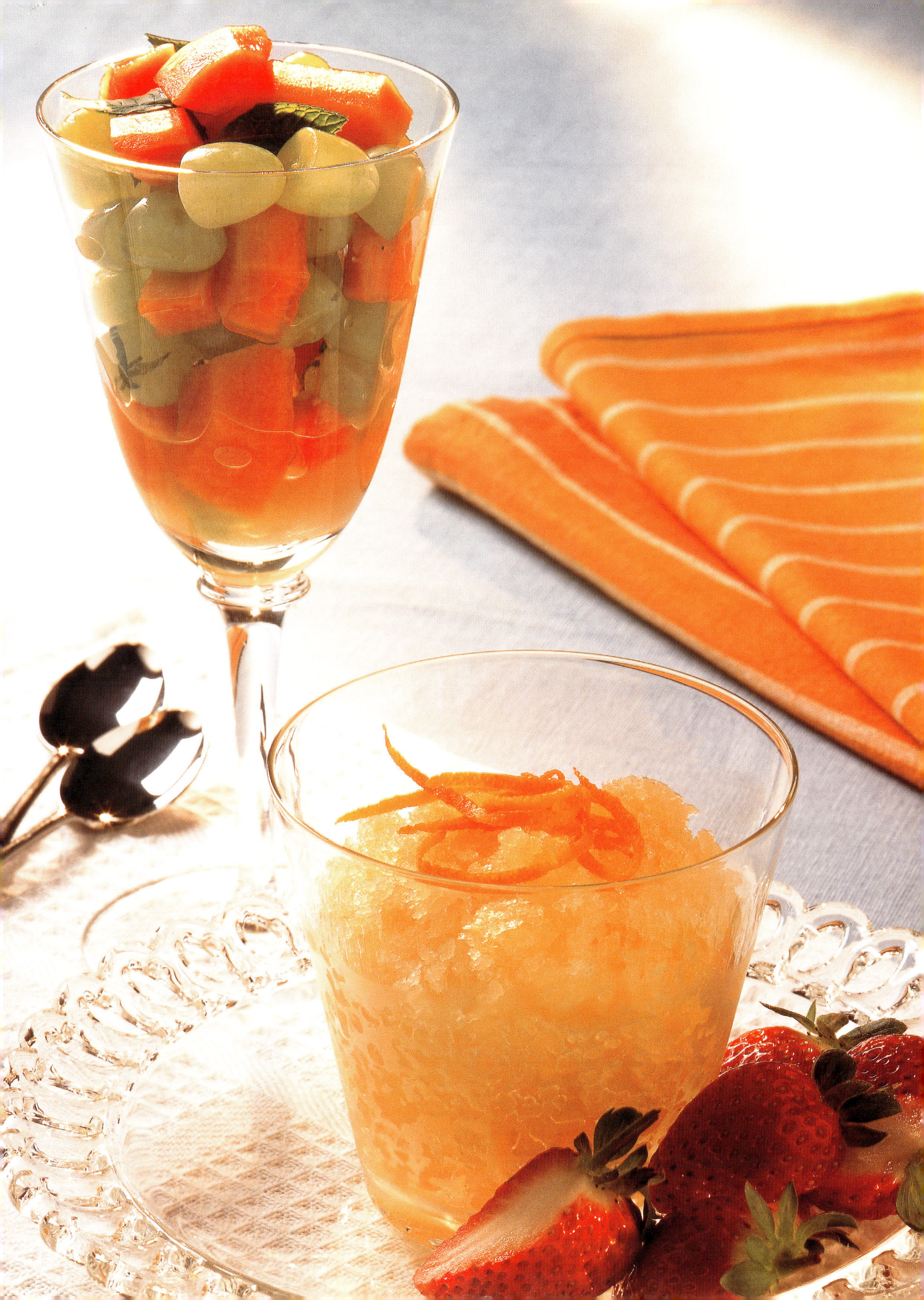

Summer berry frozen yogurt

Any combination of summer fruits will work for this deliciously creamy yet tangy dish, as long as they are frozen, because this helps to create a chunky texture. If using individual fruits, choose a mixture of red and blue currants and berries. They are all rich in vitamin C, which helps to boost the immune system and is a powerful antioxidant.

Serves 6

350g/12oz/3 cups frozen summer fruits, plus whole fresh or frozen berries, to decorate
200g/7oz/scant 1 cup low-fat probiotic yogurt
25g/1oz icing (confectioners') sugar

Variation
To make a more creamy ice cream, use Greek (US strained plain) yogurt. This will still be healthy, although slightly higher in fat.

1 Put all the ingredients into a food processor and process until combined but still quite chunky. Spoon the mixture into six 150ml/¼ pint/⅔ cup ramekin dishes.

2 Cover each dish with clear film (plastic wrap) and place in the freezer for about 2 hours, or until firm.

3 To turn out the frozen yogurts, dip the ramekin dishes briefly in hot water, taking care not to allow water to get on to the dessert itself. Invert the ramekins on to small serving plates. Tap the base of the dishes and the yogurts should come out.

4 Serve immediately, decorated with fresh or frozen berries, such as blueberries, blackberries or raspberries.

Energy 51Kcal/215kJ; Protein 2.2g; Carbohydrate 10.4g, of which sugars 10.4g; Fat 0.4g, of which saturates 0.2g; Cholesterol 0mg; Calcium 75mg; Fibre 0.7g; Sodium 32mg.

Strawberry and lavender sorbet

Delicately perfumed with just a hint of lavender, this delightful, pastel pink sorbet is perfect for a special-occasion dinner, if entertaining while following a longer detox programme. It is made with a light sugar syrup, rather than the rich custard used for making ice cream, and captures the flavours and nutrient value of fresh strawberries. It is ideal for a low-fat summer dessert.

Serves 6

150g/5oz/¾ cup caster (superfine) sugar
300ml/½ pint/1¼ cups water
6 fresh lavender heads
500g/1¼lb/5 cups strawberries, hulled
1 egg white
lavender flowers, to decorate

1 Put the sugar and measured water into a pan and bring to the boil, stirring constantly until the sugar has completely dissolved.

2 Take the pan off the heat, add the lavender flower heads and leave to infuse (steep) for 1 hour. If time permits, chill the syrup before using.

3 Purée the strawberries in a food processor or in batches in a blender, then press the purée through a large sieve (strainer) into a bowl.

4 Spoon the purée into a freezerproof container, strain in the lavender syrup and freeze for 4 hours, or until the mixture is mushy. Alternatively, churn the strawberry and lavender mixture for 20 minutes, or until thick.

5 Whisk the egg white until it has just turned frothy.

6 Scoop the sorbet from the tub into a food processor, process it until smooth, then add the egg white. Spoon the sorbet back into the tub and freeze for 4 hours, or until firm. If using an ice cream machine, add the egg white to the bowl and continue to churn until the sorbet is firm enough to scoop. Serve immediately, or transfer to a freezerproof container and freeze until needed.

7 Serve in scoops in individual glasses, decorated with lavender flowers.

Cook's tip

The size of the lavender flowers may vary; if they are very small you may need to use 8 instead of 6. The intensity of the flavour may also vary depending on the variety of the lavender. To double check, taste a little of the cooled lavender syrup. If you think the flavour is a little mild, add 2–3 more flowers, reheat and cool again before using.

Energy 123Kcal/523kJ; Protein 1.3g; Carbohydrate 31.1g, of which sugars 31.1g; Fat 0.1g, of which saturates 0g; Cholesterol 0mg; Calcium 27mg; Fibre 0.9g; Sodium 17mg.

Poached pears in scented honey syrup

Pears are among the least allergenic of foods and they contain vitamin C and provide a useful amount of potassium, essential for helping to regulate blood pressure. Delicate and pretty to look at, these scented pears, poached in a honey and lemon syrup with saffron, cinnamon and lavender, would provide an exquisite finishing touch to a detox meal.

Serves 4

45ml/3 tbsp clear honey
juice of 1 lemon
250ml/8fl oz/1 cup water
pinch of saffron threads
1 cinnamon stick
2–3 dried lavender heads
4 firm pears

Variation

If pears are not available, you can use whole, peeled nectarines or peaches instead.

1 Heat the honey and lemon juice in a heavy pan that will hold the pears snugly. Stir over a gentle heat until the honey has dissolved. Add the water, saffron threads, cinnamon stick and flowers from 1–2 lavender heads. Bring the mixture to the boil, then reduce the heat and simmer for 5 minutes.

2 Peel the pears, leaving the stalks attached. Add the pears to the pan and simmer for 20 minutes, turning and basting at regular intervals, until they are tender. Allow to cool, then serve at room temperature, decorated with a few lavender flowers.

Energy 93Kcal/392kJ; Protein 0.5g; Carbohydrate 23.6g, of which sugars 23.6g; Fat 0.2g, of which saturates 0g; Cholesterol 0mg; Calcium 17mg; Fibre 3.3g; Sodium 6mg.

Delicious healthy desserts **155**

Nectarines baked with nuts

Fresh nectarines stuffed with a ground almond and chopped pistachio nut filling are baked in orange juice until tender and juicy, then served with a fragrant sauce made by stirring passion fruit seeds into the fruity cooking juices. Peaches could be used instead of nectarines. Both fruits contain plenty of vitamin C and the nuts provide protein and vitamin E.

Serves 4

50g/2oz/½ cup ground almonds
15ml/1 tbsp caster (superfine) sugar
1 egg yolk
50g/2oz/½ cup unsalted shelled pistachio nuts, chopped
4 nectarines
250ml/8fl oz/scant 1 cup orange juice
2 ripe passion fruit

1 Preheat the oven to 200°C/400°F/Gas 6.

2 Mix together the ground almonds, sugar and egg yolk in a bowl to make a paste, then stir in the pistachio nuts.

3 Cut the nectarines in half and carefully remove the stones (pits). Pile the ground almond and pistachio filling into the nectarine halves, packing in plenty of filling, and then place them in a single layer in the base of a shallow ovenproof dish.

4 Pour the orange juice around the nectarines, then cover the dish with a lid or foil and place in the preheated oven. Cook for 15 minutes.

5 Remove the lid and bake for a further 5–10 minutes, or until the nectarines are soft. Transfer the nectarines to individual, warmed serving plates and keep warm.

6 Cut the passion fruit in half, scoop out the seeds and stir them into the cooking juices in the dish. Place the nectarines on serving plates and spoon the sauce over and around them. Serve immediately.

Energy 264Kcal/1106kJ; Protein 8g; Carbohydrate 24.8g, of which sugars 24.2g; Fat 15.5g, of which saturates 1.9g; Cholesterol 50mg; Calcium 68mg; Fibre 3.6g; Sodium 78mg.

Baked peaches

This is an excellent dessert to serve in summer, when peaches are in season and at their juiciest and most fragrant. Baking brings out their wonderful flavour, which is enhanced by the addition of a sweet apple, almond and honey juice, drizzled over the top. Serve warm from the oven or chilled with a spoonful of low-fat probiotic yogurt.

Serves 4

4 ripe peaches
45ml/3 tbsp fresh apple juice
45ml/3 tbsp clear honey
10ml/2 tsp almond extract
low-fat probiotic yogurt, to serve

Cook's tips
- You can cook these peaches over a barbecue. Place them on sheets of foil, drizzle over the fruit juice mixture, then scrunch the foil around them to seal. Cook for 15–20 minutes.
- If you are not on a detox diet, you could use Amaretto di Sarone liqueur in place of the apple juice.

1 Preheat the oven to 190°C/375°F/Gas 5. Cut each of the peaches in half and twist each of the two halves in opposite directions to separate them. Once you have separated the two halves, prise out the stones (pits) with the point of the knife.

2 Place the peaches cut side up in a roasting pan.

3 In a small bowl, mix the apple juice with the honey and almond extract, and drizzle over the halved peaches, covering them evenly.

4 Bake the peaches for 20–25 minutes, or until tender. Place two peach halves on each serving plate and drizzle with the pan juices. Serve immediately, with low-fat probiotic yogurt.

Energy 70Kcal/299kJ; Protein 1.1g; Carbohydrate 17.3g, of which sugars 17.3g; Fat 0.1g, of which saturates 0g; Cholesterol 0mg; Calcium 8mg; Fibre 1.5g; Sodium 3mg.

Baked apples with figs and walnuts

Apples help to boost the digestion and remove impurities from the liver. Their cleansing properties are further enhanced by their high fibre content, which helps to remove toxins and purify the system. Serve these delicious apples stuffed with a mixture of walnuts and dried figs with a spoonful of low-fat probiotic yogurt or an egg custard sauce made with non-dairy milk.

Serves 6

4 medium cooking apples
50g/2oz/⅓ cup dried figs, chopped
50g/2oz/⅓ cup walnuts, chopped
150ml/¼ pint/⅔ cup apple juice

1 Preheat the oven to 180°C/350°F/Gas 4. Remove the cores from the apples. Cut a slit in the skin around the middle of each. Place the apples in a small, shallow roasting pan or ovenproof dish.

2 Mix together the figs and walnuts, then stuff into the centre of each apple.

3 Pour over the apple juice. Cover the pan or dish tightly with foil and cook for about 30 minutes.

4 Remove the foil and cook for a further 10 minutes, or until the apples are tender and the juices have reduced slightly. Serve immediately with any remaining juices drizzled over the top.

Energy 56Kcal/241kJ; Protein 0.6g; Carbohydrate 14g, of which sugars 14g; Fat 0.2g, of which saturates 0g; Cholesterol 0mg; Calcium 24mg; Fibre 1.9g; Sodium 7mg.

Index

additives 11, 13, 14, 20, 23
alcohol 14, 17, 20, 30, 33, 41
allergies see food allergies
almonds 29
 Tomato and Lentil Dhal with Almonds 113
antioxidants 11, 15, 16, 19, 24, 26, 29
apples 24
 Baked Apples with Figs and Walnuts 157
apricots: Apricot and Ginger Smoothie 57
aromatherapy 34, 35
artichokes, globe 26
 Artichoke and Cumin Dip 71
 artichoke extract 19
arugula see rocket
aubergines (eggplants): Aubergine Dip 73
avocados: Avocado Guacamole 70
 Chicken, Avocado and Chickpea Soup 86
 Citrus Fruit Salad with Avocado 92
bacteria, beneficial 16, 18, 21, 30
barley 22, 27
 Chilled Tomato and Fresh Basil Soup 78
 Country Mushroom, Bean and Barley Soup 83
baths 36
beans 27
 American Red Bean Soup with Guacamole Salsa 82
 Bean Salad with Tuna and Red Onion 96
 Black-eyed Bean and Tomato Broth 81
 Butter Bean, Tomato and Olive Stew 111
 Country Mushroom, Bean and Barley Soup 83
 Minty Broad Beans with Lemon 138
beetroot 25
betacarotene 16, 24, 26, 58
blood pressure 14, 15, 20, 22, 26, 36, 37
blood sugar levels 15, 22
bread 22

Lebanese Flatbread 73
breast-feeding 7, 38
breathing 18, 19, 37
broccoli 25
 Stir-fried Broccoli with Sesame Seeds 142
bulgur wheat 22
 Bulgur Wheat Salad with Walnuts 91
butter 21

cabbages: Cabbage Salad with Lemon Dressing and Black Olives 135
 Fresh Cabbage Soup 79
caffeine 6, 13, 14, 15, 17, 19, 20, 33, 45
cakes 22
calories 17, 22, 29
 'empty' 20
caraway seeds: Potato, Caraway Seed and Parsley Salad 137
carbohydrates 19, 22, 33
carrots 25
 Date, Orange and Carrot Salad 140
 Gingered Carrot Salad 138
 Spiced Carrot Dip 72
 Tagine of Yam, Carrots and Prunes 110
cashew nuts: Stir-fried Vegetables with Cashew Nuts 106
celery 25
cheese 14, 21
 Greek Salad 93
chicken 29
 Chicken, Avocado and Chickpea Soup 86
 Chicken and Leek Soup with Prunes 87
 Griddled Chicken with Tomato Salsa 128
 Pan-fried Chicken with Pesto 129
 Warm Chicken and Tomato Salad with Hazelnut Dressing 98
 Warm Oriental Chicken and Rice Stir-fry Salad 99
chickpeas: Aromatic Chickpea and Spinach Curry 112
 Chicken, Avocado and Chickpea Soup 86
chocolate 13, 14, 20, 33
cholesterol 23, 26, 27, 29
circulation 19, 26, 32, 34, 35, 36, 41
citrus fruits 14, 24
 Citrus Fruit Salad with Avocado 92
cod 29
 Roasted Cod with Fresh Tomato Sauce 120
 Spicy Paella 127
coffee 20, 41, 45
complementary therapies 6, 16, 17, 34–7, 41

cream 21
cumin: Artichoke and Cumin Dip 71
cynarin 19, 26

dairy products 13, 21
dates: Date, Orange and Carrot Salad 140
 Porridge with Dates and Pistachio Nuts 65
dehydration 14, 20
detox diet 6, 7
 benefits 6, 16–17
 the body's natural detoxifiers 18
 complementary therapies and relaxation techniques 34–7
 exercise for body and mind 32–3
 following the detox programme 42–5
 foods to avoid 20–3
 foods to include 24–31
 how diet affects health 12–15
 how to boost your vital organs 19
 one- and two-week detox meal planners 46–9
 people who shouldn't detox 7
 preparing to detox 38–41
 toxins 10–11
dhal: Grilled Mackerel with Spicy Dhal 123
 Tomato and Lentil Dhal with Almonds 113

eggs 13, 21, 30
 Egg and Lentil Curry 119
 Spring Vegetable Omelette 118
eggplants see aubergines
essential fatty acids 19, 20
exercise 6, 7, 15, 16, 17, 19, 32, 33, 41

family meals 43
fast foods 23
fats 7, 17, 19, 23, 65
 saturated 21, 21, 23, 28
 trans 23
fennel: Grilled Fennel Salad with Niçoise Olives 136
feta cheese: Greek Salad 93
fibre 23, 24, 29
figs: Baked Apples with Figs and Walnuts 157
 Figs and Pears in Honey 60
fish 29
 Moroccan Fish Tagine 126
 see also individual types of fish
flaxseeds 29
folate (folic acid) 14
food: allergies 7, 12, 13, 15, 21, 23
 cravings/addictions 13
 diary 12

intolerance 12, 14, 15, 18
 sensitivities 7, 13, 14
free radicals 10–11, 19, 24, 31
fruit 24, 42, 43
 Citrus Fruit Salad with Avocado 92
 Dried Fruit Compote 61
 dried fruits 25
 Summer Berry Frozen Yogurt 152
 Summer Fruit Smoothie 56
 super fruits 24
 Tropical Scented Fruit Salad 59

garlic 26
 Roasted Plum Tomatoes with Garlic 143
 Spinach and Roast Garlic Salad 132
ginger 26
 Apricot and Ginger Smoothie 57
 Gingered Carrot Salad 138
 Pineapple and Ginger Juice 52
gluten 12, 27
Granola 62
grapefruit: Minted Pomegranate Yogurt with Grapefruit Salad 148
grapes: Papaya and Green Grapes with Mint Sauce 150
guacamole: American Red Bean Soup with Guacamole Salsa 82
 Avocado Guacamole 70
 Pea Guacamole 69

haddock 29
hazelnuts: Warm Chicken and Tomato Salad with Hazelnut Dressing 98
herbs: Herby Rice Pilaff 141
 Mixed Green Leaf and Herb Salad 133
 Warm Mixed Seafood and Fresh Herb Salad 94
 Wild Rocket and Cos Lettuce Salad with Herbs 134
hoki: Moroccan Fish Tagine 126
honey: Figs and Pears in Honey 60
 Poached Pears in Scented Honey Syrup 154
Hummus 68

illnesses: anaemia 14
 arthritis 24
 asthma 10–13, 20, 22, 34, 35, 61
 bloating 7, 12, 15, 18, 22, 31
 cancer 7, 11, 16, 22, 24, 26, 28, 29
 cirrhosis 18
 coeliac disease 12, 14, 22
 constipation 7, 12, 18, 22, 27, 29, 31
 depression 7, 15, 18, 34

diabetes 7, 14, 38
digestive problems 10, 12, 35
eczema 7, 12, 13, 26, 36
fluid retention 22, 31
headaches 7, 14, 15, 18, 31, 33, 45
heart disease 7, 11, 15, 16, 23, 27, 29, 36
hepatitis 18
insomnia 17, 20, 33, 34
irritable bowel syndrome (IBS) 12, 18, 30
kidney problems 14, 20, 22
osteoporosis 20, 22, 28
respiratory problems 10, 13, 18, 26
rheumatism 26
sinus problems 7, 13, 18, 21, 35
stroke 22, 27
immune system 6, 16, 26

juices 6, 19
Lime and Watermelon Tonic 53
Pineapple and Ginger Juice 52

kitchen essentials 39

lavender: Strawberry and Lavender Sorbet 153
leeks: Chicken and Leek Soup with Prunes 87
Leek and Potato Soup 84
Lemon Grass Skewers 147
lemons: Minty Broad Beans with Lemon 138
lentils 27
Egg and Lentil Curry 119
Tomato and Lentil Dhal with Almonds 113
Tomato and Lentil Soup 80
lettuce: Wild Rocket and Cos Lettuce Salad with Herbs 134
limes: Lime and Watermelon Tonic 53
Mango and Lime Lassi 58
linseeds see flaxseeds
liver 18, 19
function 14, 26
lycopene 26
lymphatic drainage massage 34
lymphatic system 18, 19, 32, 34, 36

mackerel: Grilled Mackerel with Spicy Dhal 123
magnesium 27
mangoes: Mango and Lime Lassi 58
massage 17, 19, 33–4
foot 35
lymphatic drainage 34
shoulder 35
meat products 21, 23
medication 7, 38
meditation 16, 33, 37
migraine 7, 14, 20, 26, 35
milk: non-dairy milk choices 30
millet 25

minerals 16, 21, 24, 26, 27, 29
mint: Minted Pomegranate Yogurt with Grapefruit Salad 148
Minty Broad Beans with Lemon 138
Papaya and Green Grapes with Mint Sauce 150
monkfish: Fragrant Thai Fish Soup 85
Moroccan Fish Tagine 126
muesli: Luxury Muesli 62
mushrooms: Brown Rice Risotto with Mushrooms 109
Country Mushroom, Bean and Barley Soup 83
mycoprotein (quorn) 28

Nectarines Baked with Nuts 155
noodles: Buckwheat Noodle Salad with Smoked Salmon 95
nuts 29
Nectarines Baked with Nuts 155
see also individual nut types

oats 22, 27, 62
Porridge with Dates and Pistachio Nuts 65
Raspberry and Oatmeal Blend 54
Traditional Scottish Porridge 64
oils 31, 35
olives: Butter Bean, Tomato and Olive Stew 111
Cabbage Salad with Lemon Dressing and Black Olives 135
Grilled Fennel Salad with Niçoise Olives 136
omega-3 fatty acids 29
omega-6 fatty acids 29
onions 26
Bean Salad with Tuna and Red Onion 96
oranges: Barbecued Sardines with Orange 122
Citrus Fruit Salad with Avocado 92
Date, Orange and Carrot Salad 140
Orange Granita with Strawberries 150
Rose Water-scented Oranges with Pistachio Nuts 149

papaya 24
Papaya and Green Grapes with Mint Sauce 150
parsley: Potato, Caraway Seed and Parsley Salad 137
passion fruit: Strawberries with Passion Fruit Sauce 146
pasta 22
peaches: Baked Peaches 156
pears: Figs and Pears in Honey 60
Poached Pears in Scented Honey Syrup 154

peas: dried 27
Pea Guacamole 69
Penne with Green Vegetable Sauce 104
peppers: Provençal Stuffed Peppers 117
Roasted Peppers with Sweet Cicely 74
Tofu and Pepper Kebabs 116
pineapples 24
Pineapple and Ginger Juice 52
pistachio nuts: Porridge with Dates and Pistachio Nuts 65
Rose Water-scented Oranges with Pistachio Nuts 149
plants 40, 41
polenta: Griddled Polenta with Tangy Pebre 75
pomegranates 24
Minted Pomegranate Yogurt with Grapefruit Salad 148
porridge: Porridge with Dates and Pistachio Nuts 65
Traditional Scottish Porridge 64
potassium 20
potatoes: Leek and Potato Soup 84
Turkish-style New Potato Casserole 102
poultry 6, 29
pregnancy 7, 38
preservatives 11
protein 17, 19, 21, 28, 29, 65
prunes: Chicken and Leek Soup with Prunes 87
Tagine of Yam, Carrots and Prunes 110
pumpkin seeds 29
Stir-fried Vegetables and Seeds 107
pumpkins 26

quinoa 27
quorn 28

raspberries: Raspberry and Oatmeal Blend 54
relaxation 6, 17, 33, 34
rice 27
Brown Rice Risotto with Mushrooms 109
Herby Rice Pilaff 141
Indian Rice with Tomatoes and Spinach 108
Rice Noodles with Vegetable Chilli Sauce 105
Spicy Paella 127
Warm Oriental Chicken and Rice Stir-fry Salad 99
rocket: Wild Rocket and Cos Lettuce Salad with Herbs 134
Rose Water-scented Oranges with Pistachio Nuts 149
rye 22, 27

salads: Bean Salad with Tuna and Red Onion 96
Buckwheat Noodle Salad with Smoked Salmon 95

Bulgur Wheat Salad with Walnuts 91
Cabbage Salad with Lemon Dressing and Black Olives 135
Citrus Fruit Salad with Avocado 92
Date, Orange and Carrot Salad 140
Gingered Carrot Salad 138
Greek Salad 93
Grilled Fennel Salad with Niçoise Olives 136
Minted Pomegranate Yogurt with Grapefruit Salad 148
Mixed Green Leaf and Herb Salad 133
New Spring Vegetable Salad 90
Potato, Caraway Seed and Parsley Salad 137
Salad Niçoise 97
Spinach and Roast Garlic Salad 132
Tropical Scented Fruit Salad 59
Warm Chicken and Tomato Salad with Hazelnut Dressing 98
Warm Mixed Seafood and Fresh Herb Salad 94
Warm Oriental Chicken and Rice Stir-fry Salad 99
Wild Rocket and Cos Lettuce Salad with Herbs 134
salmon 29
Buckwheat Noodle Salad with Smoked Salmon 95
Teriyaki Salmon 124
salt 15, 19, 22, 23
sardines 29
Barbecued Sardines with Orange 122
seaweeds 26
seeds 29
selenium 19, 29
sesame seeds 29
Stir-fried Broccoli with Sesame Seeds 142
shellfish 29
Warm Mixed Seafood and Fresh Herb Salad 94
side effects, possible 45
skin 18, 19
dry skin brushing 17, 19, 36
improved 6, 16
problems 7, 13, 33
sleep 6, 7, 17, 19, 33
smoking 7, 10, 11, 17, 40, 41

smoothies: Apricot and Ginger Smoothie 57
Raspberry and Oatmeal Blend 54
Strawberry and Tofu Smoothie 55
Summer Fruit Smoothie 56
snacks 7, 19, 22, 45
sorbet: Strawberry and Lavender Sorbet 153
soups: American Red Bean Soup with Guacamole Salsa 82
Black-eyed Bean and Tomato Broth 81
Chicken, Avocado and Chickpea Soup 86
Chicken and Leek Soup with Prunes 87
Chilled Tomato and Fresh Basil Soup 78
Country Mushroom, Bean and Barley Soup 83
Fragrant Thai Fish Soup 85
Fresh Cabbage Soup 79
Leek and Potato Soup 84
Tomato and Lentil Soup 80
soya 28, 30
spinach 26
Aromatic Chickpea and Spinach Curry 112
Indian Rice with Tomatoes and Spinach 108
Spinach and Roast Garlic Salad 132
sprouts 27
strawberries: Orange Granita with Strawberries 150
Strawberries with Passion Fruit Sauce 146
Strawberry and Lavender Sorbet 153

Strawberry and Tofu Smoothie 55
stress 33
sugar(s) 17, 22
sulphites 11, 13, 20
sunflower seeds 29
Stir-fried Vegetables and Seeds 107
sweet cicely: Roasted Peppers with Sweet Cicely 74

Tagliatelle with Vegetable Ribbons 103
tahini 29
tea 7, 16, 19, 20, 41
ginger 26
herbal 17, 20, 31, 33, 41, 45
Teriyaki Salmon 124
thiamin 20
tofu 28
Strawberry and Tofu Smoothie 55
Tofu and Pepper Kebabs 116
tomatoes 13, 26
Black-eyed Bean and Tomato Broth 81
Butter Bean, Tomato and Olive Stew 111
Chilled Tomato and Fresh Basil Soup 78
Griddled Chicken with Tomato Salsa 128
Indian Rice with Tomatoes and Spinach 108
Roasted Cod with Fresh Tomato Sauce 120
Roasted Plum Tomatoes with Garlic 143
Seared Tuna Steaks with Tomato Salsa 121

Tomato and Lentil Dhal with Almonds 113
Tomato and Lentil Soup 80
Warm Chicken and Tomato Salad with Hazelnut Dressing 98
toxins 7, 10–11
trout 29
Chinese-style Steamed Trout 125
tuna 29
Bean Salad with Tuna and Red Onion 96
Salad Niçoise 97
Seared Tuna Steaks with Tomato Salsa 121

vegetables 24, 42, 43
New Spring Vegetable Salad 90
Penne with Green Vegetable Sauce 104
Rice Noodles with Vegetable Chilli Sauce 105
Spring Vegetable Omelette 118
Stir-fried Vegetables and Seeds 107
Stir-fried Vegetables with Cashew Nuts 106
super vegetables 25–6
Tagliatelle with Vegetable Ribbons 103
see also individual vegetables
visualization 16, 37
vitamins 16, 21, 23, 30
vitamin A 15, 19, 20, 23, 24, 29, 58
vitamin B group 15, 23, 27, 28, 29
vitamin B12 (cyanocobalamin) 30

vitamin C (ascorbic acid) 15, 16, 19, 20, 23, 24, 58
vitamin D (calciferol) 29
vitamin E (tocopherols) 15, 19, 20, 23, 24, 26, 27, 29, 31
vitamin K 23

walnuts 29
Baked Apples with Figs and Walnuts 157
Bulgur Wheat Salad with Walnuts 91
water, drinking 6, 14, 31, 41, 45
watercress 26
watermelons: Lime and Watermelon Tonic 53
weight issues 6, 7, 13, 15, 22
wheat 12, 22, 27
wholegrains 27

yam: Tagine of Yam, Carrots and Prunes 110
yogurt 21, 30
Minted Pomegranate Yogurt with Grapefruit Salad 148
Summer Berry Frozen Yogurt 152

zinc 19, 20

Acknowledgements

Photographers: Karl Adamson; Edward Allwright; Peter Anderson; David Armstrong; Tim Auty; Steve Baxter; Martin Brigdale; Nicky Dowey; James Duncan; Gus Filgate; Ian Garlick; Michelle Garrett; John Heseltine; Amanda Heywood; Tim Hill; Janine Hosegood; Dave King; Don Last; William Lingwood; Patrick McLeavey; Michael Michaels; Steve Moss; Thomas Odulate; Peter Reilly; Craig Robertson; Bridget Sargeson; Simon Smith; Sam Stowell.

Recipe writers: Pepita Aris; Catherine Atkinson; Stephanie Barker; Ghillie Basan; Judy Bastyra; Susannah Blake; Angela Boggiano; Georgina Campbell; Carla Capalbo; Lesley Chamberlain; Maxine Clarke; Carole Clements; Trish Davies; Roz Denny; Patrizia Diemling; Stephanie Donaldson; Matthew Drennan; Sarah Edmonds; Steve England; Joanna Farrow; Rafi Fernandez; Jenni Fleetwood; Christine France; Silvana Franco; Sarah Gates; Shirley Gill; Brian Glover; Nicola Graimes; Rosamund Grant; Carole Handslip; Rebekah Hassan; Shehzaid Husain; Christine Ingram; Becky Johnson; Soheila Kimberley; Lucy Knox; Elizabeth Lambert Ortiz; Ruby Le Bois; Patricia Lousada; Gilly Love; Lesley Mackey; Norma MacMillan; Sue Maggs; Kathy Man; Sally Mansfield; Elizabeth Martin; Maggie Mayhew; Sarah Maxwell; Norma Miller; Jane Milton; Sallie Morris; Janice Murfitt; Annie Nichols; Angela Nilsen; Suzannah Olivier; Maggie Pannell; Louise Pickford; Marion Price; Keith Richmond; Rena Salaman; Anne Sheasby; Marlena Spieler; Liz Trigg; Christopher Trotter; Linda Tubby; Hilaire Walden; Laura Washburn; Biddy White Lennon; Kate Whiteman; Judy Williams; Carol Wilson; Elizabeth Wolf-Cohen; Jeni Wright.

Food stylists and home economists: Alison Austin; Eliza Baird; Alex Barker; Shannon Beare; Julie Beresford; Madeleine Brehaut; Sascha Brodie; Jacqueline Clarke; Frances Cleary; Stephanie England; Tessa Evelegh; Marilyn Forbes; Annabel Ford; Nicola Fowler; Michelle Garrett; Hilary Guy; Jo Harris; Jane Hartshorn; Katherine Hawkins; Amanda Heywood; Cara Hobday; Claire Hunt; Kate Jay; Jill Jones; Maria Kelly; Clare Lewis; Sara Lewis; Lucy McKelvie; Marion McLornan; Wendy Lee; Blake Minton; Emma Patmore; Marion Price; Kirsty Rawlings; Bridget Sargeson; Jennie Shapter; Joy Skipper; Jane Stephenson; Carol Tenant; Helen Trent; Linda Tubby; Sunil Vijayakar; Stuart Walton; Sophie Wheeler; Stephen Wheeler; Judy Williams.